Constructed Truths

Thomas Zoglauer

Constructed Truths

Truth and Knowledge in a Post-truth World

 Springer Vieweg

Thomas Zoglauer
Institute of Philosophy and Social Sciences
Brandenburg University of Technology
Cottbus, Brandenburg, Germany

ISBN 978-3-658-39941-2   ISBN 978-3-658-39942-9   (eBook)
https://doi.org/10.1007/978-3-658-39942-9

Preface

Books are a reflection of their time in which they were written. Philosophy is "its own time comprehended in thoughts," as Hegel wrote in the preface to the *Philosophy of Right*. But as Hegel rightly recognized, philosophy is always too late to instruct how the world ought to be. It can only reflect on what has already happened. Epistemology can contribute to critical thinking, it can reveal fallacies, but it cannot prevent the occurrence of errors.

The German version of this book was written during the COVID-19 crisis between March 2020 and May 2021, a time when the world was flooded by fake news, conspiracy theories, and lies spread by Trump supporters and Covid deniers. Unfortunately, this breakdown of truth is not a singular event, but a symptom of crisis in our time. The crisis prompted politicians, media experts, and IT specialists to consider how to better detect fake news and prevent its spread. But the truth crisis is also a philosophical and epistemological problem created by media, since it threatens the basis of our worldview, namely the belief in an objective truth that exists independently of subjective opinions and collective belief. With this book, I want to contribute to the rehabilitation of truth by pointing out the causes of post-factual thinking and explaining epistemological fallacies.

I received significant inspiration from the interdisciplinary conference "Post-Truth: Perspectives, Strategies, Prospects," which took place in January 2020 at the KU Leuven. At the end of February 2020, together with Peter Klimczak, I organized the conference "Wahrheit und Fake im postfaktisch-digitalen Zeitalter" (Truth and Fake in the Postfactual-Digital Age) at the Berlin-Hohenschönhausen Memorial, which resulted in the anthology of the same name (Klimczak and Zoglauer 2021). At both conferences, I was able to present my reflections on the phenomenon of "post-truth." I would like to thank the conference participants for the stimulating discussions. My special thanks go to Peter Klimczak, who was inspired by the ideas for this book and included it in his series "ars digitalis." Some of the central theses of my work were also the subject of discussion in the "Stuttgarter Philosophenkreis" (Stuttgart Philosophy Circle), in whose discussion rounds, which took place despite the lockdown due to Covid restrictions, my book slowly took shape. I received valuable suggestions and hints from Rüdiger Vaas, Harald Lorenz, and Klaus Erlach, whose critical inquiries and comments helped to sharpen my arguments.

This book originally appeared in German in 2021 under the title "Konstruierte Wahrheiten." Thanks to Springer Nature, the book has been chosen to be translated into English with the help of the AI program DeepL. I have done my best to correct and improve the computer-generated translation. If mistakes are found, they are my responsibility. I wish to thank Springer Nature and its team, especially Petra Steinmüller from Springer Vieweg, for making it possible to present my book to an English-speaking audience.

Remseck, Germany   Thomas Zoglauer
in August 2022

Contents

Introduction

Donald Trump has set an inglorious record as American president. The Washington Post's fact checkers (Kessler 2021) counted 30,573 false or misleading claims during his time in office. That's an average of about 20 fake news stories per day that he tweeted out to the world. He downplayed climate change and the COVID-19 pandemic, criminalized migrants crossing the Mexican border into the USA, disputed Russian interference in the 2016 presidential election, and claimed, without any evidence, that the 2020 presidential election was rigged and that he was fraudulently denied a second term (Kessler et al. 2020). Trump did not lie just occasionally to disguise facts or to appear in a better light. Trump's systematic lies represent a broad-based attack on truth and contributed to a polarization of American society. The intent was to construct an alternate reality in which climate change does not exist, in which the American economy is doing better than ever, and in which COVID-19 is a harmless cold. Media outlets that exposed Trump's lies were insulted as "fake news media." In an almost Orwellesque fashion, lies became truths and truths became lies (Orwell 1976).

Trump's disrespectful treatment of the truth and his ignoring of facts is characterized by the term *post-truth*. Some commentators even speak of the beginning of a post-truth age, in which truth no longer matters, and knowledge is replaced by opinion and truth by narratives. Post-truth is not a new phenomenon, but it gained a new dimension with Trump. Unlike political disinformation campaigns in the Nazi and Stalin eras, fake news nowadays spreads faster and more effectively through social media platforms and is automatically generated and personalized by bot programs. They can influence elections and the political attitude of voters. Post-truth is changing our perception of reality. When facts are ignored or no longer matter and emotions take their place, then there are only subjective truths.

As the SARS-CoV-2 virus spread across the world, so did the lies and fake news about the virus. You can protect yourself from viruses with masks and by keeping your distance, but no spam filter can protect you from fake news. Lies and conspiracy narratives are contagious. They nest in the minds of citizens, change their thinking, are retold, and shared on social media. The post-truth phenomenon is responsible for the decreasing trust in mainstream media. There is often disparaging and contemptuous talk of the "lying press." The truth crisis is thus also a media crisis. People now only trust media that reflect their own opinions. Other opinions are no longer tolerated.

The call for regulation of the large tech companies, which do not adequately fulfill their duty to delete fake news and hate messages, therefore could no longer be ignored. But the problem does not only concern Google, Twitter, Facebook, and Co. The problem was created with the new medium of the Internet itself – a medium where people can spread their own opinion and where there are no gatekeepers to check news for its truthfulness. Thanks to the Internet, we now have access to a wealth of information, but information overload has also its dark sides. The invention of the Internet set off an information bomb whose fallout spreads in the form of lies, bullshit, and half-truths, contaminating people's thinking. As the storming of the Capitol by angry Trump supporters in January 2021 shows, the spread of fake news can also become a danger to democracy.

The aim of this book is to examine post-truth from an epistemological and media-theoretical perspective. Considering the attack on truth, we need to reflect on the foundations of knowledge and ask ourselves: What is truth? How can we know it? Does truth refer to reality or is it merely a social construction? Do we possess objective knowledge of the world or is knowledge always subjective? These unresolved philosophical questions create uncertainty in our approach to truth. After all, if there are no objective facts and if truth is always relative to a perspective, does it follow that there are alternative conceptions of reality? Those who think that truth is relative and socially constructed cannot complain when post-factualists like Trump take a different view of truth. If we want to fight post-truth effectively, it is not enough to engage in fact-checking and to complain about widespread lying; first of all, we must actively defend the institution of truth. We have to show that truth is not arbitrary and not a matter of interpretation, but that there are objective truths.

In the first chapter of the book, different types of post-factualism are analyzed, and I will try to explain why many people think that their own opinions are true. Digitization and distorted thinking led to the rise of post-truth. When searching for information on the Internet, we selectively focus on content that interests us and that fits into our own worldview. This confirmation bias is reinforced by the personalization of search engines and news feeds. By these mechanisms, filter bubbles are created (Pariser 2011), which block critical content and confirm media users in their own opinions. People tend to communicate only with like-minded people. When a group is held together by ideological convictions, peer pressure takes effect, suppressing critical voices and sanctioning dissenting opinions. Dissenters, fanatics, fundamentalists, conspiracy theorists, and followers of esoteric teachings are then no longer receptive to criticism because they have isolated themselves ideologically from the rest of society. They ignore scientific facts and arguments, create their own interpretation of the world, and thus screen themselves off from the outside world, which they perceive as hostile. Such a social dynamic leads to the creation of echo chambers, which, as Cass Sunstein (2017) has shown, contribute to the polarization of society and can endanger democracy. In a society where each group lives in its own echo chamber, constructive political discourse is no longer possible. Each group defines its own truths. Truth becomes a group belief. Those who do not share this belief are excluded from the group. Hannah Arendt (1968, p. 241) defends the traditional conception of truth in saying that: "Facts are beyond agreement and consent." The truthlikeness of an assertion does not increase with the number of people who agree with it. It is, after all, the very characteristic of truth that it holds independently of people and their opinions. When society breaks down into rival groups that live in their own echo chambers, hold their own truths, and are unwilling or unable to communicate and exchange arguments with each other, then post-truth prevails and can lead to the destabilization of society.

Unfortunately, philosophy bears some responsibility for the acceptance of post-factual ideas among intellectuals. Chapter 2 presents various philosophical theories, such as relativism, social constructivism, and scientific constructivism, which have contributed to a relativization of truth. These theories assume that truth is a product of discursive practices and discourse rules determine what is true and what is false. In doing so, a close connection between truth and power is postulated: For whoever dominates discourse can impose its own truth claims. Truth, according to this view, does not exist outside discourse and social practices. Each discourse has its own truths. Such truth relativism, however, has disastrous practical consequences, which Greg Weiner (2017, p. 91) couched in the sarcastic question: "If there is no objective truth, how is it possible to say Trump lied?" Trump introduced new rules of political discourse and convinced his supporters of his version of the truth. He ignores all critical rejoinders because he can always say: Those who do not accept my rules of discourse don't have the right to criticize me. This seems to be a logical consequence of relativism, because criticism can only be formulated within discourse. Anyone who denies the existence of objective facts is playing into the hands of demagogues like Trump.

But what is truth? How can we determine whether a proposition is true? We will deal with these questions in Chap. 3. Various theories of truth have been developed in philosophy, such as the correspondence theory, the coherence theory, the pragmatic theory, and the deflationary theory of truth. The correspondence theory supports a metaphysical concept of truth: truth consists in a correspondence between a proposition and reality. The other three truth theories deny this correspondence. According to them, truth cannot be detached from its linguistic, social, and life-world context. For the coherence theory, truth is a holistic property of a belief system: statements are true if they form a coherent system. For the pragmatic theory of truth, something is true if it is useful and successful. And for the deflationary theory, truth consists merely in an approving attitude of a speaker towards a statement. Accordingly, the statement "p is true" expresses the same thing as the statement p.

Our common-sense understanding of truth is based on a correspondence theory. We check the truth of a statement by comparing it with reality. If we find a correspondence, then it is true, if not, then it is false. Fact checkers proceed in this way. However, the correspondence theory is controversially debated in philosophy, because there are some strong objections to this theory. In this respect, we face the dilemma of having to choose between an externalist, reality-based conception of truth and a contextualist, discursive conception of truth. I will present a compromise solution in the form of *perspectival realism,* in which the best of both competing approaches is united. According to perspectivism, truth depends on the current state of research and is historically variable. What we think to be true today may be false tomorrow. But not all epistemic perspectives are equally valid. Thanks to scientific progress, we can understand and explain the world today better than in the past. Truth is always relative to a theory and a perspective, but is nonetheless related to a theory-independent reality which is a neutral arbiter for our conjectures and hypotheses. If we want to know how dangerous COVID-19 is, we ask virologists, not Covid deniers. If we want to know if there is climate change, we ask climate scientists and trust what they tell us. Scientific truths, even if they are only provisional and subject to revision, provide an indispensable frame of reference that enables us to interact with the world, for example, to combat diseases and develop new technologies.

Chapter 4 examines how information becomes knowledge. There are essentially two theories that have different views of information and knowledge. According to the first theory, knowledge is a true justified belief caused by a reliable, information-conserving process that maps facts into mental representations. For example: When I see a red rose, the visual information is transmitted through my eyes and neural pathways to my brain, so that I come to know that the rose is red. Unless I fall victim to a sensory illusion or hallucination, I gain a true picture of reality. Social epistemology, on the other hand, advocates a different model: knowledge is regarded as a collective belief which has a social status (Kusch 2002, p. 109). Individuals can know something only as part of a community (Kusch 2002, p. 10). Knowledge is thus an institutionalized belief and is socially constructed (Goldman 2002, p. 186 f.). According to this theory, a belief is knowledge only when it is discursively justified and consensually accepted. A typical social definition of knowledge is the following: "any and every set of ideas and acts accepted by one or another social group or society of people – ideas and acts pertaining to what they accept as real for them and for others" (McCarthy 1996, p. 24).

Against the perceptual model of knowledge, it can be objected that information is not simply transferred from a perceived object to the brain. Cognitive science shows that the human brain is informationally and operationally closed. Perception is not a one-to-one mapping from external reality to the brain. What reaches our brain is not meaningful information but neural signals that must be interpreted and thereby acquire meaning (Roth 1997, p. 108). The brain *constructs* meanings (Roth 1992a, p. 127). Moreover, the naturalistic model of knowledge cannot be transferred from perception to other forms of knowledge. The social environment has a great influence on belief formation. Knowledge that we receive from the media is second-hand knowledge. Media are not simply technical extensions of our sensory organs. Media select, aggregate, and process information and therefore do not always produce an objective picture of reality.

On the other hand, the social knowledge model also has its weaknesses. If truth and knowledge are based only on acceptance and consensual agreement, relativism will be the consequence. For if there are no group-independent truth criteria, each group will have its own truths and will live within its own socially constructed reality. The effect be a polarization and fragmentation of society.

I will defend epistemic contextualism that presents a balanced middle position between the causal and social models of knowledge. Since knowledge is always context-sensitive, social influences play an important role in knowledge acquisition and knowledge attribution. Contextualism does not lead to relativism, because there are not different truths, but merely different degrees of knowledge. Common-sense knowledge is different from scientific knowledge and they represent different kinds of belief. There is no contradiction in stating that common-sense and scientific knowledge may refer to the same facts, since science merely extends, refines, and specifies common-sense knowledge.

According to social epistemology, we obtain our knowledge in most cases from others: from our friends or from the media. However, trust in these sources of knowledge is not always justified and can have dangerous consequences. One reason why many people believe in conspiracy theories or believe fake news is that they trust these information sources without critical reflection. Information based on hearsay is not knowledge as long as it has not been checked and confirmed. It makes a difference whether we receive the information from dubious Internet sources or from reputable scientific sources. We cannot trust what mavericks tell us about the SARS-CoV-2 virus. This kind of information is not as reliable as what virologists and epidemiologists know based on the latest research. We trust not so much the experts as the methods experts use to gain knowledge. People do not always judge in an objective and unbiased manner. Hans Albert recommends the method of critical examination (Albert 1991, p. 42 ff.) that is most likely to provide objective knowledge.

A critical reception of the media requires an open-minded consciousness and a way of thinking that does not blindly trust the opinions of others. Knowledge based on mere hearsay is not reliable. Only information that we have good reason to believe constitutes knowledge. Immanuel Kant warns us not to blindly trust others: many people are simply too dependent on others or too lazy to think for themselves. Instead they simply believe what others say. Kant therefore gives us the advice: "Have courage to make use of your *own* understanding!" (Kant 1996, p. 17) This motto is the central idea of Enlightenment and is today more important than ever.

Post-Truth Phenomenology

1

1.1   The Brave New World of the Internet

Imagine a world in which information of all kinds is freely accessible, in which news, as well as fake news, is disseminated and in which people can communicate their own opinion free of censorship. In this free information market, rumors, gossip, lies, propaganda, conspiracy myths, or just plain nonsense circulate. You are surrounded by a flood of information and can now choose and read freely what interests you. You will easily lose orientation. For every opinion there is a counter opinion, for every view there is a different account and for every truth there is an alternative truth. How can we still distinguish between true and false news? Which sources should we trust? How can we gain an objective view of reality?

This post-truth world is not real yet, but is in the offing to become reality. On the Internet and in social media you can find lots of news where you can't always distinguish whether it's true or false. False reports, fake news and disinformation campaigns have always existed, but with the Internet a new medium was created where people can shout out their own opinion and where news and rumors spread worldwide immediately. The Internet is a source of information that gives us access to the world, but that does not simply represent the world, but shows an infinite number of perspectives from which the user can choose one. If we want to know why there is so much fake news today and why so many people believe in conspiracy theories, we have to understand how the Internet and social media differ from traditional news media (newspapers, radio, television).

In the traditional media there are gatekeepers who fulfill a filter function and select news according to journalistic criteria and transmit them to the recipient. The selection criteria are truthfulness, novelty, importance, relevance, emotionality and entertainment value. In the ideal case, gatekeepers work as fact checkers and exclude false news. The invention of the Internet was celebrated by many people as a media revolution because it is a free medium without gatekeepers and where news is transmitted unfiltered from the producer to the recipient. The World Wide Web promised a democratization of knowledge, where information can be accessed freely and without charge. The Internet, it was said, would create a new culture, strengthen democracy, and contribute to intercultural understanding (Curran 2012, p. 13). Citizens could become news producers themselves, write blogs or publish their own online newspapers. At the beginning of the 1990s, in the early days of the Internet, a series of manifestos were written that praised the dawn of a new age and spread boundless optimism. The net activist John Perry Barlow published a "Declaration of the Independence of Cyberspace", in which he called for the freedom of the Internet from all state interference, surveillance and censorship:

> We are creating a world that all may enter without privilege or prejudice accorded by race, economic power, military force, or station of birth. We are creating a world where anyone, anywhere may express his or her beliefs, no matter how singular, without fear of being coerced into silence or conformity. Your legal concepts of property, expression, identity, movement, and context do not apply to us. They are based on matter. There is no matter here. (Barlow 2001, p. 29)

In this utopia the Internet was imagined as a free marketplace of ideas, like the Athenian agora, in which direct democracy could be realized (Brin 2001, p. 35; Barbrook and Cameron 2001, p. 369). In the virtual community, everyone would be free and equal, regardless of color, gender, or religion. Others create the vision of a collective intelligence that spans the world like a global brain (Lévy 1999; Halpin et al. 2014, p. 28). The "wisdom of the crowds" (Surowiecki 2004) would be more than the sum of all individual intelligences and would create new knowledge from all for all.

Soon after the initial euphoria, the dark sides of the Internet became visible: the digital divide, a lack of data protection, cybercrime and a flood of spam, hate mails and fake news. Trolls and hate preachers abuse the freedom of the Internet to influence and manipulate people's thinking. With the removal of gatekeepers, the dam that had previously held back the worst of the dirt was broken. Frankly speaking, the problems of the Internet are already inherent in the libertarian and egalitarian ideology of Internet activists. In this utopia a dilemma arises: on the one hand, freedom of information for all is demanded (Hughes 2001, p. 82; Chaos Computer Club 2020), on the other hand, private data should be protected. Hackers want to make secret information public, but on the other hand they do not want to be spied on themselves and insist on their right to anonymity (May 2001, p. 61 f.). Those who hack others should not be surprised if they themselves are hacked. The demand of hackers "All information should be free" (Chaos Computer Club 2020) can also be understood as an authorization of the state for a far-reaching surveillance of its citizens.

On the Internet, the users are confronted with a vast amount of unfiltered information and have to find their own way through the information jungle. It is not always obvious at first glance which news is true and which is false and which sources are trustworthy. The Internet users are forced to make a choice and thus become their own gatekeepers. How are they supposed to distinguish between truth, rumor and false news? The recipients have to apply their own selection criteria, which differ from the criteria of traditional news media. Their attention will be focused on those news that interest them the most.

People want to be entertained. Rumors, sensational news and fictional stories are more exciting and entertaining than political news. They fulfill the expectations of the listeners or readers (Bernal 2018, p. 239 f.). Fake news appeals to emotions and instincts. Conspiracy theories divide the world into good and evil and reveal the alleged culprits for the evils of this world. Rumors are readily retold and spread rapidly throughout the world via social media. Internet users want to hear opinions that confirm their own worldview (Tewksbury and Rittenberg 2012, p. 86). As a result, media users no longer receive the entire spectrum of news and opinions, but focus on specific sites and topics or limit themselves to specialized topics and news portals that serve their interests. Consequently, the field of vision narrows. Fragmentation and specialization of knowledge can therefore be expected to lead to less comprehensive knowledge (Tewksbury and Rittenberg 2012, p. 127). Commonalities dwindle, differences increase, and clashes of opinion intensify. A general consensus on social and political issues is lost. Each group retreats into its own media niche.

The phenomenon of fragmentation and selective news reception is not limited to the Internet. Hardly anyone reads a newspaper from the first to the last page, but picks out those news that interests him or her. Football fans skip the politics section and read the sports pages first. If someone is mainly interested in celebrity news, she or he will ignore the news from the politics section (Tewksbury and Rittenberg 2012, pp. 123, 126). Nevertheless, there is a qualitative and quantitative difference between traditional news media and news portals on the Internet. In the case of personalized news portals, certain topics are sorted out from the outset. The reader no longer has the chance to get to know other opinions and take note of other points of view. Many users confine themselves to such blogs and discussion forums that correspond to their own political views and interests. As a consequence, a shielding from criticism and an immunization effect occurs. Personalization leads to selective and subjective perception: people only see what they want to see and ignore facts that do not fit into their own world view.

Media users tend to consume mainly those media that are in line with their own beliefs and avoid media that disseminate a different worldview. This phenomenon is referred to in media psychology as *"selective exposure"* (Spohr 2017, p. 153; Schweiger 2017, p. 96). People want to avoid dissonance and contradictions and form a coherent own worldview. Therefore, they prefer those media that are ideologically close to them. Michael Oswald explains this as follows:

> Therefore, people react differently to messages and treat them selectively by ignoring or rejecting statements that are contrary to their own *beliefs*. Rejection occurs because cognitive dissonance arises when information or statements contrast with one's own ideology or when they contradict central values. (…) The better a communication frame fits with the worldview of recipients, the more likely they are to accept it. (Oswald 2019, p. 16)

Empirical studies confirm this effect (Flaxman et al. 2016, p. 317; Lewandowsky et al. 2017, p. 358; Kavanagh and Rich 2018, p. 154). In the US, Republican supporters prefer to watch Fox News, while most Democrats follow CNN (Spohr 2017, p. 152).

1.2   The Google Universe

News portals collect and select news. News reports are edited, summarized, chunked into small, quickly consumable pieces of information, accompanied by images and placed in a narrative context so that they can be accessed by a mouse click and shared with others (Coddington 2019, p. 4 ff.). In most cases, the collectors and editors of news, the so-called aggregators, only have second-hand knowledge, which they obtain from other news sources (Coddington 2019, p. 45). The filtering and selection of news is usually done by editors and internet users can act as their own gatekeepers by focussing their attention on specific topics. Besides that, there are also algorithmic gatekeepers. Search engines select content according to predetermined criteria and adapt it to the interests of users. Eli Pariser describes the effect of personalization as follows: "Ultimately, the proponents of personalization offer a vision of a custom-tailored world, every facet of which fits us perfectly. It's a cozy place, populated by our favorite people and things and ideas." (Pariser 2011, p. 12).

Google has perfected algorithmic personalization (cf. Hartmann 2020; Zoglauer 2020). If one enters a search term in Google, a list of web pages appears that provide information on this term. The order of the search results reflects the relevance and importance of the pages. How important a piece of information is depends on the user's interests. But how does Google know what value a user attributes to a piece of information? Google founders Sergey Brin and Larry Page developed the so-called *PageRank algorithm*, which determines the order of search results according to the frequency of clicks and how often a page is linked. The personal preferences and interests of the users can be inferred from the individual user behavior, e.g. how often a page is visited. The number of clicks thus becomes the measure of all things. PageRank is defined by the individual and collective preferences. The more frequently a website is linked, i.e. the more other websites refer to it, the more popular it is. Robotic programs search the Internet and cookies spy on individual user behavior. As a result, each user receives a specific listing of search results tailored to them. Google presents each user a different picture of the world, expressed in the order of search results. Since the relevance of a link is defined by the subjective assessment of its importance, the users get to see what they want to see.

The Google ranking is determined by one's own and other people's surfing behavior. Internet pages that are accessed particularly frequently by other users receive a better ranking. And the higher the PageRank, the more popular the page is and the more likely it is to be visited. The invisible work done by algorithms does not lead to a democratization of knowledge. On the contrary: the Google universe is rather plutocratically organized. PageRank represents a symbolic capital that can be converted into economic power. A higher ranking can be achieved by search engine optimization or by simple "Google bombing", by placing many links pointing to a certain website. By applying this strategy, algorithms can be duped and attention can be attained.

When listing search results, Google does not distinguish whether the information provided is true or false, or whether the sites are trustworthy or not. If you trust Google carelessly and click on a link, you run the risk of ending up on a fake news site or being redirected to a site of conspiracy theorists or pseudoscientific theories. Gérald Bronner (2016) conducted an experiment and typed five terms in Google's search site: astrology, Loch Ness monster, aspartame, crop circles, and psychokinesis. Scientific experts agree that these terms refer to pseudoscientific theories. Crop circles are supposedly the work of extraterrestrials. Psychokinesis refers to the ability of people to move objects merely by the power of thought. Aspartame is a sweetener that is suspected to cause cancer. The suspicion is based on a controversial study, but experts reject it as unscientific, because the conjecture could never be confirmed.

Bronner evaluated each of the first 30 search results and came to the following conclusion: 97% of the websites comment positively on astrology, 78% suggest the existence of the Loch Ness Monster, 70% report on the dangers of aspartame, 87% of the websites persuade the reader of the extraterrestrial origin of crop circles, and 84% present psychokinesis as a real phenomenon (Bronner 2016, pp. 24–30). By searching for "astrology," most links refer to pages with horoscopes. If one enters the keyword "Loch Ness monster", one either ends up on tourist sites advertising the Loch Ness myth or is linked to obscure You Tube videos with Nessie. And for the search term "aspartame," Google suggests the automatic word completion "poison," "cancer," or "neurotoxin," seducing to a preconceived judgment that is scientifically untenable. The results show that pseudoscientific theories are widespread on the Internet and are sometimes preferred by Google over scientific sites.

The investigation was conducted in 2010. In the meantime, Google has introduced a fact check label that indicates whether an article is classified as true, false or partially true. However, the fact check is not carried out by Google itself, but by trusted third parties. Google (2020) declares that "The publisher of the fact check must be a trusted source of information (determined by algorithm). The content must clearly tell you: which claims are being checked, conclusions about the claims, how conclusions were reached, citations and primary sources of information." If one repeats the search with the five given terms,[1] one gets a warning in the search results just in one case: for crop circles, one link shows "fact check: false". The other search results mostly refer to pseudoscientific pages where no fact check was performed. A fact check with the categories true, false or partially true seems inappropriate in these cases, because pseudoscientific theories are not falsifiable. Therefore, such sites should actually be marked as "unreliable" or "not trustworthy".

The order of search results can influence opinions, preferences and purchasing decisions because Internet users attribute greater importance and relevance to the first search

---

[1] The new search was conducted on 03/06/2020.

results than to the links further down. Psychological experiments show that elections can be influenced by manipulating search engines by directing undecided voters searching for information to specific websites that favor a particular party or candidate (Epstein and Robertson 2015).

To sum up: Google does not provide a neutral, objective picture of the world, but presents at best a perspectively distorted view of reality which is determined by the PageRank algorithm. Our perception is conducted by invisible algorithmic gatekeepers that direct our attention to higher ranked search results and thus unconsciously manipulate us.

1.3   The Blogosphere

Blogs are another source of news. A blog is an internet publication where an author (blogger) posts an article on the net and encourages comments and an open discussion. Bloggers take on the role of journalists, posting news, comments or subjective opinions and thus contribute to the diversity of opinions on the Internet. Weblogs are therefore in competition with traditional journalism. Critics complain about the neglect of journalistic standards such as objectivity, reliability, impartiality and trustworthiness. In contrast, proponents of discussion forums appreciate the possibility of a free exchange of information free of filters and gatekeepers (Coady 2011, 2012, p. 144; Munn 2012). David Coady regards blogging as a democratization of knowledge through which anyone can work as a journalist: "It is a mark of a genuine democracy that anyone can call himself or herself 'a journalist', and anyone who succeeds in informing the public of things they have a right to know is a journalist." (Coady 2012, p. 162).

Behind the call for a democratization of knowledge stands the idea that we don't need scientists and experts to arrive at the truth. It is said that everyone is an epistemic authority and every opinion is worth listening to. But, and this is the problem with post-truth, not every opinion can claim authority. There are true opinions and false opinions. False opinions are not on a par with true opinions and cannot claim the same right to be heard. Nicola Mößner and Philip Kitcher (2017, p. 4) therefore conclude: "The idea of equal epistemic status, across people and internet sites alike, is a myth."

Alvin Goldman (2008, p. 117) regards conventional news media as more reliable and trustworthy information sources than blogs, because fact checking minimizes errors and false reports. People communicating in blogs and Internet forums form a closed group of like-minded people who mostly keep to themselves and have a preconceived opinion that is not critically questioned. They develop a monoperspectival view that lacks a critical counter-instance. Counter-arguments are either not recognized or dismissed as untrustworthy from the outset (Goldman 2008, p. 119 f.). Goldman therefore considers a critical, error-correcting process of reflection to be indispensable, in which arguments and counterarguments are exchanged and weighed up. The philosopher Karl Popper has repeatedly pointed out how important criticism and corrective mechanisms are for the process of knowledge acquisition:

When I speak of reason or rationalism, all I mean is the conviction that we can *learn* through criticism of our mistakes and errors, especially through criticism by others, and eventually also through self-criticism. A rationalist is simply someone for whom it is more important to learn than to be proved right; someone who is willing to learn from others – not by simply taking over anothers' opinions, but by gladly allowing others to criticize his ideas and by gladly criticizing the ideas of others. (Popper 1999, p. 84)

Being open to criticism also means listening to the opinions of other people and not communicating exclusively with like-minded people within isolated epistemic bubbles. We must have access to reliable information in order to form our own well-founded opinion independently of others. Online news media such as blogs that don't make use of fact-checking are not reliable sources of information.

1.4   Polarization

Empirical studies show that blogs and personalized news portals contribute to a political *polarization* of society. In the USA, supporters of the Republican Party have moved further to the right in recent years, while Democrats have drifted further to the left (Tewksbury and Rittenberg 2012, p. 141; Schweiger 2017, p. 152 f.). Cass Sunstein explains the phenomenon of group polarization as follows:

The term 'group polarization' refers to something simple: after deliberation, people are likely to move towards a more extreme point in the direction to which the group's members were originally inclined. With respect to the internet and social media, the implication is that groups of like-minded people, engaged in discussion with one another, will typically end up thinking the same thing that they thought before – but in a more extreme form. (Sunstein 2017, p. 68)

Polarization causes an ideological "social distancing": citizens tend to communicate exclusively with like-minded people and no longer with people who have a different opinion. People prefer to associate with groups, in which they are recognized and where their own opinion is accepted. One feels part of a group or social movement, shares a particular group identity and thus has the chance to be heard and to feel confirmed. Groups increasingly fence off from each other, drift apart and discredit the other side.

Polarization has a self-confirming and self-reinforcing effect. For example, climate skeptics do not believe that man-made climate change exists. If you are not yet convinced by the arguments of the climate skeptics at the beginning and join one of their discussion groups just out of curiosity to learn more about their view, you are entering an epistemic bubble in which a one-sided, perspectival worldview is shared. In those forums there is no critical debate and no dissenting opinion is tolerated, but rather the already preconceived opinion is confirmed and strengthened. People in such groups protect themselves from criticism by ignoring objections (Spohr 2017, p. 151). Where critical voices are suppressed and no open debate takes place, there is a high probability that undecided people will be persuaded and eventually become climate skeptics themselves. Sunstein (2008, p. 101) describes this phenomenon as follows: "Once they hear what others believe, they adjust their positions in the direction of the dominant position." Many people simply adopt the opinion of others and join the group opinion.

The striving for dominance of individual members within an ideologically homogeneous group contributes to a radicalization of the group. Those who agitate loudest and hold the most radical views are most likely to be heard. Sunstein speaks of an information cascade if a particular theory or viewpoint attracts more and more supporters and minority opinions spread virally across the net (Sunstein 2008, p. 103 f.). He explains the emergence of an information cascade by comparing it with the spread of a rumor (Sunstein 2010). If someone in a discussion group starts a rumor, the probability is high that other group members will believe in it out of solidarity or due to peer pressure and will disseminate it not only within but also outside the group. The more sensational and emotional the news story, the higher the attention and the more people are attracted to it. Because of the lack of moderating gatekeepers, extreme and radical political views can be found in the Internet with higher probability than in traditional media. Polarization leads to a loss of consensus and reinforces the political fringes.

1.5   Framing and Narratives

There are subtle psychological mechanisms of influencing opinion. Two of these mechanisms will be presented here: framing and the use of narratives. *Framing* is a widespread phenomenon. Many terms we use in conversation are value-laden, expressing value attitudes, arousing emotions, unconsciously steering our interlocutor's thinking in a certain direction, and suggesting a certain judgment. Media scholar Robert Entman speaks of cultural framing (Entman 1993, p. 53). A frame provides an interpretative framework into which information is contextualized and which is associated with a valuation. Thus, a horizon of meaning is constructed, which gives messages and events a significance. A frame determines how something is perceived and interpreted. Depending on whether a certain fact is framed positively or negatively, different valuations and emotions can be evoked (Kahneman 2011, p. 368). For this reason, frames are often used in political rhetoric to influence citizens' voting behaviour (Oswald 2019, p. 18). Entman describes the psychological mechanism of framing as follows:

> Framing essentially involves selection and salience. To frame is to select some aspects of a perceived reality and make them more salient in a communicating text, in such a way as to promote a particular problem definition, causal interpretation, moral evaluation, and/or treatment recommendation for the item described. (Entman 1993, p. 52)

Another technique for constructing meaning horizons is the use of *narratives*. Katrin Götz-Votteler and Simone Hespers (2019, p. 108) mention the often-told and almost proverbial story of the dishwasher who works his way up to become a millionaire in the USA through his own diligence as an example of a narrative that glorifies the American Dream. It does not matter whether the story is true or not. What matters is that it seems convincing and believable, and that the listener accepts it as true. Fictional stories are often more exciting and interesting than true accounts. They seem more believable because they satisfy the listener's or reader's expectations. Important criteria for the persuasiveness of a narrative are its plausibility, coherence, precision, and probability (Oswald 2019, p. 126). A story seems more probable the more coherent it is. It must fit seamlessly into the listener's experience in order to be accepted. There must be no contradictions and no cognitive dissonance. Michael Oswald (2019, p. 127) explains how a high narrative precision is created by this means:

> In particular, a high level of narrative precision is achieved when ideology and the experiences of the recipients, cultural values and current events are interwoven into a whole. In combination with cultural-historical narratives, reference to myths or events of the past, resonance can thus be generated. (…) Narrative precision is ultimately not only a measure of the 'truth quality' of a story, but also of the extent to which it corresponds to the logic of 'good reasons'.

Many narratives have a moralizing content. Conspiracy theories often make use of such valuations (Götz-Votteler and Hespers 2019, p. 112). According to those theories there are dark forces conspiring against the population. In order not to be unmasked, the conspirators make use of camouflage and deception and operate in the background. The goal of a narrative is achieved when it is believed and retold. Myths, fake news and invented stories can also serve their purpose in this way.

Narratives appeal to emotion, not reason. They want to emotionalize. They are used to enforce certain values, perspectives and interpretations of reality. Narratives construct their own reality – it is often an alternative reality that entices the listener to accept it as reality: "As far as the social media system is concerned, it does not matter whether the news is 'real' or 'fake', it matters whether it fits the narrative – which fits the wishes and desires of the people concerned." (Bernal 2018, p. 240) You cannot tell from a text whether it is true or false. To do that, you have to compare it to reality. A narrative can be coherent, consistent, and free of contradictions, but still be false.

Narratives and framings are closely related (Oswald 2019, p. 125). A plausible narrative generates a framing because it provides an interpretation frame into which events can be placed. A story can be expanded and embellished at will, like a serial novel. The frame forms an outer shell or a framework that can be filled with a narrative.

Among media scholars, the thesis is occasionally put forward that facts and fictions cannot be so easily separated in journalism, since news is prepared and presented narratively (Hickethier 2008; Klaus 2008). Elisabeth Klaus (2008) justifies this thesis with the contextuality of facts. There is common agreement that facts are always embedded in a context of knowledge and have to be interpreted on the background of this context. Journalists obtain facts from news sources and edit them. For a better understanding and for the correct classification of the news, background information is usually included or the news is sent in the form of a report. Facts are, so to speak, the raw material and narratives are the media packaging. Knut Hickethier (2008, p. 362) writes: "Every report of the world and its events (if it does not present itself as a table of data) is therefore always also a narrative, every news item is – even in its strictly conventional forms of journalistic speech – a narrative of the world."

From a media ethics perspective this mixing of facts and fictions is problematic, since journalists are committed to the ideal of objectivity and are supposed to avoid subjective interpretations and evaluations.[2] Subjective evaluations, however, cannot always be avoided because they enter the presentation via narrative framings. Narratives have a suggestive effect. Fictional ideas are evoked in the reader that do not always correspond to reality. Fictions expand the space of reality with additional possibilities of interpretation. In media theory, fictions are therefore often represented as possible worlds (Predelli 2020).

Facts, of course, can only be presented from a particular point of view or perspective. Events must be interpreted and embedded in a meaning context. But journalists are obliged to report as objectively as possible, facts and evaluations must not be mixed. Narratives must not replace factual accounts. Otherwise there is a danger that facts will become "alternative facts". Donald Trump in particular is a master of making facts appear in a different light, thereby manipulating his listeners. His rhetoric polarizes people and has the effect that his supporters hold increasingly radical views and perceive the world from an ideological perspective. This can lead to the creation of filter bubbles and echo chambers, as will be shown in the next chapter.

1.6 Filter Bubbles and Echo Chambers

A *filter bubble* is an epistemic structure in which disturbing influences and dissenting opinions are systematically blocked out and the media user is captured in his or her own worldview. Filter bubbles can arise when people communicate and discuss only with like-minded people. Their formation is supported by a personalized information architecture that eliminates unwanted information (Pariser 2011; Schweiger 2017, p. 88 f.; Nguyen 2020). In this way, a perspectival perception is created that reinforces one's own view and ignores critical voices.

While the epistemic isolation of the subject in filter bubbles is brought about mainly *passively* through algorithmic filters, in echo chambers the flow of information is *actively* directed and manipulated through social interactions by keeping out disturbing influences (Messingschlager and Holtz 2020, p. 94). Thi Nguyen defines an *echo chamber* as follows:

---

[2]The journalistic ideal of objectivity is discussed in more detail in Sect. 2.7. On the difference between fact, fiction and fake, see Klimczak (2021).

> I use 'echo chamber' to mean an epistemic community which creates a significant disparity in trust between members and non-members. This disparity is created by excluding non-members through epistemic discrediting, while simultaneously amplifying members' epistemic credentials. Finally, echo chambers are such that general agreement with some core set of beliefs is a prerequisite for membership, where those core beliefs include beliefs that support that disparity in trust. (Nguyen 2020, p. 146)

In a way, each of us lives in an echo chamber, albeit in a weakened form. Sometimes we are so firmly convinced of our own opinion that we lightly brush aside any criticism and counter-arguments. Each of us has a subject-centered worldview and possesses unacknowledged biases. In our circle of friends we prefer to gather like-minded people around us who share our worldview. In his "New Organon" Francis Bacon explains how prejudice prevents us from gaining objective knowledge. What Bacon calls the "idols of the cave" are subjectively distorted views, as if each of us lives in a cave and is not interested in the world outside the cave:

> For (apart from the aberrations of human nature in general) each man has a kind of individual cave or cavern which fragments and distorts the light of nature. This may happen either because of the unique and particular nature of each man; or because of his upbringing and the company he keeps; or because of his reading of books and the authority of those he respects and admires; or because of the different impressions things make on different minds, preoccupied and prejudiced perhaps, or calm and detached, and so on. (Bacon 2000, p. 41)

Echo chambers are more stable and harder to penetrate than filter bubbles because they use immunization strategies to protect against criticism (Nguyen 2020, p. 153). Echo chambers divide people into insiders and outsiders. Insiders see themselves as possessing the truth. They seem to understand what really happens in contrast to the outsiders who have a false consciousness and fall prey to systematic deception. Outsiders are therefore discredited and not taken seriously.

Through group dynamic processes, dissenting opinions are deliberately blocked out from the discourse. Conformity is strengthened and criticism is suppressed. Echo chambers are particularly common among extreme political groups, terror cells and conspiracy theorists (Sunstein 2009, p. 120 f.; Nguyen 2020, p. 148). Some political observers even believe that Donald Trump and his supporters live in a cognitively closed echo chamber (Hampton 2018, p. 163). Their members remain trapped in a monoperspectival Manichean worldview and exercise unconscious self-censorship, taking note only of content that fits into their own worldview and excluding all disturbing, incompatible content. Trump supporters cannot be convinced by facts. Even when the falsity of one of his claims is exposed and Trump is convicted of lying, his supporters don't care. They stand firmly by him, no matter how much fake news he disseminates (Lewandowsky et al. 2017, p. 354).

Within an echo chamber, rumors and fake news can easily spread and are believed by insiders if they correspond to their (inter-)subjective worldview. Echo chambers have their own logic and epistemology, in which empirical evidence is irrelevant, scientific findings are ignored, facts are replaced by narratives, and one's own worldview is protected from refutation (Lewandowsky et al. 2017, p. 362).

1.7   Conspiracy Theories

Conspiracy theories are particularly well suited to demonstrate the structure and effect of echo chambers. Consider a fictional person named Oliver, invented by Quassim Cassam (2016, p. 162): Oliver does not believe in the official version of the terrorist attacks of September 11, 2001. He has read about the 9/11 conspiracy on the Internet and has become convinced that the collapse of the World Trade Center was caused by bomb explosions and not by the impact of two passenger planes. It was all the work of the CIA, he insists, and the highest government circles are involved with the aim to justify the later invasion of Afghanistan and the war in Iraq.

Cassam explains Oliver's false beliefs by his character traits: Oliver is gullible, cynical, and biased (Cassam 2016, p. 163). But this is only part of the explanation. Cassam over-looks the fact that even gullible people are able to recognize the truth if they live in an open communicative environment and not in an echo chamber. What is crucial is the epistemic position in which Oliver is situated. Let us therefore consider how he arrives at his convic-tion. Cassam (2016, p. 163) explains it as follows: "In forming his views about 9/11, the AIDS epidemic and the moon landing he relies on dodgy websites, paranoid talk radio stations, and a narrow circle of eccentric, conspiracist friends and acquaintances." So it's the Internet, social media, and his obscure friends that lead Oliver to believe in the 9/11 conspiracy. All it takes to become a conspiracy believer is to land on a website that sows doubt about the official version of events: How could the bombers enter the U.S. unchecked, pass through screening and board passenger planes? How could two planes bring down the Twin Towers? And why was Osama Bin Laden presented as the main culprit shortly after the terrorist attacks? Oliver gets curious and types "9/11" into Google to find out more. In doing so, he is redirected to conspiracy sites. In discussion forums, he meets other people who are firmly convinced that the US government is responsible. Soon he frequents these circles and acquires a firm belief that sweeps aside any doubt. His friends encourage him in his belief. Evidence that speaks against the conspiracy theory is interpreted as part of the conspiracy. In Oliver's opinion, not only did the government and intelligence agencies participate in the big cover-up, but the media was also involved and spreading lies. So Oliver is slowly drawn into an echo chamber where there is only this one truth and all other people are victims of a large-scale deception or are involved in the conspiracy themselves.

Echo chambers are a social phenomenon. No one is born as a conspiracy believer. It is not Oliver's intellectual character alone or an "epistemic vice" (Cassam 2016) that creates the 9/11 echo chamber, but the communicative interaction between him, his friends, and the media from which he draws his information. His gullibility, political attitude, and bias may predispose him to his belief, but it was the Internet and the social media that con-verted him into a devout believer.

The emergence of echo chambers is a typical side-effect of a post-truth society: "An obvious hallmark of a post-truth world is that it empowers people to choose their own reality, where facts and objective evidence are trumped by existing beliefs and prejudices." (Lewandowsky et al. 2017, p. 361) In an echo chamber, an alternative reality is constructed in which there is no man-made global warming, in which Bill Gates created the Corona virus, or in which Barack Obama is a Muslim. It is therefore useful to distinguish between a subjective, intersubjective and objective reality. The subjective reality is the world as it appears to us. We may be victims of delusion or hallucination. Subjective reality, therefore, need not be the same as objective reality. Objective reality is the world as it is described by natural science: It is a world made of atoms and elementary particles, in which there exists anthropogenic climate change and the Corona virus. Intersubjective reality, on the other hand, is a socially constructed world (cf. Berger and Luckmann 1991, p. 37). It is the world of which a group of people believe that it is real. Echo chambers create an intersubjective reality. That it need not correspond to objective reality is shown by the examples of climate skeptics and Covid deniers.

Echo chambers create a directed perception. They provide an interpretative framework into which all events are situated and through which they receive meaning. The world according to conspiracy theories is double-faced. It is determined by the ontological difference being versus appearance. The collapse of the World Trade Center *appears* to have been caused by the impact of airplanes, but *in reality* it was a result of bomb explosions. Conspiracists distrust scientific experts, the mainstream media, and government institutions. Intelligence agencies or a covert "deep state" are believed to be involved in all sorts of dark machinations and plots. It is argued that Western governments and large corporations have always acted conspirational and are involved in dirty deals, as it is expected to be the case today.

Conspiracy myths always follow the same narrative pattern: there are the conspirators who pursue a vicious goal, devise a sinister plan, and have the power to cover up their actions by manipulating the media so that the citizens don't understand what the facts are. When the conspiracy is uncovered, the conspirational veil is lifted and all the clues fit together like puzzle pieces to form a coherent picture. The facts just need to be interpreted accordingly. The conspiracy theorists make use of an epistemology that Hans Albert (1991, p. 18 ff.) calls the "revelation model of knowledge": the enlightened establish a monopoly of interpretation which gives them an aura of infallibility that legitimizes them to interpret the revealed knowledge which they share with their followers.

This sectarian, quasi-religious nature of conspiracy theories is particularly evident in the QAnon movement, which is common in conservative circles in the US. There is a prophet who is called "Q" by his followers and wishes to remain anonymous – he is supposedly a high-ranking government or military official with access to intelligence information – who sends cryptic messages (drops) to his followers via social media, which are eagerly absorbed and interpreted (LaFrance 2020). It is speculated that there is a widespread pedophile network in the U.S., including Democratic politicians, who abuse and imprison children, drink their blood, and engage in other satanic practices. Donald Trump is hailed as a savior who wants to free his people from the bondage of the "deep state" and "Make America Great Again". Some QAnon supporters identify Trump with Q. The mainstream media is seen as the enemy, constantly spreading lies and covering up the conspiracy. A "great awakening" is predicted that nothing can stop ("Nothing can stop what is coming"), which gives the movement an apocalyptic touch. According to Albert (1991, p. 18), the religious doctrine of knowledge consists in the idea "that truth is manifest, that it is open to view, and we just need to open our 'eyes' to 'see' it". To do this, he says, we have to interpret the facts "correctly." Only the believers are able to see through the veil of conspiracy, while the unbelievers live in ignorance or do not want to recognize the truth. The believers, however, take only those facts into account that fit into the conspirational worldview.

Conspiracy theorists have their own criteria to distinguish between truth and fake: Anything that contradicts their theory is fake and only the conspiracy narrative itself is true. Truth, therefore, cannot be determined by checking whether an assertion is consistent with the facts, because the facts or the apparent evidence itself may be fake. Contradictory evidence thus does not falsify the existence of conspiracies, but only shows how powerful the conspirators are that they can even manipulate the evidence. Anything that speaks against the conspiracy thus becomes evidence of its reality.

I would like to explain this immunization strategy using the example of the "Moon Hoax". Some people believe that American astronauts never landed on the moon and that the moon landing was produced in Hollywood studios and broadcast as reality TV. It is claimed that the Americans were not technically capable of sending astronauts to the moon. The television pictures were produced in order to maintain the myth of the technological and military superiority of the USA over the Soviet Union. As alleged proofs for the Apollo conspiracy the following indications are mentioned (see Wisnewski 2005):

- On the pictures shot by the astronauts on the moon there are no stars to be seen in the sky, which is seen as evidence that they were simply forgotten in the film sets.
- The American flag raised by astronauts on the moon fluttered in the wind, even though there is no atmosphere on the moon.
- The shadows of objects and the astronauts show errors.
- The hatch of the Lunar Module is too small for astronauts to pass through in their spacesuits, it is said.

Conspiracy theories use the strategy of suspicion: doubts are sown and thus uncertainty is created. Yet there is sufficient evidence that astronauts were actually on the moon (Eversberg 2013): They brought stones to earth that undoubtedly came from the moon. Mirrors were set up on the Moon to reflect laser beams sent from Earth, allowing to measure the exact distance of the Moon from Earth. Film footage of astronauts walking on the moon clearly shows that there is six times less gravity than on Earth. And above all: If there had been such a large-scale conspiracy involving thousands of people, how could it ever have been kept secret without a whistleblower leaking it?

Gerhard Wisnewski who wrote a book about "Lies in space" (2005), uncovering the Moon Hoax, presents surprisingly simple counter arguments against the alleged evidence: In order to simulate the lower gravity on the moon, he says, the film footage was broadcast in slow motion. The comparison samples needed to identify the moon rocks are said to have come from the Soviet probe Luna 15, which contrary to official reports did not crash on the moon at all, but successfully returned to Earth. And the laser reflectors were deposited on the moon by unmanned probes launched by the Soviets. But why would the Soviets help their worst enemy to demonstrate its technological superiority? And what about the scientists who confirmed the authenticity of the moonrock samples? Were they all part of the conspiracy? To the question why the conspiracy was never uncovered Wisnewski gives an astonishing answer: because it was more comprehensive than assumed and one should not underestimate the intelligence abilities of the American government because it is also involved in many other conspiracies.

The defence strategy uses a simple principle: critical arguments are dismissed by the assumption of further conspiracies. Everything that speaks against the conspiracy is turned into evidence for the conspiracy. In other words, no fact can disprove the theory. Conspiracy theories are in principle unfalsifiable.

It may come as a surprise that even in science such seemingly irrational immunization strategies are used to save theories from impending refutation. Imre Lakatos (1970, p. 116) states: "no experimental result can ever kill a theory; any theory can be saved from counterinstances either by some auxiliary hypothesis or by a suitable reinterpretation of its terms". So-called ad hoc hypotheses, i.e. additional assumptions, are introduced or the facts are simply reinterpreted so that they no longer contradict the theory. Does it mean that conspiracy theories are not as irrational as they seem at first glance, or does science use a conspirational methodology to protect itself from refutation? Sometimes it happens that unexplainable phenomena occur which stand in contradiction to an established theory. Thomas Kuhn (1970) calls such phenomena *anomalies*. In some cases an anomaly can be eliminated by the addition of an ad hoc hypothesis. Lakatos (1970, p. 100 f.) explains this method with the following example:

By using the laws of Newtonian mechanics and the law of gravity, we can calculate the motions of the planets with the highest precision. Sometimes, however, orbital anomalies are discovered, as was the case in the nineteenth century with the planet Uranus, whose observed positions deviated inexplicably from the predicted orbit. Observation and theory were at odds. From this contradiction we can conclude: Either the theory is wrong or an error was made in observation or measurement. The anomaly could be eliminated by a simple additional assumption: Astronomers postulated the existence of another planet beyond Uranus, which disturbed the orbit of Uranus by its gravitational force and thus caused the deviations. Based on the orbital deviations, it was possible to calculate the mass and orbital elements of the new planet. In fact, the new planet, later named Neptune, was discovered in 1846 by the astronomer Johann Gottfried Galle. But what would have happened if no planet had been observed at the calculated position? Lakatos speculates how history would then have proceeded. Would the laws of celestial mechanics have been discarded because the prediction had failed? Hardly. One might have assumed that the planet had been obscured by a cloud of cosmic dust and therefore could not be discovered. But even this hypothesis could be tested by sending a space probe to the suspected dust cloud, which would then be registered by the probe. Let us further assume that such a detection fails. Would the laws of Newtonian mechanics then be falsified? No! Because one could add other auxiliary hypotheses to immunize the theory against refutation. For example, a magnetic field could have disturbed the probe's measuring instruments. The chain of auxiliary hypotheses could be continued indefinitely.

This immunization strategy was successfully applied in astronomy for centuries: By introducing new auxiliary hypotheses, the geocentric worldview could be maintained from antiquity to the Middle Ages and preserved from refutation. Thomas Kuhn (1970, p. 64 f.) attributes to scientific paradigms a tendency of persistence that protects against a paradigm shift: Conceptual categories are remodelled "until the initially anomalous has become the anticipated".

This excursion to philosophy of science shows that conspiracy theories seem to have a lot in common with scientific theories. They use the same method to defend their theory against objections. However, this should not be misunderstood as a justification or ennoblement of conspiracy theories. Immunization through the introduction of ad hoc hypotheses, especially when applied repeatedly, is a pathological symptom of a degenerating theory development. The auxiliary hypotheses introduced in the planetary example are still empirically testable, whereas in the case of the Apollo conspiracy they cannot be checked and are self-confirming: Any evidence against the conspiracy is conceived as part of an even larger conspiracy. The paranoid worldview can only be sustained by a multitude of assumptions and hypotheses, each of which is quite improbable. Even if we grant some initial probability to these assumptions, each of which holds independently, mathematics tells us that the probability of a conjunction of a large number of statistically independent hypotheses tends toward zero (Zoglauer 1993, p. 209). And even if everyone involved in the conspiracy is highly unlikely to let the secret out, the more people involved, the less likely it is that the conspiracy can be kept secret.

It is surprising that even academically educated intellectuals, and among them are respected philosophers and social scientists, are sympathetic to conspiracy theories and do not want to call them irrational. They complain that conspiracy theories are stigmatized, demonized, and discredited as paranoid thinking by the public and the media (Dentith 2019; Hagen 2020; Meyer 2018; Thalmann 2019). Behind this astonishing tolerance of conspirational thinking lies a postmodern relativism and a general distrust of official government accounts. Kim Meyer quotes the conspiracy theorist Mathias Bröckers as a witness of the epistemological importance of a "critical conspirology". She argues that our highly complex and conspirational world could only be understood through an "adequate conspiracy theory" (Meyer 2018, p. 49). Thalmann (2019, p. 5 f.) and Meyer (2018, p. 184 f.) refer to Foucault's theory of knowledge as a social construct, according to which discursive practices and power relations determine what is true and what is false. What is true is, according to this theory, what is socially accepted and can be discursively enforced:

"Nothing distinguishes the conspiracist from a social critic, the conspiracy theorist from the intellectual. It is a question of recognition." (Meyer 2018, p. 34) One may conclude from this that conspiracy theories just need to be generally accepted, then they are true. Conspiracy theories are therefore not irrational, but legitimize themselves as "alternative symbolic worlds of meaning" (Walter 2014, p. 183), "competing interpretations of reality" (Fallon 2019, p. 165), or as "different epistemological commitments" (Jane and Fleming 2014, p. 128). Conspiracists are thus celebrated as fighters against hegemonic discourses of truth. These references to the academic conspiracy literature clearly show how widespread post-factual thinking meanwhile has become among intellectuals and scholars.

1.8   Science Denial and Pseudoscience

Among conspiracy theorists, but also among anti-vaxxers and climate change deniers, scientific expertise is contested. Stephen Turner writes: "expert knowledge masquerades as neutral fact, accessible to all sides of a debate; but it is merely another ideology" (Turner 2014, p. 20). Admittedly, Turner is not an anti-vaxxer or conspiracy believer, but a recognized sociologist of science, which shows that scientific skepticism is a widely held attitude in academia (see Zoglauer 2021). Steve Fuller, another sociologist of science, regards expert knowledge as a form of power: "expertise is the most potent non-violent form of power available" (Fuller 2018, p. 161). A critical attitude towards expert opinion may be justified in some cases, because experts are in principle fallible and their judgment is sometimes guided by interests. Naomi Oreskes and Erik Conway (2010) show how in the United States, from the 1970s to the 1990s, the cigarette industry paid scientists and ordered favorable reports to prove that there were no health risks from secondhand smoke. Of course, one cannot generalize such individual cases and suspect that experts are in general biased and corrupt. But when science is placed under general suspicion and scientific findings are distrusted in principle, we can speak of *science denial*, which is not only anti-scientific but also irrational.

In the COVID-19 crisis, a movement emerged with the anti-vaxxers and Covid deniers who questioned the scientific consensus on Covid and called for resistance to governmental policy in demonstrations. Besides the Covid deniers, there are also climate change deniers, evolution deniers, AIDS deniers, and Holocaust deniers who organize themselves in internet forums and advocate pseudoscientific theories. For Hansson (2017), science denial is a specific form of pseudoscience because it is in opposition to established scientific knowledge. Creationists reject Darwin's theory of evolution, anti-vaxxers often follow esoteric teachings of natural healing, and opponents of Einstein's theory of relativity persist in the Newtonian worldview, believing that space and time are absolute. Fact denial is more than just a skeptical questioning of scientific findings: it is the refusal to take any notice of empirical evidence (Washington and Cook 2011, p. 1 ff.).

John Cook characterizes science denial by five features, which he explains using the example of climate change denial (Cook 2017; Farmer and Cook 2013; Washington and Cook 2011):

1. *Cherry picking:* Climate change deniers selectively pick out those figures and trends from the statistical data on global temperature development that confirm their claim that there is no anthropogenic climate change, while they ignore or downplay contrary trends.
2. *Impossible expectations:* Another strategy is to shift the burden of proof to climate scientists and to apply excessively strict standards of accuracy and predictive power to the models. As long as there is no certain proof of climate change, it cannot be taken seriously, it is claimed. Farmer and Cook (2013, p. 454) see this as a misunderstanding of the scientific method, as climate models are always subject to uncertainty: "This strategy misrepresents the nature of science, arguing that we should wait for 100% proof before acting. This is not how science operates and is especially not how we operate in real life when managing risks. To wait for 100% certainty is to never act."
3. *False experts:* In order to counter the broad consensus among climate researchers, pseudo-experts are cited who hold a different opinion and support the view that there is no man-made climate change. The supposed experts usually turn out to be amateur scientists or scientists from other disciplines who are not competent in the field of climate research.
4. *Logical fallacies:* One argument of climate change deniers is that there has always been natural climate change, that the current global temperature increase has natural causes and is merely a statistical fluctuation. This is a false inference from an effect to a specific cause. Farmer and Cook (2013, p. 452 ff.) detect many such false conclusions in the arguments of climate change deniers.
5. *Conspiracy theories*: Science deniers like to see themselves as victims of a conspiracy, claiming that the truth is suppressed and that the experts are corrupt or follow political interests.

Good science is characterized by objectivity, empirical adequacy, falsifiability, reproducibility, explanatory power, accuracy, coherence and systematicity. For Popper (2002) there is a clear dividing line between science and pseudoscience: scientific theories are falsifiable, pseudoscientific theories are not falsifiable. A theory is falsifiable if it is possible in principle to find empirical data that contradict the theory. Theories must be able to fail in the face of experience. Popper (1962, p. 37) presents three examples of theories that he believes are not falsifiable: astrology, the Marxist theory of history, and psychoanalysis. Astrological predictions, such as those found in horoscopes, are usually so vague and imprecisely formulated that, with a little good will, one can always see them confirmed. The same holds of the theory of historical materialism: Marx and Engels predicted a socialist revolution, in the wake of which capitalism will be replaced by a dictatorship of the proletariat and afterwards by a class-free society. Since no concrete date is given for the announced revolution, this event can be postponed further and further into the future, so that the prediction cannot be refuted. Popper also accuses Freudian psychoanalysis of avoiding empirical verification. He compares Freud's theory of the ego, id, and superego with Homeric myths, which have little in common with science. Other examples of pseudoscientific theories are alchemy, ufology, parapsychology, phrenology, homeopathy, Lyssenkoism, esotericism, occultism and Intelligent Design.

Popper's criterion of demarcation has been criticized because the history of science has shown that contradictions between theory and experience do not always lead to the rejection of a theory; rather, as we have seen, theories can protect themselves from refutation and evolve in an "ocean of anomalies" (Lakatos 1976, p. 24). Falsifiability is an important but not the only decisive criterion to distinguish science from pseudoscience. To distinguish both, it is better not to use criteria for the scientific character of theories but to list characteristics of pseudoscience. Besides non-falsifiability, pseudoscience can be marked by the following features: anecdotal justifications, simplifications, and also the lack of progress, verifiability, criticizability, and reproducibility (Lack and Rousseau 2016; Mahner 2007; Vollmer 1993). Often, adherents of pseudoscientific theories are characterized by a selective perception that only takes into account those phenomena that fit into their own worldview, while contradictory evidence is ignored. Gerhard Vollmer (1993, p. 22) sees the lack of critical thinking as the main reason for the inclination to pseudoscience:

> One feature that is particularly common in pseudoscience is the attempt to protect one's theory from criticism. This can be done by dogmatic adherence to assertions, by weakening the claims ("mostly"), by redefining the terms, or by downplaying the problems. It is also possible that a theory is constructed from the outset in such a sophisticated way that it cannot be tested at all and, above all, cannot be refuted.

What pseudoscientific theories do not lack is their amazing ability to explain phenomena: Some esoteric theories even claim to be able to explain *everything*. It is precisely this absence of self-restraint and modesty that distinguishes them from serious scientific theories.

Sociologists of science, on the other hand, focus on a different demarcation criterion: They claim that the distinguishing feature of pseudosciences consists in their rejection and stigmatization as unscientific by the scientific community (Hecht 2018, p. 8). It is argued that the standards of science have changed historically, therefore the above-mentioned demarcation criteria have no objective status, but are merely the result of a social practice. Implicit in this argument is the accusation that scientists, because of their position of power, exclude unwelcome competitors and thereby discriminate against them. Frequently, this critique of science is also linked with the call to open up to alternative views and to accept indigenous knowledge in order to overcome latent eurocentrism. However, if objective methodological standards no longer count and subjective beliefs, feelings and anecdotal accounts are to be recognized as "extended facts", as Silvio Funtowicz and Jerome

Ravetz (1993, p. 115 f.) demand in their draft of a "post-normal science", or if an "anything goes" (Feyerabend 1976) is propagated, an anti-scientific trend is created that leads to post-truth.

1.9 Fake News

People with a skeptical attitude towards science and the mainstream media are particularly susceptible to conspiracy narratives and fake news. Especially in times of crisis like the COVID-19 pandemic, when the citizens are disturbed and are looking for culprits that can be made responsible for the crisis, pseudoscientific explanations fall on fertile ground. Many people cannot cope with such complexities and are searching for simple explanations. Who knows what a spike protein is and what an R_0 number is and how a virus damages human cells? Rumors circulate: Corona viruses were allegedly bred in a Chinese laboratory. Or wasn't it a secret American lab funded by Bill Gates? Does the Corona virus exist at all or is it just a fabrication of our politicians and the "lying press" to restrict our basic freedoms in the name of fighting a pandemic? Or it is claimed that the vaccines could cause genetic mutations and make us sick. If such fake news is believed to be true and becomes entrenched in people's minds, alternative patterns of interpretation can arise and reality is perceived differently.

Fake news is defined as news that is spread with the intention to deceive or influence opinion (Götz-Votteler and Hespers 2019, p. 19; Hendricks and Vestergaard 2019, p. 63; Schmid et al. 2018, pp. 74, 77). Consequently, it is characterized by the features of falsity and the intention to deceive.[3] Fake news often mix truth and falsity, with the effect of confusion and disinformation. Unlike a lie, fake news is not only addressed to the immediate listener or reader, but it wants to be shared and retold (Rini 2017, p. E44). This viral element is the third distinguishing feature of fake news. Fake reports are released out into the world like a virus, mainly on social media, in the hope that they will spread quickly and more people will take it at face value. Axel Gelfert (2018, p. 94) distinguishes fake news from other types of false news such as rumors, gossip, hoaxes, and urban legends. He defines fake news as follows: "Fake news is the deliberate presentation of (typically) false or misleading claims as *news,* where the claims are misleading *by design.*" (Gelfert 2018, p. 108) One characteristic of fake news that distinguishes it from other types of misinformation and disinformation is its design. Fake news is like a Trojan horse: it imitates the news format, giving itself a serious appearance, thus gains the trust of the recipients and is gratefully received and further disseminated (Rini 2017, p. E45).

Fake news is not a new phenomenon. It existed even before the invention of the Internet (Frank 2018b; Gelfert 2018, p. 90 f.; Gorbach 2018; McIntyre 2018, pp. 97–104; Schmid et al. 2018, p. 72 f.). Due to its communicative structure, social media act as a propagator

---

[3] Various definitions of fake news circulate in the literature. On the question of which of these definitions are adequate see: Zimmermann and Kohring (2018).

and accelerator for the dissemination of false information (Bernal 2018, pp. 241, 244 f.). *Trolls* are often involved in the spread of fake news, deliberately setting out fake news as bait and waiting for gullible people to bite and spreading the message further (Bernal 2018, p. 228). *Fake people* can open fake accounts, create a fake profile, and infiltrate a social network undetected to influence people's thoughts and actions. For example, entire troll networks and troll farms worked to manipulate the Brexit referendum in the UK and the 2016 US presidential election (Bernal 2018, p. 241).

Fake news makes use of a post-truth epistemology: to appear more credible it is embedded in a narrative context and a frame, so that truth and falsity merge and become indistinguishable. Fake news creates a feeling of being true. This is why they are also called *fake narratives*. Paul Bernal explains how fake news and fake narratives work:

> Creation of a fake narrative is subtler and can be both more dangerous and more damaging. It might start with a real story and take it out of context, or show only some parts of it and use this to create a narrative that is in essence false, though that falsity is hard to pin down, let alone conclusively prove. (...) Fake news can be more 'believable' than the real thing: the aphorism that truth is stranger than fiction has some logic behind it. When a story is created – whether an individual piece of fake news or a fake narrative – it can be worked upon to ensure that it is logical, coherent and easily followed. Holes in the plot can be filled. Twists in that plot can be signposted and counter arguments predicted and opposed. A carefully crafted story is not as messy as reality. It does not have so many seemingly inexplicable warts – so it can make 'sense' where reality or the real explanation seem counterintuitive. (Bernal 2018, pp. 235, 239)

The readiness to believe fake news is based on second-hand knowledge. Regina Rini (2017, p. E46) therefore speaks of an "epistemology of testimony": "A person counts as believing a proposition on the basis of testimony when she believes it *because* the proposition was presented to her by another person." Some people trust what they read on the Internet or what good friends tell them and they do not critically question a report. Untruthfulness is not detected because people do not look closely enough. A report is considered credible if it fits coherently into an existing belief system. For example, if a supporter of the Republican party who has always been suspicious of Barack Obama and has never agreed with his politics hears a rumor that Obama is in fact a Muslim, born in Kenya, and is therefore not an American citizen, and thus was never legitimately president, he will believe that rumor more readily than a Democratic supporter. The seeds of doubt thrive best in people who already possess a biased ideological worldview. Rini calls this an "epistemic partisanship" (Rini 2017, p. E50). One is more likely to value like-minded friends as trustworthy sources of knowledge than strangers who hold different beliefs, which in turn reinforces conformist thinking within an echo chamber.

Fake news and fake narratives have a truth-destroying effect. They entice recipients to take false reports as true. However, an increased and systematic dissemination of fake news can also have more far-reaching consequences: People or social groups may interpret facts and events differently which has the effect that they can no longer distinguish between true and false, and fall prey to epistemic disorientation. Fake news has the long-term effect that news is generally distrusted (Mathiesen 2019, p. 168).

1.10 Democracy and Truth

Surprisingly, some people do not see fake news as a threat to democracy, but regard it as a legitimate expression of free speech. For example, Joshua Habgood-Coote (2019, p. 1054) writes: "It is a familiar liberal idea that people have a right to believe what they want to, which generates a correlative duty for individuals and states not to interfere with others' beliefs." If one wanted to prevent the spread of fake news, one would, in his opinion, prevent the free exchange of information. Habgood-Coote therefore sees a thought police at work in the fight against fake news and speaks of "epistemic policing". The term "fake news" supposedly stigmatizes and discriminates against people who simply want to express their own opinion and their own point of view. Hence the title of his essay, "Stop talking about fake news!" He gives the advice to avoid the term at all costs: "If you use weaponized terms, you run the risk of hurting people." (Habgood-Coote 2019, p. 1054).

Like Habgood-Coote, David Coady (2019) also believes that the real danger doesn't come from fake news but from the pejorative use of the term "fake news" and that we should therefore stop using this term. Both see it as a discriminatory use of language that seeks to discredit and suppress oppositional expressions of opinion. Coady even sees fake news in a positive light: media users today have access to more information than ever before. And more information means: more true and more false information (Coady 2019, p. 51). Therefore, Coady argues, we should be happy about this increase in information. The accompanied increase in misinformation seems for him to be a small price to pay for the benefit of free access to knowledge: "That's part of the price we pay, and it seems to me that it's been a price worth paying." (Coady 2019, p. 51).

One objection to Coady's argument is this: Free access to more information does not automatically lead to an increase in knowledge. This is because information is not the same as knowledge (Zoglauer 2020, p. 78). Knowledge presupposes the ability to distinguish between true and false information and to place it correctly in a context (Zoglauer 2020, p. 80). The removal of gatekeepers has fundamentally changed the epistemic situation of media users. Not only do we receive more false news, in a post-truth world filter effects and echo chambers make it increasingly difficult for us to distinguish between truth and falsehood. Coady and Habgood-Coote are arguing self-contradictory when, on the one hand, they see a "policing device" in the term "fake news" (Coady 2019, p. 40), but on the other hand, they themselves act as language police and want to ban the use of this term.

Fake news cannot be justified by appealing to the freedom of information. Anyone seeking information wants to receive *true*, not false information. Fake news is also not protected by the right to freedom of expression. After all, its producers do not want to contribute to an open and unbiased debate on controversial issues or unorthodox opinions. Rather, they seek to prevent free debate by operating not through the means of factual argument, but through the means of deception. The aim here is not to give a voice to oppressed groups, but to suppress the voice of truth (Mathiesen 2019, p. 174 f.).

Does fake news pose a threat to democracy? One might think not. After all, democratic elections are based on majority decisions. Even if some citizens are misinformed, a minority cannot decide elections. This argument is based on what is known as the *Condorcet Jury Theorem*. The French philosopher, mathematician, and politician Antoine Condorcet (1743–1794) was an ardent supporter of the revolution and a fighter for democracy. He set up the following thought experiment (Goodin and Spiekermann 2018, p. 17 ff.): a jury consisting of n persons is to reach a verdict. It is assumed that the persons decide independently of each other and that there are only two possibilities for the decision, namely to judge true or false. If each jury member reaches a true verdict with a probability higher than 50%, then the probability of reaching a correct overall decision increases with the number of jury members. With two people, there is always a risk that one or both of them will make a wrong decision. But with three or more people, the risk of a collective wrong verdict decreases. Democratic elections therefore have an equalizing tendency.

However, the result can easily flip as soon as the probability of a single voter making the right decision falls below 50%. Then the probability of a wrong verdict by the whole jury tends towards 1 when the number of votes increases. Therefore, when fake news occurs on a massive scale and influences the opinion of a large number of voters, it may well have a damaging effect on democracy. Indeed, the Brexit vote in the UK and the 2016 US presidential election were influenced by a massive disinformation campaign. Robert Goodin and Kai Spiekermann (2018, p. 331) conclude:

> False information designed to alter political attitudes is likely to undermine the reasoning of otherwise competent reasoners, leading them to incorrect conclusions and to vote in incorrect ways. Political lies, after all, attempt to change the way people behave in the voting booth. If those people are 'otherwise competent reasoners' (i.e. voters who would otherwise be likely to vote correctly), the lies changing their votes would most often change them for the worse, epistemically speaking.

Fake news increases the likelihood that individual citizens will judge wrongly. The more fake news is spread and the more citizens believe it, the greater the danger. Perhaps the tipping point at which collective opinion tilts has not yet been reached. But this consideration shows how dangerous fake news is. Cass Sunstein (2008, p. 100) sees the increasing polarization and balkanization of the public sphere as a threat to democracy:

> If the public is balkanized, and if different groups design their own preferred communications packages, the consequence will be further balkanization, as group members move one another toward more extreme points in line with their initial tendencies. At the same time, different deliberating groups, each consisting of like-minded people, will be driven increasingly far apart, simply because most of their discussions are with one another. Extremist groups will often become more extreme.

A pluralism of opinion is important for democracy. A healthy culture of debate is based on dissent and factual discussion, but also on the ability of rational argumentation and communication. When people live in epistemic bubbles, they are no longer willing or able to engage in rational discourse. In a world where each group lives in its own echo chamber, everyone will believe they are in possession of the truth. This leads to epistemic relativism, in which there are only group-specific views, but no overlapping consensus. John Rawls sees an overlapping consensus as a basic condition for a functioning democracy (Rawls 2001, p. 32 f.). According to Rawls, this includes the recognition of fundamental rights and freedoms, the principle of tolerance, a conception of justice that is shared by all, and loyalty to state institutions. When everyone lives in a different reality, this overarching consensus ceases to exist and democracy comes under threat.

Jennifer Kavanagh and Michael Rich (2018, pp. 21–40) cite four alarm signs of impending truth decay: an increasing dissent over the interpretation of facts and empirical data, a blurred distinction between opinion and factual assertion, the primacy of subjective opinions over objective facts, and a dwindling trust in and lack of respect for once generally accepted reliable sources of information. Vincent Hendricks and Mats Vestergaard (2019, p. 104) speak of a "post-factual democracy" "when politically opportune but factually misleading narratives form the basis for political debate, decision, and legislation." In a post-factual society, citizens cannot recognize the truth, either because they are trapped in an echo chamber or because they are inundated with fake news and the truth submerges in it. We are not yet living in a post-factual society. But there are dangerous social and political trends pointing in that direction, perhaps more so in the US than in Germany. These symptoms include the increasing acceptance of conspiracy theories and pseudoscientific theories, widespread science denial among anti-vaxxers, covid deniers, and climate change skeptics, and the strengthening of extremist groups on both the right and left side of the political spectrum.

As we have seen, Coady (2019) and Habgood-Coote (2019) defend fake news by arguing that democracy is based on pluralism of opinion and that there can be no right or wrong in democratic elections; rather, the citizens must decide for themselves what they believe to be right. In the 1920s, the Austrian legal philosopher Hans Kelsen (2013, p. 103) put forward the thesis that democracy presupposes relativism and truth pluralism. For him, truth absolutism, i.e. the view that there is a universally valid truth, is autocratic. Dictators believe to be in possession of a blissful truth, thinking always to decide correctly, and legitimize their leadership with it. Human knowledge, however, is always fallible. Therefore, there can be no absolute truths. People, especially politicians and governments, can be mistaken. If in a democracy every vote has equal weight, Kelsen argues, every voter opinion must therefore also be equally true.

Kelsen's relativism argument is based on a fallacy. For he confuses opinion with truth and pluralism with relativism. Democracy presupposes only a pluralism of opinion, but not a relativism of truth. Kelsen himself assumes that we can never be in possession of definitive truths, but only have more or less well-founded opinions that can turn out to be wrong at any time. Disagreement does not imply relativism, at least not relativism in the strong sense.[4] The democratic ideal consists in a rational exchange of arguments and a common search for consensus.

Theories of deliberative democracy see rational discourse as the source of democratic legitimacy. Habermas formulates the discourse-theoretical principle "that a regulation may claim legitimacy only if all those possibly affected by it could consent to it after participating in rational discourses" (Habermas 1998b, p. 259). A democratically constituted society is based on the ability and willingness of its citizens to resolve disputes and conflicts peacefully through the exchange of arguments and by consensus. Relativism precludes a free, undogmatic discourse because everyone sees himself in possession of the truth. Truth can only be the goal of discourse, but not its starting point.

Jürgen Habermas (1990, p. 58 ff.; 1984, p. 99) counts truth, rightness and truthfulness among the basic conditions of discourse. Fake news violates these conditions of a free exchange of opinions and thus endangers consensus building. In an essay published in 2006, Habermas (2006, p. 18) almost prophetically describes the split in American society that later became reality under the Trump presidency: "The polarization of world views in a community that splits into fundamentalist and secular camps, shows, for example, that an insufficient number of citizens matches up to the yardstick of the public use of reason and thereby endanger political integration." Habermas concludes that "a 'post-truth democracy' (…) would no longer be a democracy." List and Goodin (2001, p. 277) see the goal of democracy in the search for truth. Revealing the truth is a powerful tool in the fight against abuse of power, corruption and conspiracies. If the truth dies, democracy dies. Dictatorships are typically characterized by censorship and state control of the media, because dictators want to control people's thinking and suppress the truth.

In contrast to the Habermasian model of a deliberative democracy, Chantal Mouffe (2000) proposes an agonistic theory of democracy. In her view, the objective of a political discourse cannot be the creation of a general consensus, but rather, in a pluralistic society marginalized groups must be given a voice. Consensus excludes alternatives and only serves to stabilize hegemonic power structures, as Mouffe affirms:

> It is for that reason that the ideal of a pluralist democracy cannot be to reach a rational consensus in the public sphere. Such a consensus cannot exist. We have to accept that every consensus exists as a temporary result of a provisional hegemony, as a stabilization of power, and that it always entails some form of exclusion. The ideas that power could be dissolved through a rational debate and that legitimacy could be based on pure rationality are illusions which can endanger democratic institutions. (Mouffe 2000, p. 104)

While for Habermas democracy can only function on the basis of a rational discourse respecting truth, Johan Farkas and Jannick Schou (2020, p. 155) place rationality and truth under suspicion of ideology: "They are not mere descriptions of a world that is already assembled and created 'out there', but discursive weapons used to intervene and shape both the state and future of democracy." Elsewhere they say: "Democracy (…) is not just

---

[4] For the difference between strong and weak relativism see Sect. 2.2.

about facts, reason and evidence. (…) It is about affect, emotions and feelings." (Farkas and Schou 2020, p. 7) This assertion grants feelings an equal status as truths. The subjective experience of disadvantaged groups should be taken into account in discourses just as objective facts. But if subjective feelings can outweigh, neutralize or even trump rational arguments, then consensus is no longer possible, then the polarization of society is reinforced. Instead of appealing to common interests, differences and disagreements are emphasized. Mouffe may tacitly accept political conflict or even welcome it as a democratic struggle, but she does not provide any proposals for a pacification of society. The utopian belief in a peaceful struggle seems unrealistic. A dispute can only develop a positive democratic function if solutions are searched and a reasonable consensus is found that is acceptable for all sides. When feeling stands against feeling, or alternative facts against empirical evidence, then competing power claims remain, which are fought out by other means than good arguments. An agonistic democracy thus becomes a post-factual democracy, in which objective truths are no longer respected and each group lives in its own socially constructed reality.

1.11 Post-Truth

In 2016, the Oxford English Dictionary elected the term "post-truth" as the word of the year. The choice was explained by the fact that with the Brexit referendum in the UK and Donald Trump's presidential campaign, the previously rarely used word suddenly became a key political term. The term denotes "circumstances in which objective facts are less influential in shaping public opinion than appeals to emotion and personal belief."[5] In the same year, the Gesellschaft für deutsche Sprache named "postfaktisch" (post-factual) word of the year. In that year, the term was mainly associated with Donald Trump's political rhetoric and his distortion of facts. But Trump is not the inventor of a post-factual politics. Lies and a loose handling of the truth have always existed in politics. Yet post-truth or post-factualism takes on a new quality with Trump. For Trump is not simply a liar or a truth-twister. A liar wants the hearer to believe the truth of his claims. But the strategy of post-factual politics goes beyond that. Its aim is that at some point citizens will no longer be able to distinguish between truth and falsehood, they will simply accept opinions unquestioned, and belief will replace knowledge. A post-truth society is a world in which truth no longer matters and serves only a rhetorical function. Post-truth operates as a strategy of detaching discourse from reality. Facts are ignored and empirical evidence is disregarded. If facts don't count, assertions cannot be tested for their truth. Post-truth thus makes critical discourse impossible. Vittorio Bufacchi (2021, p. 350) defines post-truth as follows:

---

[5] https://languages.oup.com/word-of-the-year/2016/ (last accessed 07/13/2020).

Post-truth is a deliberate strategy aimed at creating an environment where objective facts are less influential in shaping public opinion, where theoretical frameworks are undermined in order to make it impossible for someone to make sense of a certain event, phenomenon, or experience, and where scientific truth is delegitimized.

A few years before post-truth was chosen as the word of the year, the American philosopher Harry G. Frankfurt (2005) drew attention to the phenomenon of "bullshitting". According to Frankfurt, a bullshitter is someone whose speech is insubstantial and devoid of informational value: empty talk without content. Frankfurt compares what comes out of the bullshitter's mouth to human excrement.[6] The bullshitter does not care whether what he says is true or false, he just wants the listener to believe what he says (Frankfurt 2005, p. 55; Stokke 2019, p. 265). For Frankfurt bullshitting is more dangerous than lying. A liar acknowledges the difference between truth and falsehood because he knows the truth but still tells the falsehood. The bullshitter thinks in other categories. What matters to him is not content but effect. Bufacchi (2021, p. 349) draws attention to an important difference between bullshitting and post-truth:

While bullshitters choose to ignore the truth, advocates of Post-Truth (henceforth, post-truthers) are more devious: they are in the business of subverting truth. Also, while bullshitters are disrespectful towards the truth, post-truthers feel threatened by truth, therefore they want to undermine or emasculate truth. Bullshitters find truth inconvenient, so they circumvent it, although they would have no problem with embracing truth again, the moment truth serves them well. Post-truthers are different: their aim is to delegitimize truth, since this is the best way to disarm the threat truth poses to them.

To better understand the implications and consequences of post-factualism for our notion of truth, we need to compare it to *factualism,* our common-sense theory of truth. The common view is that there is a real world and objective facts. True statements are those that correspond to the facts. The common-sense theory of truth may be philosophically naive, but it gains general acceptance because we can use it to orientate ourselves in the world and determine the truth content of assertions. In a post-truth world, on the other hand, we can no longer distinguish between true and false statements because facts are no longer relevant. This leads to a detachment of the universe of speech from the world. It is even possible to create alternative facts and construct alternative realities. In factualism, a lie can still be recognized as such by comparing it to reality. In a post-truth world, however, such a comparison is no longer possible because facts and empirical evidence no longer matter. Post-truth systematically undermines trust in scientific experts, the media and political institutions (Cosentino 2020, p. 139).

---

[6]"There are similarities between hot air and excrement, incidentally, which make *hot air* seem an especially suitable equivalent for *bullshit.* Just as hot air is speech that has been emptied of all informative content, so excrement is matter from which everything nutritive has been removed." (Frankfurt 2005, p. 43)

There are various explanations for the emergence of post-truth (MacMullen 2020): One can ignore the truth contrary to one's own knowledge, out of pure naivety or ideological delusion. One can also adopt a skeptical attitude and say: we do not know the truth and persist in faith and belief. Or one knows the truth, but nevertheless lies and instrumentalizes truth and lies for political purposes. A fourth option is to retreat to the position: There are no objective facts and therefore no definite truths; instead, there are many different equally valid truths. I will call these four attitudes truth ignorance, truth skepticism, truth cynicism and truth relativism.

Truth ignorance occurs when people are mistaken, misinterpret things or events, or have a completely false understanding of the facts. A typical example of a truth-ignorant is Cassam's Oliver (cf. Sect. 1.7), who believes in conspiracies. Out of sheer gullibility, Oliver believes what he reads in obscure internet blogs or what his friends tell him. He ignores facts that might refute his conspiracy theory or he thinks they are fakes. Thus he is epistemically biased and disregards the rules and methods on the basis of which we usually gain knowledge.

Although truth-ignorants adhere to factualism, they misjudge the truth and are subject to a systematically distorted perception of reality. MacMullen (2020) classifies this attitude as "unconscious post-factualism." Ignorants follow their gut feelings instead of their reason and are unreceptive to the truth. Group loyalty contributes to a selective perception of the world. All these psychological factors create echo chambers and alternative interpretations of the world, which are promoted by post-factual politics and ultimately lead to the consequence that truth is becoming less important. Only the promotion of critical thinking and the orientation towards scientific methods of knowledge acquisition can help to fight truth ignorance.

Another attitude toward truth MacMullen calls "epistemic post-factualism." The epistemic postfactualist is a *truth skeptic* who says, "There are facts here, but I have no way of knowing them." (MacMullen 2020, p. 100) When asked for his opinion, a skeptic doesn't want to be pinned down and is likely to waver and talk bullshit. Harry G. Frankfurt (2005, p. 64 f.) therefore considers skepticism to be the cause of bullshit:

> The contemporary proliferation of bullshit also has deeper sources, in various forms of skepticism which deny that we can have any reliable access to an objective reality, and which therefore reject the possibility of knowing how things truly are. These "anti-realist" doctrines undermine confidence in the value of disinterested efforts to determine what is true and what is false, and even in the intelligibility of the notion of objective inquiry.

The skeptic distrusts scientific experts. This distrust undermines the authority of science and leads to science denial. Many truth skeptics argue that even experts disagree on some issues, e.g. on the question whether or not man-made climate change exists. And even when they do agree, the skeptics say, they are interest-driven and therefore untrustworthy. When confronted with the latest scientific findings, they just shrug and say, "Who knows? No source can really be trusted, not even the ones that we like." (MacMullen 2020, p. 110)

The truth skeptics capitulate to the complexity of the world that hopelessly overwhelms them. They abstain from judgment or decide according to feeling and group affiliation: "For them, politics is fundamentally about identity and group loyalty (and perhaps also ideology), not factual accuracy, and there is nothing regrettable or second-best about this state of affairs." (MacMullen 2020, p. 111).

The skeptics prefer to trust friends and good acquaintances. Their knowledge is based on hearsay. Facts play no role for them. They judge according to feeling. Due to their indifferent attitude and their inclination of being easily influenced the truth cynic become submissive victims of post-factual politics. The proto-type of the truth skeptic is the undecided voter who does not know which politicians he or she should trust and vote for, but is nonetheless captured by populist sentiments and then votes against the political establishment in protest. Donald Trump won the 2016 election due to his anti-establishment agenda, which mobilized protest voters, who ultimately helped him to win.

Is Donald Trump a post-factualist? One might think that Trump is simply a bullshitter. Kristiansen and Kaussler (2018, p. 18) call Trump a "bullshitter-in-chief." But unlike the bullshitter, truth-ignorant, and skeptic, he knows the truth very well and subordinates it to his political goals. Trump promotes post-factualism, making it a media strategy and a political program. For him, truth and untruth are interchangeable terms that can be readjusted according to situation and opportunity. His strategy is more than a mere disinformation campaign. He wants to construct a different reality by social means. In his world, there is no climate change, the Corona virus was bred in a Chinese lab, and the 2020 presidential election was won not by Joe Biden but by himself, "the real Donald." According to the Washington Post, Jan. 19, 2021, one-third of Americans believe the 2020 U.S. presidential election was rigged, despite any lack of evidence (Del Real 2021).

Trump has an Orwellian understanding of truth: whoever has the power determines what is true. Ian MacMullen (2020, p. 105 ff.) calls this attitude "motivational post-factualism". One can also call it *truth cynicism*. Trump's typical character traits are his anti-intellectualism, his hostility to science, and his lack of respect for truth. Stewart Lockie (2017, p. 1) describes this cynical play with truth as follows: "The post-truth politician manufactures his or her own facts. The post-truth politician asserts whatever they believe to be in their own interest and they continue to press those claims, regardless of the evidence amassed against them." This creates alternative facts. The facts are simply adjusted to suit the political goals at hand. The truth cynic does not necessarily need to lie. There are many gradations of truth, from tendentious reporting, loose handling of the truth, creating a false appearance, and concealing important facts, to outright lying, which the truth cynic may use to manipulate his audience (Haack 2019).

In George Orwell's "1984" words are given a new meaning: "War is peace, freedom is slavery, ignorance is strength." (Orwell 1989, p. 6) In "newspeak" the concept of freedom no longer exists, oppositional thoughts are eradicated or can no longer be thought. The truth cynic does not have to invent a new language or a new grammar. Trump simply creates a new reality for himself by constructing alternative facts. If a lie is repeated often enough and spread in politically-affiliated media, it will eventually be believed. A media echo chamber is thus created that captures more and more citizens.

In Trump's case, one may wonder whether he himself believes in what he says. Numerous political observers and commentators see Trump as a boastful narcissist craving for power who cannot tolerate criticism or dissent (Frank 2018a). Members of the government who express different opinions are fired. Trump surrounds himself with opportunists who don't contradict but reinforce him in his views. Those who live in such an echo chamber, where their own opinion is always confirmed, finally fall prey to self-deception.

It would be wrong to limit truth cynicism to Trump alone. Motivational post-factualism can be found in both right-wing and left-wing political circles that bend reality to suit their ideology. Colin Wight (2018) and Ian MacMullen (2020) blame identity politics for the current spread of post-factualism: "Identity politics is a plea for us to give up on any notion of objectivity in the sense of trying to remain unbiased. This is because identity politics privileges social location over facts. Identity politics demands that we see group loyalty as taking priority over facts. Loyalty under identity politics is to the group, not the facts." (Wight 2018, p. 20).

In identity politics, group membership plays a decisive role. Only members of one's own social group are believed to possess an objective view of reality. Standpoint theory holds that particular social standpoints and their views, preferably those of an oppressed minority, are epistemically privileged (Ashton 2020a; Crasnow 2014). Other viewpoints are dismissed as biased or interest-driven, or are assumed to be based on a false consciousness. As a consequence, the truth content of a statement depends not only on the statement itself, but also on *who* is saying something. But if group membership determines what is true and what is false, then there exist no longer universal truths that are binding for everyone; rather, truth becomes a question of group loyalty.

Post-factualism implies the precedence of values over facts and solidarity over objectivity. That means: Facts are viewed and interpreted from a normative perspective. When Donald Trump, for example, insults media that report negatively about him as fake news media, the term "fake" is for him not a synonym for falsehood, but stands for everything he rejects. The line of demarcation is not between truth and falsehood, but between self and other, friend and foe. In this way Trump's Twitter message can be understood:

> The Fake News is working overtime. Just reported that, despite the tremendous success we are having with the economy & all things else. 91% of the Network News about me is negative (Fake). Why do we work so hard in working with the media when it is corrupt? Take away credentials? (@realDonaldTrump, May 9, 2018)[7]

We have to distinguish between descriptive and normative post-factualism. *Descriptive post-factualism* describes a state or at least a dangerous tendency in politics and society:

---

[7] Quoted from Schubert (2020, p. 196).

- the spread of fake news and conspiracy theories,
- the discrediting of facts and empirical evidence,
- a lack of trust in the mainstream media and scientific experts,
- science denialism and pseudoscience,
- the emergence of echo chambers.

The growing number of truth ignorants, truth sceptics and truth cynicists is an alarming symptom of this development.

Normative post-factualism gives descriptive post-factualism a philosophical legitimacy. It says: There are no objective facts, but only different interpretations. Truth is relative and socially constructed. MacMullen (2020) also calls normative post-factualism "metaphysical post-factualism" and holds postmodern philosophy responsible for the rise of post-factual politics. This accusation is not new and is also made by other critics of post-factualism. Lee McIntyre (2018, p. 150) calls postmodernism the "godfather of post-truth". Matthew D'Ancona (2017, p. 96) takes the same line: "post-modernist texts paved the way for post-truth". However, one must be careful with such sweeping accusations. For postmodernism is not a homogeneous philosophical movement. Its representatives have developed quite different conceptions of truth and objectivity, and they also take up divergent political and social standpoints. Among postmodern philosophers there are many who have been very critical of post-factualism and Trump's politics. Even Ian MacMullen does not want to equate postmodern philosophy with post-factualism, but moderates his critique of postmodernism in a footnote when he writes that he merely intends to characterize a style of thinking associated with post-factual politics.[8]

Nevertheless, there are recurring theses and attitudes among the various groups and advocates of postmodern philosophy that at least come very close to post-factualism. One could even claim that post-factualism did not come into the world with Donald Trump, but was always latently present in postmodern philosophy. Typical postmodern theses include *truth relativism,* doubt about the existence of objective facts, social constructivism, anti-realism, and a critical attitude towards science.

Postmodern truth theory is characterized by C.G. Prado (2018, p. 4 f.) as follows:

Postmodern relativistically conceived truth essentially has it that propositions are true when they are sanctioned by established discursive practices and are generally accepted as true. Being true is held to be a function of the communal construals and practices of the members of a society or culture, construals and practices sanctioned by those individuals respected as authoritative figures in those cultures and societies. (...) 'True', then, is a description that applies only to propositions articulated in a rule-bound, communicative context. This essential point precludes conception of truth as wholly subjective. That is, it rules out propositions

---

[8]"I make no claims about how best to understand the variety of theories and philosophies that are sometimes called postmodern. I mean only to describe a certain way of thinking that has some affinity to those views and that has been linked with post-factual politics." (MacMullen 2020, p. 203, fn. 20).

being true when held or voiced only by individuals and regardless of others' responses or indifference.

Prado refers to Foucault (1980), who postulates a close connection between truth and power: Every society represents a "regime of truth" that determines by its discursive power what is true and what is false. According to this model, there is no such thing as objective truth; instead, there is a "truth war" (Lee 2015) in which each group seeks to impose its own view of truth. If one takes this theory seriously, then descriptive post-factualism is a consequence of normative post-factualism. Echo chambers function according to the principles postulated by Prado: Truth, accordingly, has nothing to do with reality. What truth ignorants believe to be true is the product of a group's social practices, and this group makes sure that its members believe in the socially constructed truth. Dissenters are sanctioned. Individual opinions do not count; only the group opinion is binding. The community of Trump supporters is held together according to these principles. And Trump is a master at using this group dynamic to his advantage. Trump supporters, QAnon followers, and other conspiracy believers think as a collective, not as individuals. For individualism threatens the stability of the post-factual regime of truth. If there were such a thing as an objective truth that was individually recognizable and existed independently of group opinion, that would undermine the authority of the group.

Colin Wight (2018) believes that postmodernism, which is dominant in sociology and cultural studies, has created an intellectual climate in which post-factualism has flourished: "Of course, academics are not the only source of post-truth. But in a significant way, they have contributed to it." (Wight 2018, p. 25) Gabriele Cosentino (2020, p. 19) is even more explicit: "In my reading, postmodern epistemic relativism and the trust crisis of mediating authorities are inherently related, and the deterioration of objective truth in public discourses is linked to both factors."[9]

Postmodern philosophy is confronted with the reproach that it provided the metaphysical and epistemological foundations for a post-factual politics, even if it may distance itself from such a politics. This charge is not entirely unjustified, what can be seen from the fact that some philosophers openly defend post-factualism. With the end of grand narratives, also an end of truth is proclaimed: "Truth is old, outdated, battered by lies with no eyes to see, suffering the tragedy of never being heard." (Koro-Ljunberg et al. 2019, p. 587) Giovanni Maddalena and Guido Gili (2020, p. 50) regard truth as an antiquated relic of a bygone age that prevents pluralism of opinion and open discourse: "Twentieth-century philosophy reached the conclusion that truth always leads, unfortunately, to authoritarianism and violence." Some postmodern thinkers reject the binary true-false dichotomy because it allegedly reflects power structures (Susen 2015, p. 42). Truth claims are interpreted as an act of discursive violence that impedes open debate: "truth talk enacts a kind of discursive violence" (Alcoff 2005, p. 339). Instead of criticizing and fighting post-factualism, it is declared, we should welcome it as a liberating force that resists hegemonic

---

[9] Susana Salgado (2018, p. 321 ff.) makes a similar point.

power structures: "a post-truth world could enable individuals to resist inflexible realities" (Koro-Ljunberg et al. 2019, p. 588). The very warning of the dangers of post-factualism is interpreted as a kind of panic reaction and "masculine hysteria" (Coady 2019, p. 50; Myres 2018). Post-truth critics are suspected of subliminal racism: "post-truth criticism runs the risk of absolving whiteness of its social status by positioning it as just another victim of the post-truth era" (Mejia et al. 2018, p. 112).

Steve Fuller, a leading scholar in science and technology studies and social epistemology, praises post-factualism as contributing to a more liberal and democratic society: "I believe that a post-truth world is the inevitable outcome of greater epistemic democracy." (Fuller 2018, p. 61) As the subtitle of his book "Post-Truth. Knowledge as a Power Game" (2018) suggests, he views science as a power game in which power relations and rules of discourse decide what is considered true or false (see Zoglauer 2021). Consensus among scientists, he continues, acts as a principle of exclusion that suppresses other opinions (Fuller 2018, p. 49 ff.). It may therefore come as no surprise that Fuller is sympathetic to the intelligent design movement and advocates a radical truth relativism: for him, truth is always discourse-relative. He sides with the "post-truthers" who want to change the rules of discourse:

> Unlike the truthers, who play by the current rules, the post-truthers want to change the rules. They believe that what passes for truth is relative to the knowledge game one is playing, which means that depending on the game being played, certain parties are advantaged over others. (Fuller 2018, p. 53)

Post-factualism wants to break the power of experts and democratize science: "In a post-truth utopia, both truth and falsehood are themselves democratized." (Fuller 2018, p. 182) According to this view, not the experts, but the citizens should decide for themselves what is true. As far as his critique of science and his view of truth is concerned, Fuller has a political ally in Trump. For Trump has an extremely anti-science stance: during his time in office he has deliberately curtailed the influence of expert panels, cut research funding and ignored the advice of experts in the fight against the Covid crisis and climate change. Trump has – in the spirit of Fuller – changed the rules of political discourse and "democratized" truth: What is true is what he and his supporters believe to be true. Whoever has the power can enforce his own view of truth.

This short selection of quotations shows that some philosophers are quite sympathetic to post-factualism or even defend it openly. In the following chapter, I will examine various philosophical theories and ideas that advocate post-factualism or at least come close to it. Truth ignorance, truth skepticism and truth cynicism can be easily countered. Truth ignorance is best treated by critical thinking. The truth skeptic and the science denier have to understand that scientific truths, even if they are fallible and provisional, provide a reliable frame of reference which is superior to alternative worldviews. And in democracies truth cynics can be easily voted out of office. But the greatest challenge is posed by truth relativism. Against it only good philosophical arguments can help.

Post-Truth Epistemology

2

2.1 Friedrich Nietzsche: Perspectivism as Post-Factualism

Post-factualism is not only a media and political phenomenon. Philosophical truth relativism has contributed significantly to the delegitimization of factualism and thus supported post-factualism. Friedrich Nietzsche is probably the first philosopher to advocate a decidedly post-factualist position, and he influenced many thinkers after him.

As explained in the previous chapter, truth relativism represents a form of post-factualism. Truth relativism claims that truth is relative to a perspective, worldview or interpretation. Accordingly, a proposition can be true in one perspective and false in another (Hales 2006, p. 1). For Nietzsche, there are no facts, only interpretations (NB, p. 139; KSA 12, p. 315).[1] Just as there are different interpretations for one text, there are infinitely many different ways of looking at the world (NB, p. 63; KSA 12, p. 39). Nietzsche writes:

> But I think that today we are at least far away from the ridiculous immodesty of decreeing from our angle that perspectives are *permitted* only from this angle. Rather, the world has once again become infinite to us: insofar as we cannot reject the possibility that it *includes infinite interpretations.* (GS § 374; KSA 3, p. 627)

> There are many kinds of eyes. The Sphinx also has eyes: and consequently there are many kinds of "truths," and consequently there is no truth. (UF, p. 67; KSA 11, p. 498)

---

[1] In the following, quotes from Nietzsche's writings refer to the Kritische Studienausgabe (KSA), indicating the volume number (e.g. KSA 12). In addition, the abbreviations commonly used in the Nietzsche literature are used to identify his works: GS = The Gay Science, GM = On the Genealogy of Morals, BGE = Beyond Good and Evil, HA = Human, All Too Human, etc.

T. Zoglauer, *Constructed Truths*, https://doi.org/10.1007/978-3-658-39942-9_2

Even physics is for Nietzsche only one world interpretation among others (KSA 13, p. 373). Thus he writes, "that physics too is only an interpretation and arrangement of the world (according to ourselves! If I may say so) and *not* an explanation of the world" (BGE § 14; KSA 5, p. 28). According to this view, logic, too, is merely an instrument for the "*falsification* of all events" by postulating identities where there are only differences (KSA 11, pp. 505, 633 f.). Nietzsche assumes that there is no privileged God's eye point of view from which we can perceive the world as it really is. We only see the world as it *appears* to us. Our view is always subjectively distorted, biased, and depends on assumptions by which we make up the world for our convenience, simplify it, and make it comprehensible. In an early writing, "On Truth and Lie in an Extramoral Sense" (TL), Nietzsche describes how human beings use concepts and abstractions in order to successfully cope and survive in the world. It does not matter whether the man-made image of the world is true or false, because illusions can also serve their purpose. The only important thing is that the ideas are *useful* and make our lives easier: "*Truth is the kind of error* without which a certain species of living being could not live. Ultimately the value for *life* decides." (UF, p. 75; KSA 11, p. 506)

Truth is for Nietzsche "a mobile army of metaphors, metonymies, anthropomorphisms (…): truths are illusions that are no longer remembered as being illusions" (TL, p. 257; KSA 1, p. 880 f.). The concepts of truth and illusion, fact and fiction, are therefore interchangeable; they have nothing to do with reality. Truth suggests a closeness to reality that, according to Nietzsche, does not exist. In Twilight of the Idols, Nietzsche boasts himself that he has abolished the idea of a "true world" (KSA 6, p. 81). Rather, the pursuit of truth springs from the desire to become master of the world. Maudemarie Clark (1990, p. 236) describes this striving for truth as follows: "What the knower wants is not truth, but the feeling of intellectual appropriation or command over the world." Since the world can only be perceived in perspective, truth and falsity can also only be thought of relative to a perspective. The idea that there could be an absolute truth that transcends perspective is revealed as a delusion.

Nietzsche understands a perspective as a way of interpreting the world. It determines whether a proposition is true or false (Hales and Welshon 2000, p. 21). One might think that one only has to look at a thing from many different perspectives, to see it with "more eyes", so to speak, in order to arrive at an objective view:

> There is *only* a perspectival seeing, *only* a perspectival 'knowing'; the *more* affects we are able to put into words about a thing, the *more* eyes, various eyes we are able to use for the same thing, the more complete will be our 'concept' of the thing, our 'objectivity'. (GM III, § 12; KSA 5, p. 365)

"Objectivity" is put in quotation marks in the above quote, because objectivity is for Nietzsche only a relative objectivity. Even if one could change perspective and see with many eyes, so to say, nothing would be gained. A multi-perspectival, supposedly objective view is also only *one* perspective among others and must succeed against other perspectives. The question, which of two world perspectives is more correct, is meaningless, "because the answer would require the prior application of the standard of *correct perception*, i.e. a *non-existent* standard" (TL, p. 260; KSA 1, p. 884). Since for Nietzsche there is no criterion for truth and objectivity, it is ultimately success that decides which perspective is given preference.

Robert Fogelin (2003, p. 73) characterizes *perspectivism* by the following statements:

- There are a plurality of different perspectives.
- Every judgment is made within a certain perspective and is therefore only true within or relative to that perspective.
- All perspectives are equal, none is superior to others.
- The system of perspectives does not contain an Archimedean point or "God's eye view" from which all perspectives can be surveyed and compared.

Nietzsche, however, would disagree with the third thesis that all perspectives are equal. This is because utility determines which perspective we adopt. Truth or falsity do not matter. False assumptions can also be useful: "Not the truth, but the usefulness and susceptibility of opinions has had to be proven in the course of empiricism; it is a delusion, which also our present experience contradicts, that the most possible adaptation to the *real* situation is the most favorable condition for life." (KSA 9, p. 565).

Steven Hales and Rex Welshon (2000, p. 31) believe that Nietzsche only holds a *weak perspectivism*, according to which there is at least one statement that is true in one perspective and false in another. Weak perspectivism is thus a *local* relativism that is limited to a few perspectives and does not rule out the possibility that there are statements that are true in *all* perspectives. *Strong perspectivism*, on the other hand, claims that for *every* statement, there is a perspective in which it is true and another perspective in which it is false (Hales and Welshon 2000, p. 31).

Alexander Nehamas (1985) accuses Nietzsche of advocating such a strong perspectivism and objects that it is self-contradictory. For if every statement were perspective-relative, this would also apply to the thesis of strong perspectivism itself. Then Nietzsche's theory could not claim absolute validity, but would only be a relative truth:

> This view is perspectivism, Nietzsche's famous insistence that every view is only one among many possible interpretations, his own views, particularly this very one, included. But if the view that there are only interpretations is itself only an interpretation, and therefore possibly wrong, it may seem to follow that not every view is after all an interpretation and that Nietzsche's position undermines itself. (Nehamas 1985, p. 1)

But why would it be so bad if there were no absolute truths? In this case strong perspectivism would merely be a hypothesis, a sort of thought experiment that one makes to see if it can be useful for epistemology. Strong perspectivism is not self-contradictory as long as one does not claim that there are truths independent of any perspective. In Nietzsche's view, philosophy should be playful in character, in which one can test daring hypotheses. Nietzsche often restricts his theses, provides them with caveats, or presents them as conjectures. A contradiction arises only if one declares strong perspectivism as an absolute truth. One can understand Nietzsche's perspectivism as a hypothesis that does not even claim to be absolutely true, according to the motto: let us assume that everything is relative and then see how far we get with this assumption.

However, it seems paradoxical to claim that there is no absolute truth and to present this claim itself as a relative truth and mere opinion. In doing so, Nietzsche feeds skeptical doubts and weakens his own position. Kai-Michael Hingst (1998, p. 328) concludes: "He asserts something he cannot know if he is right." Nietzsche is well aware of the problem of the self-referentiality of his perspectivism: "Granted, this is only an interpretation too – and you will be eager enough to make this objection? – well then, so much the better." (BGE § 22; KSA 5, p. 37) But would Nietzsche not thereby weaken his own position by making it a mere conjecture and hypothesis? Doesn't he make a truth claim with his philosophy? (cf. Hingst 1998, p. 29)

It would be problematic if we were to regard all perspectives as equally valid, with the consequence that people could claim whatever they wanted. Such relativism would be self-destructive. People could then insist on their own personal truth without even taking notice of other perspectives. Dissent would be unresolvable because there would be no perspective-independent standard by which we could compare perspectives and determine which truth is "truer." Each person would be trapped in his or her own perspective. To escape this relativism, Nietzsche introduces utility as a criterion for comparison and decision. Usefulness represents a perspective-independent standard of value against which different perspectives can be compared. If two perspectives are in contradiction, the one that is more useful is to be preferred: its usefulness is its truth (KSA 13, p. 283).

> That which corresponds to the necessary living conditions of the time, of the group, will always prevail as 'truth': in the long run *the sum of opinions* will be *incorporated into* mankind, in which it has greatest benefit, i.e. the possibility of the longest duration. (KSA 9, p. 541)

Nietzsche wants to show that truth in the sense of adequacy to reality and truth as usefulness have nothing to do with each other. Often it is precisely the wrong ideas that are particularly successful:

> The falseness of a concept is for me not yet an *objection* to it. Perhaps our new language sounds strangest in this respect: the question is, how far is it life-promoting, life-preserving, species-preserving. I am even fundamentally of the belief *that the falsest assumptions are precisely the most indispensable* to us, that without an acceptance of logical fiction, without measuring reality against the *invented* world of the absolute, self-identical, human beings cannot live, and that a renunciation of this fiction, a practical dispensing with it, would amount to the same thing as a renunciation of life. (UF, p. 95 f.; KSA 11, p. 527; cf. also BGE § 4)

Nietzsche doesn't intend to define truth by means of utility. Usefulness is not a criterion or sign of closeness to reality. Nietzsche does not propose the equation truth = usefulness, because falsehood can also be useful. Rather, usefulness is for him the more fundamental category, while he rejects truth as correspondence. In this pragmatic sense, Georg Simmel (1895) explains how truth can be beneficial to life: Certain ideas turn out to be suitable and useful for action. The principle of utility acts as a selection principle. The ideas that are useful for life are called true, and ideas that turn out to be inappropriate are called false. This pragmatic conception of truth coincides with the radical constructivist concept of *viability* (von Glasersfeld 1987, p. 140 f.): viability means something like usefulness, suitability for life, expediency. The individual creates ideas, hypotheses and theories and as long as they prove successful, they are viable. Viability has nothing to do with truth in the correspondence-theoretical sense. Ernst von Glasersfeld (1985, p. 20) explains this with the example of the fitting of a key into a lock: One might think that the reason why a key can be used to unlock a door is that the shape of the key matches the shape of the lock, that is, that there must be a structural correspondence between key and lock so that we can successfully open the locked door. But a burglar does not need a "matching" key to open the door. A suitably shaped wire is also sufficient for a successful break-in.

The common-sense notion of truth is a correspondence-theoretical notion. As we have seen, viability does not presuppose a correspondence-theoretic notion of truth. Conversely, however, falsity can also turn out to be useful, i.e., viable. This is especially true in the moral realm. Nietzsche encourages us to admit "the necessity of lies" (KSA 12, p. 354): "*We need lies* in order to achieve victory over this reality, this "truth", that is, in order to *live* … The fact that lies are necessary in order to live is itself still part of this terrible and questionable character of existence …" (KSA 13, p. 193).

But if the pursuit of truth is reduced solely to the goal of usefulness, the question arises: what does "useful" mean? And above all: useful *for whom*? Is there an absolute value standard of usefulness or is the assessment of the usefulness of an idea or conception also only relative to a perspective?

What is useful can only be judged within a perspective. Nietzsche admits that usefulness is "also just a belief, a fiction" (GS § 354; KSA 3, p. 593). He thus relativizes the concept of utility and casts doubt on the existence of a perspective-transcending standard. If two people hold different views and argue about which view is better or more useful, each may insist on his or her own perspective. Agreement will not be possible. Further, success and usefulness criteria have only temporary validity: a perspective may be successful and prevail for one moment, but may fail in the next. However, if there is no cross-perspective standard, Nietzsche's perspectivism amounts to a radical relativism, according to which there are different perspectives, but we cannot say which is the best one. Each perspective may claim to be useful and successful. If we assume a competition of perspectives, then it is possible that sometimes one perspective prevails, other times the other. Such relativism is anarchic and destructive because everyone can claim to be right and in the possession of truth, and there is no authority that can decide. Nietzsche creates the image of an agonal struggle for truth, which is in fact a struggle for power. The will to truth thus turns out to be a hidden *will to power* (KSA 13, p. 282):

> the methodology of truth has *not* been found from motives of truth, but from *motives of power, of the wanting to be superior.* (KSA 13, p. 446)

> Knowledge works as a *tool* of power. It's obvious, therefore, that it grows with every growth in power .... (NB, p. 257; KSA 13, p. 302)

> then one arrives at this solution: the "will to truth" develops in the service of the "will to power": on close scrutiny its actual task is helping a certain kind of untruth to victory and to duration, taking a coherent whole of falsifications as the basis for the preservation of a certain kind of life. (UF, p. 247; KSA 11, p. 699)

This striving for power is not simply soberly stated, but explicitly welcomed: "What is good? – Everything that increases the feeling of power, the will to power, power itself in man." (KSA 13, p. 480) Individuals can be seen as foci of power struggling for dominance and supremacy. They act in an affect-driven manner, although affects are also only epiphenomena and creations of the will to power (KSA 13, p. 300). Lust conveys a "feeling of power" (KSA 13, p. 291). Ultimately, the will to power acts as the driving force that uses affects as a means.

The image Nietzsche describes is disillusioning: we cannot recognize reality. Truth in the sense of a correspondence between proposition and fact is an illusion. Facts do not exist, only interpretations. Each person has her own "truths." And the claim to be in possession of the truth is ultimately only a rhetorical means to gain power of opinion. Nietzsche's perspectivism is therefore the prototype of *post-factualism*.

Morality, too, is in the service of the will to power. A lie is justified for Nietzsche, if it serves the preservation or the increase of power. He calls lying and deviousness a character trait of "great men" (KSA 12, p. 202): "deviousness belongs to the *essence* of the elevation of man" (KSA 12, p. 550). For "immorality belongs to greatness" (KSA 12, p. 428). The great man must place himself "beyond morality" (KSA 12, p. 225). For him, the end justifies the means: "he *wants* the great aim and therefore also its means" (KSA 12, p. 406). Politicians are therefore above morality, beyond good and evil, because: "The state and the politician really need a more *supermoral* way of thinking" (KSA 12, p. 532). Nietzsche advocates a Machiavellianism of power and admires "great men" with a strong will who make promises to the citizens and thereby enjoy popularity. The character profile of a "great man" is described by Nietzsche as follows: He must be "violent, envious, exploitative, scheming, fawning, cringing, arrogant, all according to circumstances" in order to be successful (HA I, § 460; KSA 2, p. 298). Even if a politician commits a crime, it can be excused, because, as Nietzsche says, "crime belongs to greatness" and "*all great men have been criminals*" (KSA 12, p. 406). The character traits Nietzsche ascribes to "great men" – the use of lies, deviousness, obsession with power, and a willingness to place one-self "outside morality" – apply in a special way to Donald Trump. Nietzsche thus becomes a mastermind and advocate of post-factual politics.

2.2 Relativism and Incommensurability

Nietzsche's philosophy was like an ignition spark, which significantly influenced the development of relativism at the beginning of the twentieth century and left deep traces not only in epistemology, but also in aesthetics and cultural philosophy. Perhaps one day, when a retrospective history of ideas of the twentieth century is written, we will speak of a century of relativism. It was at the turn from the nineteenth to the twentieth century that many people became painfully aware of the disintegration and dissolution of traditional values. The philosophical systems of the past were shattered and a multitude of divergent styles and new paradigms rose from the ruins. While many people found this loss of orientation disturbing and frightening, others welcomed the gain of new freedoms and celebrated relativism as an expression of pluralism, diversity, and tolerance. Not coincidentally, Albert Einstein developed the theory of relativity at the same time, in which there is no longer an absolute and universally valid frame of reference. There are an infinite number of equally valid coordinate systems with which the world can be described equally well.

In analogy to Einstein's theory of relativity, the American linguists Edward Sapir and Benjamin Lee Whorf (1957) formulated a linguistic relativity principle – also called the *Sapir-Whorf hypothesis* – according to which every language expresses its own worldview and every person is tied to a particular ontology by learning a language and thinking in grammatical categories. Whorf studied the language of the Hopi Indians and found that the grammar of this language is fundamentally different from all Indo-European languages and that the Hopi describe their world with different ontological categories. The world of the Hopi is thus different from the world in which Europeans live. From the Sapir-Whorf hypothesis follows the *untranslatability thesis:* words or sentences of the Hopi language cannot be completely and adequately translated into English because their meaning is determined by the culture and worldview of the Hopi Indians, to which there is no equivalent in our world.

In epistemology and philosophy of science, a similar tendency towards relativization can be observed. Since the meaning of concepts is always context-dependent, every shift in context is accompanied by a change in meaning. This is true not only for the terms of our ordinary language, but also for fundamental physical concepts such as space, time, motion, etc. After a scientific revolution the meaning of concepts changes. When Isaac Newton and Albert Einstein speak of space and time, they mean different things.

There is no God's eye point of view from which one could describe the world objectively and truthfully, rather, seen from a relativistic point of view, there is a plurality of different perspectives, descriptions, and worldviews of which one cannot claim that one is better than another. In relativism, there is no truth across perspectives, but only truths in the plural that are exclusively valid within or relative to a perspective. The question which of two world perspectives is the correct one or better than the other is meaningless, since there is no absolute standard of comparison by which to compare the two perspectives. Every judgment is made within a perspective and is therefore only valid within or relative to that perspective.

Relativism can be described by a simple scheme. Relativity denotes a binary relation and means that something is relative with regard to something else: X is relative to Y. In *conceptual relativism,* X denotes the truth of judgments or the meaning of concepts. Y can be a conceptual scheme, perspective, language, theory, or paradigm. In *ethical relativism,* X is a norm, law, or moral judgment, which is relative to a society, a group of people, or an individual person. *Cultural relativism* is a special form of ethical relativism, where Y here represents a way of life or culture. Culture is seen as the ultimate frame of reference, which cannot be questioned further and to which moral norms and values refer. A moral norm can be valid in one culture and invalid in another, but it makes no sense to speak of an absolute validity of norms independent of a cultural frame of reference.

I want to discuss *conceptual relativism* in more detail because it plays an important role in both analytic and postmodern philosophy and provides the epistemological basis for other forms of relativism. Michael Krausz and Jack Meiland (1982, p. 8) explain conceptual relativism as follows:

> In one of its most common modern forms cognitive relativism holds that truth and knowledge are relative, not to individual persons or even whole societies, but instead to factors variously called conceptual schemes, conceptual frameworks, linguistic frameworks, forms of life, modes of discourse, systems of thought, worldviews, disciplinary matrices, paradigms, constellations of absolute presuppositions, points of view, perspectives, or worlds. What counts as truth and knowledge is thought to depend on which conceptual scheme or point of view is being employed rather than being determinable in a way which transcends all schemes or points of view.

Concepts and their meaning are considered relative to a *conceptual scheme.* A conceptual scheme is a classification system, which is used to structure and interpret perceptions and experiences. Here is a quote from Donald Davidson on this topic (1984, p. 183):

> Conceptual schemes, we are told, are ways of organizing experience; they are systems of categories that give form to the data of sensation; they are points of view from which individuals, cultures, or periods survey the passing scene. There may be no translating from one scheme to another, in which case the beliefs, desires, hopes, and bits of knowledge that characterize one person have no true counterparts for the subscriber to another scheme. Reality is itself relative to a scheme: what counts as real in one system may not in another.

That means: a conceptual scheme is like a pair of glasses through which we perceive the world, but which we cannot take off in order to see the things as they are in themselves. "Objects do not exist independently of conceptual schemes," as Hilary Putnam (1981, p. 52) says. Only with the help of our concepts we can refer to objects, distinguish, classify, count, attribute properties to, or establish relationships between objects. William James (1959, p. 172) compares a conceptual scheme with a "tally by which we 'keep tab' on the impressions that present themselves. When each is referred to some possible place in the conceptual system, it is thereby 'understood'." Conceptual relativism means that if we were to use a different conceptual scheme as a basis, the world would look different to us, it would be an entirely *different* world. James suggests for the first time the possibility of alternative conceptual systems. Different conceptual systems are conceivable with which we can bring sense impressions into congruence with concepts and thus rationalize them. James (1959, p. 171) makes the following thought experiment: If we were lobsters or bees, we would perceive the world differently and organize our experience differently. He concludes that other conceptual categories, even if we cannot imagine them, can be just as useful and successful as those we actually use.

The question which of the various conceptual systems is the true or the correct one loses its meaning, because truth itself is relative to the underlying conceptual system. In this sense, scientific theories are also nothing but conceptual classification schemes by which we interpret the world. Thomas Kuhn (1970) calls such an interpretive scheme for theoretical world orientation a *paradigm*. In a scientific revolution, one paradigm is replaced by another.

According to Kuhn, different paradigms cannot be compared directly because each paradigm represents its own conceptual scheme with which the world is described, ordered and quantified. Even space and time are part of this conceptual scheme. In a paradigm shift not only the content of a theory changes, but also the meaning of its terms. Kuhn describes it as a "displacement of the conceptual network through which scientists view the world" (Kuhn 1970, p. 102). For example, the meaning of the terms space, time, and mass is different in special relativity than in Newtonian mechanics (Kuhn 1970, p. 101 f.). Similar to the Sapir-Whorf hypothesis, we can speak of an untranslatability of concepts. The representatives of two competing paradigms cannot agree on scientific matters of fact because they use different incompatible conceptual schemes. According to Kuhn, the paradigms are therefore *incommensurable,* that means, "there is no language, neutral or otherwise, into which both theories, conceived as sets of sentences, can be translated without residue or loss." (Kuhn 1982, p. 670) The incommensurability thesis is an important feature of conceptual relativism. It can be characterized by three theses:

1. *Plurality thesis:* There is a multitude of different conceptual schemes. There is no absolutely valid conceptual scheme.
2. *Relativity thesis:* Truth is relative to a conceptual scheme.
3. *Incommensurability thesis:* Conceptual schemes are incommensurable (incomparable, untranslatable).

The incommensurability thesis is stronger than the plurality and relativity theses. For it would be conceivable that different conceptual systems overlap and that concepts of one system and the other system are intertranslatable and thus the truth of certain propositions can be acknowledged in both systems. The incommensurability thesis rules out such a possibility. Therefore, concepts are untranslatable. If a proposition p is true in one conceptual system or epistemic perspective, this does not mean that it is also true in another perspective. And even if it were, the propositions can have different meanings and then, strictly speaking, there are two different truths. Similar to perspectivism, we must distinguish between strong and weak relativism. The plurality and relativity theses lead to weak relativism. Together with the incommensurability thesis we get a strong relativism.

The comparability of conceptual schemes or paradigms is ruled out by the incommensurability thesis. Therefore, one cannot say that one system is truer or describes the world better than another system. Applied to cultural relativism, one could not compare the values and morals of different cultures, nor speak of higher or lower cultures. One could not even claim that two conceptual systems or cultures are *equal* or have equal value, because even the determination of equality presupposes the comparability of the two systems and a common standard of value. Adherents of different paradigms would not be able to communicate, they wouldn't understand each other. It is as if they lived in different worlds.

Weak relativism, the harmless variant of conceptual relativism, asserts only local relativity, but does not exclude the possibility of overlapping perspectives and partial translatability of concepts. Steven Hales (2006, p. 1) defines his view of relativism as follows: "Philosophical propositions are true in *some* perspectives and false in others." (emphasis mine) This holds at least for *some* propositions and need not be true for all propositions and *all* perspectives. There can be truths that are acknowledged in many perspectives and there may be disagreement only in a few perspectives about the assessment of the propositions. In this way cultural relativism would lose its rigidity and would not obstruct intercultural understanding and agreement on fundamental issues, because insurmountable disagreement would remain only on a few points. Weak relativism is thus the opposite of absolutism, according to which *all* true judgments are absolutely true.

John MacFarlane (2010, p. 129) explains relative truth as a truth that depends on the context of judgment: "Relativism about truth is the view that there is at least one judgment-sensitive sentence." According to MacFarlane, *one* example suffices to confirm the assessment-sensitivity of sentences. He uses the sentence "Licorice is tasty" as a standard example (MacFarlane 2014, p. 72). As we all know, there is no accounting for taste. Tastes are different. Not everyone likes licorice. Licorice lovers will agree to MacFarlane's statement; others will deny it. The same is also valid for aesthetic truths. Not everyone will find Picasso's "Les Demoiselles d'Avignon" beautiful. Yet, no one will deny that it was painted by Picasso. The former is a subjective judgment of taste, the latter an objective truth. Merely admitting the subject-dependence of aesthetic judgments does not make one a relativist. Kant (2007, p. 35) also acknowledged the subjectivity of judgments of taste. Such a weak relativism as Hales and MacFarlane defend is therefore not only harmless, it is trivial.

Besides strong and weak relativism, we can distinguish local and global relativism. In global relativism, *every* statement is only relatively true and none is absolutely true, whereas local relativism allows for truths that hold in multiple perspectives. Locally it would be possible that individuals, social groups, or cultures judging from different perspectives and on the basis of different conceptual schemes agree on common truths because their perspectives overlap locally. Therefore, members of two cultures might acknowledge the truth of simple empirical propositions such as that the sun rises in the east, that a day has 24 hours, and that there is a full moon approximately every 29.5 days. This presupposes, of course, that the terms east, hour, day and full moon have equivalent meanings in the other languages. The incommensurability thesis is much more radical and excludes such a translatability of terms or an understanding across languages with different conceptual schemes. Incommensurability therefore inevitably leads to global relativism.

The incommensurability thesis was developed independently by Thomas Kuhn and Paul Feyerabend in the early 1960s. One of its consequences is that in case of a theory change, not only the content of the theory changes, but also the entire conceptual framework. The terms that appear in the theory take on a new meaning. As a result, the two theories, the precursor theory and the successor theory, are not comparable, they are incommensurable, because a profound meaning change occurs, which changes, besides the scientific worldview, also the perception and theoretical description of the world. Communication between the adherents of the two theories or paradigms is no longer possible because the semantics has changed. The vocabulary may still consist of the same terms, but they are used differently or defined operationally different. The different interpretation of phenomena and experiments leads to an inability of mutual understanding. Incommensurability for Kuhn therefore means the untranslatability of concepts and theories:

> Most readers of my text have supposed that when I spoke of theories as incommensurable, I meant that they could not be compared. But 'incommensurability' is a term borrowed from mathematics, and it there has no such implication. The hypothenuse of an isosceles right triangle is incommensurable with its side, but the two can be compared to any required degree of precision. What is lacking is not comparability but a unit of length in terms of which both can be measured directly and exactly. In applying the term 'incommensurability' to theories, I had intended only to insist that there was no common language within which both could be fully expressed and which could therefore be used in a point-by-point comparison between them. (Kuhn 1976, p. 190 f.)

We can imagine an extreme case of incommensurability if we consider how we might communicate with aliens, presupposing that they exist and communication is technically possible (Zoglauer 2016). Nicholas Rescher (1999, p. 201) doubts that communication with aliens can be established, because they would probably operate with conceptual schemes that are completely alien to us, and "the taxonomic and explanatory mechanisms by means of which their cognitive business is transacted might differ so radically from ours that intellectual contact with them would be difficult or impossible." In a sense, this is also true of terrestrial cultures. Feyerabend (1976, p. 310 f.), in his exposition of the incommensurability thesis, points to the Sapir-Whorf hypothesis, which states that different languages imply an incomparable conception of the world and a different cosmology.

Meaning incommensurability, according to Feyerabend, leads to ontological incommensurability. Untranslatability has the effect that different cultures acknowledge different facts: What is a fact in system A need not hold in system B, and vice versa (Feyerabend 1976, p. 370 f.). The conceptual systems thus describe different worlds:

> For one certainly cannot assume that two incommensurable theories are dealing with one and the same objective state of affairs (…). If, therefore, one does not want to assume that they are dealing with nothing at all, one must admit that they are dealing with different worlds, and that the change has come about through the transition from one theory to the other. (Feyerabend 1976, p. 386)

In incommensurable systems, one cannot think beyond the boundaries of one's own conceptual horizon. Cultural incommensurability thus leads to an inability to engage in a dialogue across cultural boundaries. If one takes the incommensurability thesis seriously, we would have to regard members of foreign cultures as aliens, so to speak, with whom we cannot communicate and whom we cannot understand. In order to claim that there is genuine incommensurability and that an alien language cannot be translated because of contextual meaning differences, we would have to know the meaning of alien terms and be able to compare them with the terms of our language. But then languages cannot be incommensurable as Feyerabend claims. "On the contrary, if translations were impossible, we would not be able to say that and to what extent conceptions differ from one another," as Putnam (1981, p. 117) critically remarks.

When Feyerabend (1976, p. 357 ff.), for example, explains that archaic cosmology and more recent cosmology are incommensurable, this shows that he has a profound knowledge of archaic natural philosophy and that it is apparently possible after all to gain a deeper understanding of the other culture. Consequently, the languages in which these worldviews are described must be at least partially translatable. Donald Davidson (1984, p. 184) also emphasizes the contradictory character of the incommensurability thesis: "Different points of view make sense, but only if there is a common co-ordinate system on which to plot them; yet the existence of a common system belies the claim of dramatic incomparability." If there were indeed incommensurable conceptual schemes, we should be able to compare these schemes. But every distinction presupposes a common scheme on the basis of which the comparison is made.

Feyerabend understands incommensurability as an all-or-nothing notion: either two conceptual systems are incommensurable or they are not. However, if incommensurability is explained in terms of (un)translatability, then we have to take into account there are degrees of translatability and understanding. The culture of an extraterrestrial life form may indeed be so radically different from ours due to biological differences that understanding becomes impossible (Zoglauer 2016). But our earthly cultures have so many similarities and commonalities that one can hardly speak of incommensurability.

In his later writings, especially in "Science in a Free Society" (1978), Feyerabend expounds a "democratic relativism". In this context he doesn't speak of cultures, or worldviews, but of a plurality of different "traditions" representing different values and forms of knowledge. He outlines a vision of a free society in which all traditions have equal rights and equal access to the institutions of education and other centers of power (Feyerabend 1978, p. 82 f.). Science is for Feyerabend just one of many traditions besides natural healing, creationism, astrology and witchcraft beliefs. Each tradition has its own values that are unique to it. There is no universal standard for all traditions by which we could judge the value of a tradition (Feyerabend 1978, p. 83). We can easily imagine how a libertarian society would look like in Feyerabend's sense: parents could decide whether their children would be taught evolutionary theory or creationism at school (Feyerabend 1978, p. 87). Populists, fundamentalists, and conspiracy theorists would have equal access to the media. At this point relativism, which claims to be tolerant of other forms of thought and traditions, reaches its limits. For in order to protect traditions and avoid conflict, an "efficient police force" is needed (Feyerabend 1978, p. 84). The police force acts like zookeepers to ensure that the traditions do not break out of their enclosures and threaten other traditions.

Similar to Feyerabend, Carol Rovane (2013, 2016) also argues for a strong relativism. Even before Rovane, Feyerabend (1976, p. 371) remarked that there can be no logical relations between incommensurable theories or worldviews. Rovane (2016, p. 268) agrees and puts it this way: "To say that claims are neither consistent nor inconsistent is to say that they do not stand in *any* logical relations – they are, as I shall put it, *normatively insulated* from one another." Suppose A claims that in her perspective (or relative to her perspective), p is true. B claims that in her perspective, which is incommensurable to A's perspective, p is false. Usually, if we hold absolutism, we would conclude that either A's or B's assertion is false, since of two contrary assertions, at most one can be true. But this would place the two statements in a logical relation. Now, according to the thesis of relativism, there is no cross-perspective standard by which the truth claims of incommensurable statements can be compared. Truth is always relative to a perspective, and claims can only be judged, verified, and criticized within that perspective. There are no trans-perspectival logical relations.

I will illustrate this with an example from Baghramian and Coliva (2020, p. 71): Suppose we want to determine how many sheep are in an enclosure. Mary counts 28 sheep, Jane comes up with 30 sheep. We are inclined to believe that at least one of them has counted incorrectly and that the true number can be determined objectively. But suppose Mary and Jane belong to different cultures and traditions, each with a different mathematics and a different way of counting. According to the incommensurability thesis, both are right relative to their own views. Rovane (2016, p. 266) calls this a "metaphysically irresolvable disagreement." There is an "epistemic barrier" between these incommensurable perspectives: "the truths on the other side of it would not be truths-for-me even though they would be truths-for-others" (Rovane 2016, p. 269). Rovane concludes that people who believe in different truths live in different worlds and names her philosophy *"multimundialism,"* which is a kind of "many-worlds theory." But if Mary and Jane live in different worlds, one must ask whether they actually see the same enclosure and count the same sheep. Mary and Jane would then be epistemically and ontologically isolated, each dreaming and counting sheep in their own solipsistic world.

If one takes relativism seriously, according to which everything is perspective-relative, then it follows that the incommensurability thesis cannot claim absolute validity. It is a thesis by relativists for relativists, which need not be accepted by non-relativists. Relativists cannot expect to convince their philosophical opponents with it. Even rules of discourse and principles of argumentation apply only to members of a social community who share an epistemic perspective. What a relativist regards as a valid argument, an anti-relativist need not accept. The relativist thus remains trapped in her own epistemic perspective, from which she cannot break out.

It seems to me that relativists are not aware of the consequences of their own theory. For how should inhabitants of different worlds be able to communicate with each other if they don't share a common conceptual system nor a common logic? For them, it wouldn't be consistent to criticize anyone who held a different opinion. Trump supporters could no longer argue with Democrats because they each believe in different truths. For Trump voters, Trump won the 2020 presidential election, while for Democrats, Biden won the election, and so both groups live in their own reality. A sincere relativist will remain in his epistemic niche and tolerate other people's opinions, especially those of non-relativists, without trying to persuade them or change their minds, "instead he may simply be presenting his position in a logically ordered manner" (Meiland 1980, p. 125), where we have to add that the relativist has his own logic. The crucial question is whether anyone listens to him in his soliloquy and takes him seriously.

Martin Kusch defends a *social relativism*. In his opinion, the social community is the supreme authority and judge of questions of truth and determines whether someone applies the truth concept correctly: "The accepted beliefs of a community cannot be false if by 'being false' we mean something like 'false independently of what anyone says or thinks'." (Kusch 2002, p. 249) Consequently, the community cannot be wrong. What it believes to be true is true. This gives the group a right to claim infallibility, which has the consequence that individuals can err, while the community is infallible. Social relativism elevates the collective over the individual and thereby degrades the individual. When Kusch says that knowledge is always a collective truth, this means for the individual: you know nothing, therefore trust the community! The judgment of the community can at best be criticized from an external perspective. Another group B can conclude that the judgment of group A is wrong (Kusch 2002, pp. 250, 259). But this judgment, too, is only valid relative to the social judgment perspective and has validity only within group B. There is no neutral judge who is able to decide between the competing truth claims. As a result there are as many truths as there are groups that establish a regime of truth through their discursive practices. These groups will engage in an endless ideological power struggle over who is right and who can claim interpretive sovereignty over truth issues.

The Finnish philosopher Antti Hautamäki (2020, p. 172) defends relativism against the accusation that it favors or supports post-factual politics: "There are no causal links from epistemological relativism to the maxims of the post-truth era." He is convinced that relativism does take truth very seriously: "Truth is taken seriously in relativism." And he asserts that a relativist also respects the truth imperative: "tell the truth, look for evidence for all you believe and say" (ibid., p. 173). But what truth is meant by this?

> According to relativism, there is no absolute answer about whether a belief is true because truth-value is relative to points of view. But every statement has a definite truth-value in each point of view. Therefore, to evaluate the truth of a statement, one has to identify a point of view behind it. (Hautamäki 2020, p. 172)

What truth a relativist is committed to depends on his or her epistemic perspective. "Always tell the truth" means for a relativist: "I always tell *my* truth, no matter what other people think is true". That means: even Donald Trump is allowed to tweet *his* truth out to the world. A relativist can't actually object to that. Relativism thus provides a philosophical justification and legitimation for post-factual politics.

2.3   Cultural Relativism

Nearly at the same time as Kuhn and Feyerabend presented their incommensurability thesis, Peter Winch (1964) developed his concept of cultural relativism, which radically questions the superiority of scientific rationality. According to this approach, each culture has its own understanding of rationality that is not comparable to that of other cultures. As an example of an alien concept of rationality Winch mentions the belief in witches and the magical rituals of the Azande, a people living in Central Africa. Scientifically educated people regard witchcraft beliefs and demon oracles as irrational and culturally inferior. We do not believe that diseases can be cured by magical rituals and exorcising demons because we are used to think in terms of scientific cause-and-effect relationships. A demon incantation cannot be the cause of a miraculous healing because we cannot detect a causal relation between an incantation and physiological processes. We also do not believe that rain dances can bring about rain. Spirits and demons have no place in our material world. Our scientific standard is the empirical testability of hypotheses, and testable is for us only what is observable, measurable, and quantifiable. The fact that ghosts and demons do not exist is for Peter Winch not an argument against the Azande's worldview because, as Sapir and Whorf have shown, our conception of reality is determined by culture and language. The Azande have a different language and culture, and therefore a different conception of reality.

According to Winch, we have no right to criticize the alleged irrationality of Azande beliefs, because a critique of the Azande's conception of rationality presupposes a deeper understanding of the alien culture of this people. We could only understand a culture if we shared its way of life: "the concepts used by primitive peoples can only be interpreted in the context of the way of life of those peoples" (Winch 1964, p. 315). Therefore, from our Eurocentric point of view, we should not condemn the rituals of the Azande as irrational:

"Something can appear rational to someone only in terms of *his* understanding of what is and is not rational. If *our* concept of rationality is a different one from his, then it makes no sense to say anything either does or does not appear rational to *him* in *our* sense." (Winch 1964, p. 316)

Rationality, just like moral concepts, is bound to an evaluative perspective. The magical rituals of the Azande may seem irrational to *us,* but to the Azande they are habitual. We must not apply *our* standards of value to foreign cultures, but judge them from *their* point of view. We would have to engage with other ways of life and open our understanding to other points of view and rationalities: "Since it is we who want to understand the Zande category, it appears that the onus is on us to extend our understanding so as to make room for the Zande category, rather than to insist on seeing it in terms of our own ready-made distinction between science and non-science." (Winch 1964, p. 319)

Against cultural relativism is often raised the objection of self-contradiction. This argument was first developed by the ancient skeptics. The Pyrrhonian skeptic counters every dogmatic assertion that claims absolute truth in denying its validity by setting up counter-arguments or demonstrating the relativity of the standpoint. But the skeptic, too, makes an assertion, which he believes to be true. If one claims that everything is relative and doubtful, that includes one's own claim. For the relativist judges from a perspectival view. Thus perspectivism weakens its own position. Sextus Empiricus answers to the question whether he holds a dogmatic doctrine with the following remark:

> If you say that a school involves adherence to a number of beliefs which coher both with one another and with what is apparent, and if you say that belief is assent to something unclear, then we shall say that Sceptics do not belong to any school. (Sextus 2000, p. 7)

The Pyrrhonian skeptic teaches *abstention from judgment* (epoché). Only if one consistently abstains from an opinion can one attain tranquility. For he who strives for knowledge and pursues knowledge lives in permanent restlessness. Only when one abandons every doctrinal opinion can one attain inner peace. But does not skepticism itself represent a doctrine? The skeptics understand their doctrine as a practice and attitude to life. Skepticism and doubt are a kind of therapy for purifying the soul from any kind of dogmatism.

Unfortunately, the cultural relativists have not followed this abstention from judgment. Whoever claims that there are no universally valid norms is himself making a claim with universal validity. If, on the other hand, it is only an assertion with limited validity, which need not be shared by others, then the relativist cannot assume norms that apply to all cultures or that could prescribe how we should behave towards representatives of other cultures. Cultural relativists speak of the right to cultural self-determination and the duty to preserve cultural heritage, thus postulating universal values that, according to cultural relativism, cannot exist (Rippe 1993, p. 61 f.). On the one hand the relativity and cultural boundedness of all norms and values is asserted and on the other hand the tolerance towards other cultures is raised to a universal, transcultural demand. That does not fit together.

In order to compare the values and rationality conceptions of other cultures, a cross-cultural perspective is required, which in turn contradicts the principles of cultural relativism. Presumably, the concept of rationality or a concept comparable to our occidental understanding of rationality does not occur in the language of the Azande. The assertion that the Azande possess a *different* conception of rationality than we do is based on pure speculation or the wishful thinking of some anthropologists. It therefore makes no sense to classify the magical practices of the Azande as rational or irrational. Nicholas Rescher (2006, p. 6 f.) expresses this very aptly when he writes:

> If their conception is not close to a conception of what *we* call rationality, then it is just not a conception of *rationality* – it does not address the topic that *we* are discussing when we put the theme of rationality on the agenda. (…) So it is literally nonsense to say 'The X's have a different conception of rationality from the one we have'. For, if they do not have ours, they do not have any.

Peter Winch describes the magical rituals of the Azande very sensitively and sympathetically. He speaks of the "Zande category of magic". But again, "magic", like "rationality", is a term of our language, it is therefore in fact *our* categories that Winch unjustifiably transfers to the Azande culture. Here again the main problem of cultural relativism becomes visible: on the one hand, relativism claims that the representatives of alien cultures think in different conceptual schemes that have nothing in common with our conceptual categories. On the other hand, the reports of ethnologists and anthropologists suggest a deep understanding of other cultures, as if they can see the world through the eyes of the Azande. Cultural relativism cannot avoid this dilemma: Either cultural views are indeed incommensurable and incomparable, in which case we cannot understand other cultures even approximately. Or there are commonalities and cultural universals after all, in which case cultural relativism in the strong sense Winch advocates cannot be correct. Even if the Azande perceive the world differently and describe it in different terms than we do, we all live in the *same* world and share common hopes, desires, and values.

The cultural relativist views the world from an "eagle perspective" because she wants to overcome the ethnocentric "frog perspective" and believes that she can competently judge the significance of alien cultures from her universal standpoint (Stagl 1992, p. 150 ff.). But this ethnological eagle perspective is not unbiased and value-neutral. Although the relativist assigns all cultures equal value, she criticizes the arrogance of Western culture and rejects "Eurocentrism" as a "postcolonial" way of thinking.

The "Statement on Human Rights" (1947, p. 543) published by the American Anthropological Association states: "man is free only when he lives as his society defines freedom". That means, freedom is defined by society, ultimately by the government of the country in question. In North Korea and in China, freedom will be understood differently than in the United States. For a regime critic languishing in a North Korean prison, such a view may sound cynical and like sheer mockery. Slavery would therefore also be simply an expression of a different understanding of freedom. However, it would be absurd if we had to tolerate all cultural practices, no matter how cruel. Michael Ignatieff rejects the cultural relativists' criticism of the supposedly Western-oriented human rights discourse by saying: "Relativism is the invariable alibi of tyranny." (Ignatieff 2001, p. 74). It is shameful that the right of cultural self-determination is repeatedly claimed by dictators to excuse the brutal repression of opposition members.

The modern conception of human rights was developed in Europe at the time of the Enlightenment and is thus of Eurocentric origin. But genesis must not be confused with justification. The fact of their historical and political-regional origin must not lead to the conclusion that they are only valid for European culture. Human rights are a means of combating tyranny and oppression. They were born out of the desire to live in dignity. This desire is shared by all people in the world.

If – as claimed – people can only be happy in their own culture, then migration would be harmful to cultural identity in the long run. Cultural relativism is therefore the opposite of cosmopolitanism. Instead of overcoming cultural boundaries, intellectual walls are erected between cultures. Indigenous people who leave their homelands would no longer be "authentic". Justin Stagl (1992, p. 152) compares the world of the cultural relativist to an ethnological zoo where the "natives" are locked up and the "keepers" make sure that they don't break out of their prison.

In the age of globalization, individual cultures no longer live in isolation, but are connected through communication, trade relations, and mobility. Globalization leads to an intercultural understanding. The task of cultural studies should therefore be to recognize not only the particularities but also the commonalities of cultures. For Hans Küng (1992, p. 49) the world community needs a basic ethical consensus, because only in this way conflicts can be settled, wars prevented and global justice realized. In his project "Global Ethic" he identifies "maxims of elementary humanity" which are valid in all great world religions and to which the five commandments belong: do not kill, do not steal, do not commit adultery as well as respect parents and love children (Küng 1992, p. 82). Michael Walzer recommends a moral minimalism that emerges as the lowest common denominator from the diversity of cultures. The core morality contains first of all negative obligations such as the prohibition of murder, torture, oppression, and tyranny (Walzer 1994, p. 10). The minimal morality is an expression of a world-wide solidarity, which expresses our compassion for the disadvantaged and oppressed of this world. Torture, tyranny, and political oppression cannot be excused as expressions of a different moral code or cultural peculiarity. Without this minimum standard, humanity would disintegrate into a multitude of cultures that separate from each other.

Cultural relativism assumes that human beings are shaped by society and culture. Their values are seen as products of socialization and environment. According to this model, culture and society determine what is true, good and right. This means as a consequence that our categories of thinking are socially conditioned or socially constructed. There is no doubt that our perception and thinking are influenced by unconscious assumptions, ideas, and concepts. But is *everything* just a social construction? This is what we want to examine in the next chapter.

2.4 Social Constructivism

Traditional epistemology assumes that the world is independent of our thinking and that we can gain an objective view of the world. According to this theory, our knowledge is a more or less realistic representation of the world. In contrast to such "representationalist" theories, various constructivist theories of knowledge were developed in the twentieth century, which postulate that our image of the world is not a representation of reality, but a construct of our mind or society. As a consequence, the world and the facts are *made*.

There are different forms of constructivism: social constructivism, radical constructivism, media constructivism and scientific constructivism, which is represented by David Bloor and Barry Barnes in the "Edinburgh Strong Programme" and has been further developed into laboratory constructivism by Latour, Woolgar and Knorr-Cetina. All these constructivist theories reject factualism, i.e. the existence of objective facts, and differ only in explaining how our view of the world is constructed. In radical constructivism, the world of experience is *cognitively* constructed by our brains; in social constructivism, it is a *social*, discursive construction; and in media constructivism, it is a *media* construction. Scientific constructivism and laboratory constructivism can be considered as special forms of social constructivism because in this case it is the scientific community that produces knowledge as a collective. We will deal with scientific constructivism separately in the next chapter. In this chapter, the focus will be on social constructivism because it is currently the dominant paradigm in the social sciences.

Usually we assume that facts are found or discovered. In contrast to that, for social constructivism there are no "raw facts". Rather, facts are the result of how we interpret the world. And the interpretation therefore depends on the social and cultural context in which we live. This is explained as follows:

> Social constructionism denies that our knowledge is a direct perception of reality. Instead, as a culture or society we construct our own versions of reality between us. Since we have to accept the historical and cultural relativism of all forms of knowledge, it follows that the notion of 'truth' becomes problematic. Within social constructivism there can be no such thing as an objective fact. All knowledge is derived from looking at the world from some perspective or other, and is in the service of some interests rather than others. (Burr 2015, p. 9)

In constructivism, a state of affairs becomes a fact only when it is recognized as a fact by people. The process of recognition is a social process in which social conventions, interests and prejudices play a role. Cognition is thus the result of a social activity. Social constructivism therefore advocates *anti-individualism*. For Ludwik Fleck (1979), it is not an individual but a *thought collective* that is the bearer of knowledge. He defines a thought collective as a "community of persons mutually exchanging ideas or maintaining intellectual interaction" (Fleck 1979, p. 39).

Social constructivism is very much influenced by Wittgenstein's contextual theory of meaning, which he explained in his Philosophical Investigations (PI). According to Wittgenstein, the meaning of a word is determined by its use and the linguistic context. He calls the pragmatic context in which a language is embedded a language game. Communicative action is like a game defined by social rules. The meaning of a word is not the object or state of affairs it denotes. Words do not refer to a world outside language; rather, language is a referentially closed construct.

We classify things by applying conceptual categories, whereby – according to the constructivist view – these categories are socially shaped. Sally Haslanger (2000, p. 34) explains the process of social construction with the example of gender and race: "On this approach, the world by itself can't tell us what gender is, or what race is: it is up to us to decide what in the world, if anything, they are." Through our socialization we adopt concepts and categories, but also values and prejudices. If an individual lives in a group that attributes the property P to an object X, then the individual will believe, or tend to believe, that X does indeed have the property P. Through such attributions and ascriptions, property P is discursively constructed (Haslanger 1995, p. 99). By exposing the mechanisms of social construction, constructivism is able to unmask prejudices and show that supposedly "natural" facts are value-laden. This debunking project also pursues a political goal: it wants to reveal hidden power structures, condemn discrimination and fight for more social justice.

Social constructivism can be characterized by the keywords *contingency* and *convention*. If something is socially constructed, it is contingent and based on a social convention. Contingency means: it is not inherently so, but could be otherwise. Ian Hacking explains the concept of social construction as follows: X is socially constructed if it holds that "X need not have existed, or need not be at all as it is. X, or X as it is at present, is not determined by the nature of things; it is not inevitable." (Hacking 1999, p. 6) If Hacking's definition is taken seriously, everything would be socially constructed. To take an example: Even the existence of the moon is contingent in natural history: it could have been that it never came into existence. We could live in a world where there is no moon, or where there is a moon other than the one visible in our skies at night. But does it follow that it is socially constructed? To be frank, we did not create the moon.

The demonstration of contingency is often accompanied by the disclosure of an implicit valuation and the moral demand for a value change: "X is quite bad as it is. We would be much better off if X were done away with, or at least radically transformed." (Hacking, ibid.)

Since the world can only be viewed from a socially situated perspective, constructivism is closely connected to *perspectivism*. There are no true or false constructions. But not all constructions or perspectives are equal. This is because some constructions can have the effect that some social groups are disadvantaged or discriminated against. Therefore, social constructivism recommends to favor those constructions that lead to more social justice: "When deciding what social categories are, we should just pick the carving that best suits our social and political goals." (Barnes 2017, p. 2419)

Ian Hacking wants to refute a widespread misunderstanding: According to constructivism, it is not individual things and material objects that are socially constructed, but ideas, categories and classifications. Hacking explains this with three examples: "What is socially constructed is not, in the first instance, the individual people, the women refugees. It is the classification, *woman refugee*." (Hacking 1999, p. 10) Similarly, it is not children watching television who are socially constructed, but "the idea of the child viewer" (p. 26). And in physics, it is not the quarks as objects that are constructed, but the *idea* or *conception* of quarks (Hacking 1999, p. 68). However, this still does not answer a crucial question: are ideas, concepts and their semantic contents arbitrarily constructible or are they subject to some constraints? Obviously, it makes a difference whether we are analyzing social or natural concepts. Let us consider the examples of women refugees and quarks mentioned by Hacking. What intuition we have of women refugees depends on the psychological and social attitude of the observer. Hacking calls the term "woman refugee" an interactive kind because the meaning we attach to the term depends on how we interact with women refugees (Hacking 1999, p. 104). In contrast to that, quarks are natural kinds. Their physical properties do not depend on how we interact with them. Admittedly, definitions, units of measurement, and methods of measurement can be freely chosen and are therefore conventional. But once we agree upon a method of measurement, units of measurement, and a framework of theory, the masses, electric charges, and other properties of quarks are unalterably fixed. John Searle (1995, p. 9) calls these properties intrinsic to nature. Intrinsic properties are not socially constructed. Women refugees have, besides socially constructed properties, also natural intrinsic properties. If social constructivism is to be taken seriously as a theory, it must be able to explain the difference between natural and socially constructed properties and make a clear distinction between nature and culture.

In the 1920s, Wilhelm Jerusalem (1982, p. 29 ff.) put forward the thesis that Kant's categories are socially constructed. But what would remain of the world if one subtracted all constructed categories from our description of the world? People without properties? Things without properties? Sally Haslanger warns us not to make the mistake of seeing the whole world as a social construction:

> But once we come to the claim that *everything* is socially constructed, it appears a short step to the conclusion that there is no reality independent of our practices or of our language and that "truth" and "reality" are only fictions employed by the dominant to mask their power. (Haslanger 1995, p. 96)

One must therefore distinguish between strong and weak social constructivism. Haslanger (1995, p. 100) explains the difference as follows: A term is socially constructed in the *weak* sense if its use is only *partially* determined by social factors.[2] And a concept is

---

[2] Thus, the existence of the moon would not be socially constructed because its existence does not depend on social factors.

socially constructed in the *strong* sense if its use is *completely* determined by social factors. For example, weak constructivism says that sex differences are partly biologically determined, while *gender* is socially constructed. But there are also voices critical of the sex/gender distinction. Strong constructivism claims "that the physical differentiations into two sexes are not inherently given, but form a culturally specific classification" (Riegraf 2010, p. 73). According to this theory, sex differences are discursively constructed and we should therefore give up the conception of a gender binary, which opens the possibility of a free choice of gender identities. This position is a form of culturalism according to which human beings are mainly culturally and socially shaped and nature has only a minor influence on their development and behaviour.

In contrast to weak constructivism, which is plausible and widely accepted today, strong constructivism is highly controversial. My critique will therefore be limited to strong constructivism in the following.[3] I will show that this theory amounts to post-factualism, because according to strong constructivism there are no objective facts and also truth is ultimately a social construction and based on conventions.

Constructivism has often been accused of supporting anti-realism and casting doubt on the existence of a subject-independent reality. Constructivists made it easy for their critics because they often used imprecise formulations and did not correctly distinguish between reality that is independent of us and our (socially constructed) *conception* of reality. For example, Peter Berger and Thomas Luckmann (1991, p. 13) write "that reality is socially constructed." Siegfried Weischenberg and Armin Scholl (1995, p. 220) affirm that: "Reality is socially constructed." Siegfried J. Schmidt defines media constructivism as the thesis: "Media do not provide an objective image of reality; rather, they are used to construct realities." (Schmidt 1994, p. 268 f.) And Kenneth J. Gergen (2015, p. 5) draws the bold conclusion: "if everything we consider real is socially constructed, then *nothing* is real unless people agree that it is". Immediately afterwards, Gergen weakens his own thesis by adding appeasingly: "Social constructionists do not say, 'There is nothing', or 'There is no reality'. The important point is that whenever people define reality (…) they are speaking from a particular standpoint." (Gergen 2015, ibid.) We can conclude from this that reality can only be viewed from a particular epistemic perspective or social standpoint and that we cannot conceive what reality is in itself. The crucial question is: Does there exist a mind-independent reality independent of our particular subjective point of view? If one says that reality is constructed, one might think that we can make reality as we like. But we can't turn water into wine, and we can't just wish away things we don't like. So what is constructed is not the world itself, but our *interpretation* of the world: that is, what we mean when we speak of "reality".

Nietzsche already realized that there are many different interpretations of reality. Like Nietzsche, Gergen also advocates a pluralism of perspectives. But not all perspectives are equal; some constructions are more useful than others: "Constructions gain their significance from their social utility. (…) All descriptions are not equal; some seem accurate and

---

[3] When constructivism is mentioned in the following, I mean strong constructivism.

informative while others are fanciful or absurd." (Gergen 2015, p. 10 f.) But what does useful mean? Ultimately, each interest group decides for itself which constructions are useful for them. Elizabeth Barnes presents a criterion for this: We should choose those constructions that best serve our social and political interests (Barnes 2017, p. 2419). For Nietzsche, it is always power interests that determine which perspective is taken. Max Scheler takes up Nietzsche's theory of power and applies it to the sociology of knowledge:

> Neither the so-called pure reason (rationalism and Kant) nor – as the empiricists thought – sensual experience (…) is the *ultimate* basis for the conviction of the existence of spatio-temporal laws of nature which guide all scientific research, but the biological (and not the rational or "spiritual") drive to *dominion and power,* which itself determines both the intellectual behaviour towards the world in perception, imagination and thinking, *and* the practical behaviour of acting in the world and in moving things in our environment. (Scheler 1982, p. 71 f.)

Constructivism retreats to the position that words have no referential meaning, but merely play a role in a language game. The meaning of "reality" is discursively constructed and context-dependent. Therefore, there can be no "reality" (singular), but only "realities" (plural). Lincoln and Guba (2013, p, 39) believe that the existence of objects is merely a matter of definition and convention: "they exist only in the minds of the persons contemplating them. They do not 'really' exist. That is, they have ontological status only insofar as some group of persons (…) grants them that status." Truth is also socially constructed: "Truth is a quality of a construct or construction." (Lincoln and Guba 2013, p. 51) The concept of truth is thus deprived of any reference to reality. A statement is true if it is accepted as true. Ultimately, this amounts to a consensus theory of truth: "If the social consensus is that X is real, it is; if the consensus is that X is not real, it is not." (Walsh 2013, p. 21) What is true or false is therefore not decided by good arguments or empirical evidence, but solely by the majority opinion and thus ultimately by power relations. Such a view of truth leads to *post-factualism.*

According to constructivism, the world cannot be viewed from a neutral objective standpoint outside the world. All knowledge is bound to a standpoint and cannot be detached from a social perspective. Viewpoints are always subjective, value-laden and interest-driven (Harding 2003, p. 302). Scientists also occupy an epistemic standpoint and have interests. For Sandra Harding, there can be no value-free science. Lorraine Code demands that epistemology must distance itself from the myth of objectivity and take subjective points of view into account: "I maintain that a constructivist reorientation requires epistemologists to take subjective factors – factors that pertain to the circumstances of the subject, S – centrally into account in evaluative and justificatory procedures." (Code 2008, p. 722) Francis Fukuyama (2018) criticizes this subjectivization because it would contribute to an emotionalization of politics: with the commitment to subjectivity, feelings would be placed above rational deliberation and thus prioritize the view of one's own group against other views: "The focus on lived experience by identity groups prioritizes the emotional world of the inner self over the rational examination of issues in the outside world and privileges sincerely held opinions over a process of rea-soned deliberation that may force one to abandon prior opinions." (Fukuyama 2018, p. 101).

If one cannot detach oneself from this situated perspective, the question arises as to how sociologists can abstract from their own or their group's perspective and arrive at an objective view. Sharon Crasnow emphasizes that the goal of a feminist *standpoint theory* is to change existing power relations: "Feminist standpoint theory highlights the collective and, hence, political interests of women, and so those features of the social world that contribute to maintaining the power relations that keep women in subordinate positions are relevant given the goal of transforming those power relations." (Crasnow 2014, p. 156) Sandra Harding calls for a new politics, a rejection of the dominant point of view and a partisanship for the socially disadvantaged (Harding 2015, p. 34 f.) The goal is to end oppression and create an egalitarian society.

Feminist standpoint theorists like Nancy Hartsock, Sharon Crasnow, and Natalie Ashton believe that socially disadvantaged groups are epistemically privileged (Ashton 2020a, p. 77; 2020b, p. 331; Crasnow 2014, p. 159). Oppressed minorities could reveal the "true" social conditions and power structures due to their experience. The epistemic privi-lege thesis has its roots in Marxist epistemology, according to which only the proletariat is capable of recognizing the social reality and bringing about change, while the bourgeoisie has a false consciousness (Ashton and McKenna 2020, p. 32). What Marx and Engels call class consciousness, is in standpoint theory the identity consciousness of the social group that determines its thoughts and actions.

It is undoubtedly true that the epistemic perspective of the dominant group is also socially dominant and that minorities cannot gain attention against the hegemony of the majority. But why should the perspective "from below" be superior to the perspective "from above" or be epistemically of advantage? One has to wonder why so many women and people of color in the US voted for Donald Trump when, according to Ashton, they should be politically enlightened as socially disadvantaged groups. Either their sense of identity does not give them an epistemic advantage, or their views depend on other factors than their social position.

Susan Hekman (1997, p. 349) states that women have different points of view and therefore there are also several truths and multiple realities and none of these points of view is privileged. The viewpoint of a disadvantaged minority is just one discursively constructed perspective among many others and cannot claim to have access to the reality 'in itself'. Epistemic privilege is an evaluative term that presupposes a perspective-independent standard of value.

How is the thesis of epistemic privilege justified? According to Ashton, there can be no justification independent of perspective, since every justification is itself tied to a socially situated perspective. Ashton explains this *justificatory relativism* as follows: "Justification depends on "socially situated" perspectives." (Ashton 2020b, p. 330) This means, in con-sequence, that any social group can claim to be epistemically privileged. Even if the thesis of epistemic privilege can be justified, it need not be accepted by members of another social group, e.g. the socially dominant group, since they have their own standards of epistemic justification. Ashton (2019, p. 588) says that "all standpoints are equally correct". Paul Boghossian objects to this justificatory relativism that it is circular:

> The claim "Nothing is objectively justified, but only justified relative to this or that epistemic system" must be nonsense, for it would itself have to be either objectively justified, or only justified relative to this or that particular epistemic system. But it can't be objectively justified, since in that case it would be false if true. And it can't be justified only relative to the relativist's epistemic system, since in that case it is just a report of what he finds it agreeable to say. If he also invites us to join him, we need not offer any reason for declining since he has offered us no reason to accept. (Boghossian 2006, p. 66)

Ashton responds to this objection by supplementing epistemic relativism with additional assumptions (Ashton 2019, p. 601 f.):

- An epistemic relativist should be able to share the perspective of her critics.[4]
- An individual should be able to take on multiple perspectives.
- There must be an overlap between the different epistemic perspectives.

But these additional assumptions do not solve the central problem of relativism: for different perspectives are based on different criteria of truth and justification. What is true in one perspective may be false in another. Suppose there is an overlap between perspectives A and B. If a statement p is true in perspective A and false in perspective B, what is the truth value of p in the overlap between A and B? If a person is able to take on a different perspective, does that also mean that she accepts a proposition of the other perspective as true, even if it is false in her own perspective? And last but not least: If the epistemic relativist shares the perspective of her critics, does this mean that she also shares the claim of her critics that relativism is false?

Ashton (2019, p. 599) constructs a fictional example to illustrate her position: Suppose a person claims that some people have less worth because of their skin color or their gender, while you yourself are convinced that all people are equal, i.e., have equal worth. Undoubtedly, there are conflicting perspectives here. How can we convince a racist that he is wrong? If one assumes, as Ashton (2019, p. 588) does, that all perspectives are equally correct and that each perspective has its own standards of justification, then we could not criticize the racist. How can a relativist convict Donald Trump of lying if she has to concede that Trump simply has a different view of truth, especially one that may be just as correct as her own view? How can you convince climate change deniers of global warming when even constructivists believe that climate change is socially constructed (Pettenger 2007) and that there are no objective facts?

---

[4] Ashton speaks of "epistemic frameworks". I understand it as a kind of perspective.

2.5   Scientific Constructivism

Social constructivism is a central component of the sociology of knowledge, whose central thesis is "that in principle *all* knowledge (the false and the true consciousness) is socially conditioned" (Maasen 1999, p. 13). The founders of the Edinburgh School, David Bloor and Barry Barnes, developed a strong constructivism according to which scientific beliefs are caused by social factors. The *causal thesis* states that the sociology of science is causal, that is, it is "concerned with the conditions which bring about belief or states of knowledge." (Bloor 1991, p. 7) The task of the sociology of science, it is argued, is to explain why scientists hold certain views and theories and have certain beliefs. It does not matter whether these beliefs are true or false: both true and false beliefs must be explainable in the same way. Bloor calls this the *symmetry thesis* (Bloor ibid.).

Barry Barnes postulates a *social determinism* which claims that scientific beliefs are socially determined (Barnes 1974, p. 75). He compares a human being to a machine whose actions are determined by its software (Barnes 1974, p. 78 ff.). A person is programmed by her socialization, whereby culture and society act like "programmers." If we knew how the program works, we could fully explain people's beliefs and actions. In this model, the social influences represent the input that acts on a scientist, and the output is the result of his or her research achievements.

This model of scientific research is in sharp contrast to the traditional rationalist model of explanation, according to which scientific hypotheses and theories can be rationally explained: A scientist adopts the hypothesis that provides the best explanation for observed phenomena, and she chooses the theory that coheres best with empirical data. The traditional model assumes that scientists can work uninfluenced by society and politics and are not guided by interests.

Hans Reichenbach (1961, p. 7) distinguished between a *context of discovery* and a *context of justification*. A scientific discovery may be historically contingent: Isaac Newton could have discovered his law of gravitation a few years earlier or later. For physics it is not relevant *who* discovered something, to which social class a scientist belongs or in which culture he lives. Nor does it matter what mental processes were going on in Newton's mind when he first formulated the law of gravitation. The only thing that matters for a physicist is how the law of gravity is *justified*. Only logical and empirical arguments count for a rational justification. The context of discovery may therefore be of interest for the history and sociology of science, but it is irrelevant for the scientist who wants to justify a hypothesis or a theory.

In the traditional model of science, there is a clear division of tasks between the philosophy of science and the sociology of science: philosophy of science describes how research should ideally be conducted, i.e. independently of external social factors, while the sociology of science is concerned with the context of discovery and takes the social context into account. For the justification of a scientific hypothesis, so the argument goes, the social context plays no role.

Barnes and Bloor reject the distinction between the context of justification and the context of discovery. For them, there can be no autonomous research free of social influences. They refer to the thesis of social constructivism, according to which scientific facts are socially constructed. The followers of the Edinburgh School assume that internal epistemic reasons are socially determined or based on social conventions. David Bloor contends that he can explain why scientists prefer certain hypotheses and theories: the reasons are social causes.

Let us consider an example: the Marxist historian of science Boris Hessen published an essay in 1931 in which he examined "The Social and Economic Roots of Newton's Principia" (1974). He shows how the rise of industrial capitalism created the technical problems that the new mechanics wanted to solve. The cultural and social environment in which Newton worked can indeed contribute much to understand the context of discovery of the law of gravitation. But this does not explain why the gravitational force of two masses is inversely proportional to the square of the distance between them, and not according to some other law. This can only be explained physically. Social explanations can be useful in cases of scientific controversy, where alternative interpretations exist, or where scientists have to decide which line of research they want to pursue. Research can sometimes indeed be influenced by interests, for example when external values and aims become guidelines for scientific research. But there are also disciplines where such external social and political influences are negligible, for example in logic, mathematics or theoretical physics. Here, too, some research aims may be externally imposed, but in most cases the problems are primarily of theoretical nature.

The assumption of a social determination of mental beliefs is a strong thesis with far-reaching consequences. For it denies the apparent rationality of science. Applying the principle of causality to the sociology of science itself means that its theses are also socially determined. Bloor regards the possibility of reflexive self-application as a basic principle of the sociology of science: "In principle its patterns of explanation would have to be applicable to sociology itself." (Bloor 1991, p. 7) Let us therefore ask how Bloor justifies his theses. Bloor presents a number of reasons and arguments and refers to historical case studies. But in his own view, all such reasons are merely epiphenomenal. For whatever theses he holds and no matter how he justifies his theses: His beliefs were caused by social factors. Bloor cannot help but hold these theses because he has been so socialized and because he has grown up in an academic milieu in which such theses receive recognition. This social background may explain why he holds these theses. But it says nothing about whether these theses are true or false, convincing or poorly founded. According to his symmetry thesis, his theses could even be false or simply irrational and still be accepted because we cannot draw any conclusions from the social circumstances to the truth of a theory. It would therefore be pointless to appeal to reasons or try to convince. Bloor is actually undermining his own scientific claim, namely the claim to hold a well-founded theory. Why should we believe Bloor? According to the causal thesis, we would be compelled by causal factors to believe it. But in this respect we are free: We are not forced to take his theses seriously.

Mathematics seems to be largely free of social influences and to present a prime example of a strictly rational science. If Bloor wants to defend his theses of social externalism and conventionalism, he has to show that mathematics is also based on conventions and is socially determined. Admittedly, in one point we have to agree with Bloor: Mathematical theorems are derived from axioms, and the choice of an axiom system is indeed arbitrary and based on convention. For example, one can do geometry with or without the *parallel postulate*.[5] The parallel postulate is an essential part of Euclidean geometry. If you drop the parallel postulate, you will get a non-Euclidean geometry. The postulate therefore represents a convention. In the nineteenth century there was a controversial dispute on the question whether the parallel postulate represents an a priori truth or whether there are alternative non-Euclidean geometries. The dispute over the parallel postulate was not only a mathematical, but also a philosophical dispute. This example shows that the development of mathematics may well be determined by external, in this case philosophical, influences.

The choice of an axiom system provides a theoretical framework, within which mathematicians conduct research autonomously, following the inner logic of the system, by deriving conclusions from the axioms. The choice of the framework may indeed depend on social and cultural influences. We can compare the work of a mathematician to a game: The rules of the game are given by the axioms, proofs are like moves, and the theorems are the resulting configurations of the game. The rules determine how theorems can be derived from axioms. At this point Bloor takes up a consideration of Wittgenstein to show that rule-following in mathematics is also based on social conventions: "Mathematical necessity is just a species of the moral necessity that frequently attaches to the more important social conventions." (Barnes et al. 1996, p. 183) Wittgenstein describes mathematical rule-following with the example of an addition exercise: The exercise is to continue a sequence of numbers by repeatedly adding two to the last number. For example, if the number 20,000 is given, then the sequence 20,002, 20,004, 20,006, … etc. results. Wittgenstein presents the following dialogue between a student and a teacher to explain how rule-following works in mathematics:

> *How do I know* that in working out the series + 2 I must write "20004, 20006" and not "20004, 20008"? (The question: "How do I know that this colour is 'red'?" is similar.)
> "But you surely know for example that you must always write the *same* sequence of numbers in the units: 2, 4, 6, 8, 0, 2, 4, etc." – Quite true: the problem must already appear in this sequence, and even in this one: 2, 2, 2, 2, etc. – For how do I know that I am to write "2" after the five hundredth "2"? i.e. that 'the same figure' in that place is "2"? And if I know it *in advance,* what use is this knowledge to me later on? I mean: how do I know what to do with this earlier knowledge when the step actually has to be taken? (Wittgenstein, RFM, p. 3e)

---

[5] The parallel postulate states that for every line and every point outside the line, there is exactly *one* parallel line through that point that does not intersect the given line.

Bloor interprets Wittgenstein's remarks as follows: Wittgenstein's point is that rule-following is a habit or practice (PI § 199, 202).[6] Mathematics is like a game: mathematicians agree on certain rules and then play according to these rules. Learning the rules is done by example. The teacher explains the task "add 2" using the example of numbers in the number range up to 1000, e.g. 100, 102, 104, 106, etc., and then lets the student continue the series beyond 1000 (cf. Wittgenstein PI § 185). It is inductive learning. The student is supposed to learn the rule from simple examples and then apply it to other examples. Such inductive learning is susceptible to error. This is because finite number sequences cannot uniquely be continued. For example, the sequence 2, 3, 5, 8, ... can be continued by the numbers 12, 17, 23, 30, ... The underlying rule is: add to the first number 1, add to the second number 2, add to the third number 3, add to the fourth number 4 and so on. But you can also see another rule in the first four numbers: The n-th number in the sequence is the sum of the two preceding numbers. For example, 8 is the sum of 3 and 5. The continuation of the sequence will then be: 13, 21, 34, 55, ...

Bloor concludes: "When we are confronted with a finite set of examples we do not extract from them any general idea, rather, we instinctively pass on to what strikes us as the next step or the next case. There is no rational basis for this, nor one that can ever be formulated in terms of propositions assented to by the rule follower." (Bloor 1997, p. 13 f.) To eliminate ambiguity we have to agree upon a unique interpretation of the rule. In the student example, the teacher repeatedly corrects the student when he gets something wrong. In science, it is the *consensus* of the scientific community that determines the application of rules (Bloor 1997, p. 16). According to Bloor, rules have a *normative* character: the social community is the authority that controls the correct rule-following:

It is necessary to introduce a sociological element into the account to explain normativity. Normative standards come from the consensus generated by a number of interacting rule followers, and it is maintained by collectively monitoring, controlling and sanctioning their individual tendencies. (Bloor 1997, p. 17)

Due to this social control there can be no autonomous science that makes research completely independent of society. For it is always the social or scientific consensus that decides whether standards of correctness are obeyed and whether certain theses and theories are accepted. But Bloor's reasoning also has some weaknesses. His interpretation of Wittgenstein is highly controversial (cf. Child 2011, p. 142 ff.; Glock 1996, p. 329). When Wittgenstein says that following a rule is a practice (PI § 202), he does not explain whether he means a *social* practice or claims that rule-following is only possible in a social community. Hans-Johann Glock (1996, p. 329) writes: "firstly, there is no plausible rationale for restricting rule-following to a community; secondly, the *Nachlass* explicitly condones the possibility of a solitary person like Robinson Crusoe following and inventing rules." But even if we impute to Wittgenstein the view attributed by Bloor, it does not follow that

---

[6] PI = Philosophical Investigations

this view is also correct and convincing, because Wittgenstein represents an extreme outsider position within philosophy of mathematics which, if we apply Bloor's central criterion, is not consensually accepted. If consensus is taken as a criterion for correctness, then Wittgenstein's view cannot be correct and cannot be used as a justification for Bloor's thesis.

Learning by examples may be a good didactic method to teach students correct rule-following, but it is not characteristic of how professional mathematicians learn and apply rules. In arithmetic, the rules of counting and addition are explained by the *Peano axioms*. The mathematical rules are not introduced by exemples or inductively, but are defined *deductively*. There is no uncertainty about the correct application. The addition of numbers is performed purely mechanically as in a computer program without reference to a social community. A computer that performs the operation "+ 2" does not have to ask the human community whether it is applying the algorithm correctly. There is no ambiguity or contingency in the application of mathematical rules. Logical reasoning follows an internal necessity which is given by the axioms. The rules of inference, such as modus ponens, can also be introduced axiomatically. The rules of mathematics are therefore fundamentally different from the rules of ordinary language. Language rules are not as fixed and rigidly defined as the rules of logic. Language games have freedom for individual expression. Colloquial language is not a mathematical calculus.

Of course, it is always possible to introduce other rules and, for example, to define an arithmetic in which 2 + 2 does not equal 4, but 5, for example. Barnes, Bloor and Henry (1996, p. 170 f.) mention the example of a modular arithmetic in which 3 + 3 = 1. Which arithmetic and which addition rules one chooses is the result of an agreement or consensus. But within a theoretical framework, once agreed upon, the correct rule-following is uniquely defined.

Bloor rejects the correspondence theory of truth (Bloor 1991, p. 40). Truth in the sense of a correspondence between assertion and reality cannot exist for him, since reality in the sense of an existence of objective facts is socially constructed. For Bloor, truth has only a rhetorical function (Bloor 1991, p. 40). Sociologically, truth is determined by authority: "In as far as any particular theoretical view of the world has authority this can only derive from the actions and opinions of people." (Bloor 1991, p. 41) According to his theory, truth and knowledge are based on social consensus. Let's assume that some day in the future the USA will be governed by a president who believes that the earth is flat and he makes sure that the Flat-Earth Theory will be taught in all schools and universities, so that the majority of Americans will believe in this theory and only a small minority of scientists will remain convinced of the spherical shape of the earth, then according to Bloor the sentence "The earth is flat" would be true.[7] Bloor's social conventionalism thus leads to *relativism:* another society might adopt other conventions and stipulate, for example, that 2 + 2 = 5. Barnes et al. (1996, p. 169) mention a scene from George Orwell's novel "1984" in which

---

[7] Daniel Loxton (2019) estimates that about 1–2% of American and British citizens believe in the Flat Earth theory.

Winston Smith is tortured by O'Brien, the representative of a totalitarian regime. O'Brien explains to him the philosophy of the Party:

> Reality exists in human thought and nowhere else. Not in the individual mind, which can make mistakes, and in any case soon perishes: only in the mind of the Party, which is collective and immortal. Whatever the Party holds to be truth, *is* truth. (Orwell 1989, p. 261)

The omnipotent Party thus advocates a kind of social constructivism, according to which truth is something that is constructed by the Party. Therefore, anything what the Party says, is true, even if it claims that 2 + 2 = 5 (Orwell 1989, p. 262 f.). Unfortunately, Barnes and Bloor seem to agree with O'Brien, whereby in their case society takes the role of the Party: If other social conventions hold, then 2 + 2 could also add up to 5 (Barnes et al. 1996, p. 184). Bloor (1991, p. 5) writes: "knowledge for the sociologist is whatever people take to be knowledge. It consists of those beliefs which people confidently hold to and live by." Thus Bloor advocates a radical *post-factualism*. Evidence does not count. All that matters is what people *believe*. Belief replaces knowledge, and knowledge is nothing else than consensual belief.

2.6 Objectivity in Science

According to the traditional view, research is determined solely by internal epistemic values and is free from external social influences. The representatives of the Edinburgh School sketch a different picture of science. In their view, scientists are driven by external goals and interests (Barnes et al. 1996, p. 120 ff.; cf. Yearley 2005, p. 43 f.). Jürgen Habermas also doubts that there is an interest-free knowledge. For the empirical-analytical sciences, Habermas (1965) diagnoses a technical exploitation interest that aims at the prediction and control of phenomena. In his view, there can be no such thing as an unbiased, impartial, and disinterested subject. Because knowledge and human interests are inseparably tied together, also facts and values cannot be separated. This calls the ideal of scientific objectivity and rationality into question. Sandra Harding and other feminist philosophers of science doubt that a value-free, subject- and passionless science is possible. For them, science as it is currently practiced is sexist and androcentric (Harding 2015, p. 26 f.).

Objectivity is often equated with an aperspectival view, a "god's eye view" (Putnam 1981) or a "view from nowhere" (Nagel 1986). Since human cognition is always perspectival, there cannot be a god's eye point of view, but "only the various points of view of actual persons reflecting various interests and purposes that their descriptions and theories subserve" (Putnam 1981, p. 50). This perspectivity is characteristic not only of our perception but also of our thinking, judgments, and values: A person's judgments are biased, prone to error, and sometimes based on fallacies. The goal of science is to overcome the subjectivity and perspectivity of cognition and to replace the different individual viewpoints by a unified objective view, which Thomas Nagel calls the "view from nowhere". The view from nowhere is a perspective-less and holistic view that is not bound to a thinking subject, not spoiled by prejudices, and not limited by cognitive boundaries. It is a seeing without eyes, a thinking without brain, but nevertheless a cognition of reality.

While human subjects only see how the world appears to them, objective knowledge wants to reveal the world as it is in itself, that is, independent of our cognition. We believe to arrive at objective knowledge by purifying our judgments of all subjective ingredients, and in this way objectifying them. But how can we know which components of a judgment are of subjective and which are of objective origin? Does not the ability to make such a distinction already presuppose an objective standpoint which finally has to be attained?

Knowledge is never independent of human subjects. Everything that is known is known by a subject. Schopenhauer emphasizes this inescapable subject-dependence of human cognition when he says: "Thus, no truth is more certain, no truth is more independent of all others and no truth is less in need of proof than this one: that everything there is for cognition (i.e. the whole world) is only an object in relation to a subject, an intuition of a beholder, is, in a word, representation." (Schopenhauer 2010, p. 23 f.) Statements about objective facts are based on judgments made by human subjects. Every judgment is necessarily subjective, hypothetical, and fallible. Subjective sources of error can never be completely eliminated. But we can learn from errors and at least come closer to objective knowledge. The success of science shows that our hypotheses and theories are not entirely wrong.

Objectivity is not an all-or-nothing concept. Rather, there is a continuum between the subjective and the objective (Nagel 1991, p. 206). Thomas Nagel says that objectivity is a goal that we can get closer to, but never reach. Even if there is no such thing as a perspective-less view, we should not abandon the pursuit of objectivity in the sense of a regulative idea. The goal of science is to provide a description of the world which has to be as realistic as possible.

In the debate about the possibilities and limits of scientific objectivity, different concepts of objectivity are used, which must be carefully distinguished. Objectivity is often associated with truth: a statement is objective if it is true independently of us (Brown 2001, p. 101). Or it is said that a thing exists objectively if it exists independently of us. Elisabeth Lloyd (1995) speaks of *ontological objectivity* when a statement is made about reality as opposed to mere opinion. Ontological objectivity assumes realism and postulates that there are things that exist independently of us and that we come to know reality at least approximately. Lloyd doubts that this is possible. Ontological objectivity, she argues, starts with a false premise. Lloyd speaks of an "ontological tyranny" and justifies this by saying that we cannot detach ourselves from our subjective views and interests. But I think Lloyd goes too far with her critique of the ideal of objectivity. For if we abandon a connection between scientific knowledge and reality and deny the possibility of objective knowledge, then we become victims of post-factual thinking. Joseph Hanna (2004, p. 340) accuses Lloyd of being biased in her judgments:

How can one coherently reject the claim that science is "aimed at" an independently existing, objective reality, while maintaining that scientific methods can (and ought to) be neutral, non-ideological, and unbiased? If we cannot make sense of the notion of an external reality that is independent of our expectations, interests, and intentions, then how can we maintain that scientists ought to follow a method of investigation that is neutral and disinterested?

The possibility of objective knowledge is based on the assumption that the objects of research are real, that means that electrons, planets, or black holes, for example, exist. What Lloyd calls ontological objectivity, Hanna (2004, p. 343) calls external objectivity: "external objectivity amounts to independence from subjective or inter-subjective factors or influences". External objectivity determines what is a correct description of the world. To represent a fact objectively means to represent it truthfully, i.e. as close to reality as possible. If there were no external or ontological objectivity, we would have no access to reality. Science would be detached from the real world and everything would be mere opinion and conjecture.

According to common usage, objectivity is the opposite of subjectivity. Persons engaged in scientific work therefore judge objectively when they are unbiased, impartial, and rational. Lorraine Daston and Peter Galison (2007, p. 17) explain this notion of objectivity as follows: "To be objective is to aspire to knowledge that bears no trace of the knower – knowledge unmarked by prejudice or skill, fantasy or judgment, wishing or striving." Nevertheless, this pursuit of objectivity is called into question and discredited because it allegedly demands "the scientific self to be eliminated" (Daston and Galison 2007, p. 197). Objectivism is accused of suppressing "some aspect of the self" (Daston, Galison 2007, p. 36). This pejorative use of words shows that Daston and Galison themselves do not judge without bias and pretend that objectivity is a bad thing. But it may be doubted that abandoning the ideal of objectivity and allowing more subjectivity (Code 2008) will improve science.

Sometimes objectivity is identified with *intersubjectivity*. It is therefore important to distinguish the three terms subjective, intersubjective and objective.[8] Subjectivity, intersubjectivity and objectivity can be seen as three stages in the process of knowledge acquisition by which we overcome our own subjective view and come closer to an objective description of the world. In the beginning there is a subjective opinion: a person believes to be in possession of the truth, but does not realize or does not want to admit that other people see the world differently and have their own truths. What is subjectively true need not be intersubjectively or objectively true. For example, if Smith believes that Jones owns a Porsche, then it is a subjective truth for Smith. But Smith may be mistaken. It could be that the car belongs to someone else. In this case, Smith's claim can be objectively verified, for example, by inspecting the car's ownership documents.

Other truths, however, are only subjectively true, such as the sentence "Vanilla ice cream tastes better than walnut ice cream." This sentence may be true for Smith but false

---

[8] On the difference between subjective, intersubjective, and objective truths, see Vaas (2020).

for Jones because they have different taste preferences. The truth of such subjective opinions cannot be verified, since we cannot look inside other people's minds. Sensation judgments can only be introspectively verified by the person who has those sensations: I know my mental states by "looking inside myself." In a sense, one cannot be deceived in this. For what does deception mean in this case? The determination of a deception presupposes a comparison of true and false. But judgments of sensation have no basis of intersubjective comparison. Wittgenstein writes: "One would like to say: whatever is going to seem correct to me is correct." (Wittgenstein, PI § 258)

Subjective opinions can be shared by other people. If several people believe that Smith owns a Porsche, then a subjective truth becomes an *intersubjective truth*. But also intersubjective truths need not be objectively true. Smith could deceive his neighbors and pretend that he owns the Porsche. In reality, he just rented it. Intersubjective truths are based on consensus and represent the prime example of socially constructed beliefs. The judgment of the community represents a corrective to subjective opinions. Nevertheless, even if all people believe that a proposition p is true, that does not mean that p is also objectively true. In the past people used to believe that the earth is flat. As we know today, this belief is objectively false. The social mechanisms that lead to an intersubjective consolidation of a belief despite contrary evidence are typical of echo chambers, because those epistemic bubbles gain their stability and strength from mutual support and confirmation.

Intersubjective truths are often overestimated. A common fallacy is the belief that the probability of a proposition p to be true increases with the number of people who are convinced that p is true. It is argued with the "wisdom of the crowds" (Surowiecki 2004) and the cleverness of the masses. But the alleged "wisdom of the crowds" can also turn out to be a populist stupidity. What matters, after all, is not what the majority believes, but whether there are *good reasons* to believe it and whether that belief can be empirically confirmed. Truth is not determined by vote or consensus.

What distinguishes an *objective truth* from a merely intersubjective truth is the way of justification. Arguments and evidence must be put forward, people must be *convinced* and not simply persuaded. According to Popper, the scientific approach is characterized by the *objectivity of its method*. Scientific statements are open to criticism, they are based on empirical methods, and are intersubjectively verifiable. A clairvoyant may arrive at unbiased and impartial judgments, and what she predicts with her prognostic abilities may be correct *by chance*, but her approach is unscientific and therefore not objective. Risjord explains the objectivity of method (2014, p. 23) as follows: "A method is reliable insofar as it provides results that are likely to be true. (…) In the reliability sense, objectivity has to do with how well we trust our methods to be free from error." This procedural conception of objectivity defines objective truths as the outcome of the research process by the use of scientific methods (Hammersley 2011, p. 82). Popper therefore characterizes objectivity not by the epistemic virtues of the scientist or by the intersubjective consensus of the scientific community, but by its critical tradition: "What may be described as scientific objectivity is based solely upon a critical tradition." (Popper 1976, p. 95)

Popper (1976, p. 93 ff.) tells an anecdote to support his view of objectivity: Popper joined a scientific conference, where a social anthropologist participated and attentively followed the discussions of the other participants. When asked if he could also contribute something to the discussion, he replied that he was merely following the debate "from the outside and from a more objective point of view". Indeed, he observed how individual speakers tried to dominate the group and thus exercised discursive power. The debate, he said, was merely "a group ritual of verbalization." Popper then asked him if he were to believe that there is such a thing as factual reasons or arguments that could be valid or invalid. The anthropologist replied that it is a subjective illusion to believe that one can distinguish between arguments and other verbalizations, or between objectively valid and invalid arguments. What Popper is describing here is the practice of ethnomethodology which is popular especially in scientific constructivism: sociologists are not interested in truth; they are just researching social phenomena, which belong to the realm of the intersubjective.

In the natural sciences, a proposition p is said to be *objectively true* if the best available theories and the best available data imply that p is true. Truth in this sense is merely a *temporary* truth, since with increasing knowledge even generally accepted truths can turn out to be false. A similar conception of objectivity can be found in the historical sciences: A historical statement is objectively true if it has been evaluated by established research methods and if it coheres with all available historical sources (Faber 1975, p. 24).

In the sociology of science and feminist philosophy of science, on the other hand, there is a widespread tendency to reduce objectivity to intersubjectivity. This is explained by the interactive social character of science (Longino 1990, p. 68). Scientific knowledge is regarded as a special kind of social knowledge (Longino 1990, p. 75). In the process of scientific discourse, so the story goes, different subjective assessments of empirical data and hypotheses would be replaced by a uniform consensual belief, which would improve the reliability and objectivity of research results:

> From all this it follows again that the greater the number of different points of view included in a given community, the more likely it is that its scientific practice will be objective, that is, that it will result in descriptions and explanations of natural processes that are more reliable in the sense of being less characterized by idiosyncratic subjective preferences of community members than would otherwise be the case. (Longino 1990, p. 80)

Thus, truth is what receives intersubjective approval. If truth consisted only in social recognition, this would lead to relativism and each social group could postulate its own truths. A dialogue or an exchange of arguments between these groups would not be possible, because intersubjective truth is established by *recognition* and not by arguments or objective criteria. Suppose group A acknowledges the truth of proposition X and group B holds X to be false. Then there are at least two intersubjective truths, because truth exists only within a group. And each group has its own standards of rightness and truth. There are the Trump supporters and Trump opponents, the Covid deniers, racists and conspiracy theorists. All these groups interpret the world differently and defend different values. When all perspectives are equal, you can no longer criticize someone who holds a different opinion than you.

Helen Longino is well aware of this problem and therefore takes up Jürgen Habermas' idea of defining truth not simply as an unqualified consensus, but as a justified discursive consensus that emerges as the result of an argumentative debate (Longino 1990, p. 78 f.; cf. Habermas 1995, p. 160). Since discourse is a social process, the scientific community is the ultimate authority on matters of truth. Discourse theory rejects an ontological conception of objectivity: It is not reality that determines whether an assertion is true, but the scientific community. Justification is understood as a dialogical process in which subjective factors and social values contribute to the result. To justify an assertion means to justify oneself toward a community. According to this view, justifications are always relative to an audience (Rorty 1995, p. 283).

Like Longino, Thomas Kuhn (1977, p. 329) argues that individual factors enter into the decision between competing theories, which depend on the biography and personality of the scientists. Martin Kusch (2002, p. 148) also does not acknowledge the difference between the context of justification and the context of discovery and categorically asserts that "justification is a social status". For him, there is no truth and objectivity independent of social institutions (Kusch 2002, p. 258).

Robert Brandom (1994, p. 599) criticizes this identification of objectivity with intersubjectivity: "The identification of objectivity with intersubjectivity so understood is defective in that it cannot find room for the possibility of error regarding that privileged perspective; what the community *takes* to be correct *is* correct." Such a view leads to extreme relativism and post-factualism. If one decouples truth from reality and defines it as the consensual opinion of a social group, then each group can hold its own truth without fear of being refuted by reality. Argument and reasoning may be important for Longino, but what must be added to make an assertion true is the *agreement* of the community. Longino's conception of truth can be called an authoritarian model of truth. For example, if Copernicus believes that the earth moves around the sun, then this would be false until the scientific community decides to accept the Copernican doctrine. The truthmakers are therefore not the facts, but the scientific community.

For Longino (1990, p. 67), science is a social practice in which many individuals work together on a project and justify their hypotheses and theories discursively. It seems as if individuals alone are not capable of doing science and producing results. But sometimes scientific revolutions are initiated by researchers who work and research as lone wolves outside the scientific community. To provide an example, consider how Albert Einstein developed the special theory of relativity. In 1905, Einstein was a patent examiner at the Swiss Federal Patent Office in Bern, working isolated from the scientific community on a theory that he published in the same year in the Annalen der Physik under the title "On the Electrodynamics of Moving Bodies" and which was later celebrated as a scientific revolution. Einstein was not part of a scientific network. He explained his ideas only to his colleagues Michele Besso and Joseph Sauter, who were also employed at the Bern Patent

Office. He didn't join a scientific discourse, i.e. he didn't communicate his ideas to other scientists. Einstein could have lived on a desert island and worked out his theory of relativity there. In his article he didn't mention the important works of Lorentz, Fitzgerald, and Poincaré, which paved the way to Einstein's theory, so it is not clear, how much he owes his ideas to the work of others. In contrast to today's academic customs, Einstein's publication didn't contain a bibliography.

If one takes Longino's and Kusch's thesis seriously that justifications have a social status and can only be established by a thought collective, then one could not call Einstein the founder of the special theory of relativity. The theory would only be objectively valid if it gained general recognition. Einstein had to wait many years for this recognition. But this view is counterintuitive. An approval does not make a theory true or objectively correct. Justification is done by argument, not by the assent of other scientists. Laws of nature, unlike legal laws, do not have to be approved and signed by an authority.

Longino (1990) and Harding (2015, p. 37) reject the claim of value freedom and value neutrality in science. The value freedom thesis is regarded as an obsolete relic of positivist philosophy of science. They simultaneously refuse to accept the distinction between the context of justification and context of discovery. For Elizabeth Lloyd (1995, p. 352), cognition depends on gender. And Sandra Harding (2015, pp. 27, 34) blames widespread sexism, androcentrism and Eurocentrism for the lack of objectivity in scientific research. In her view, there is no separated rational realm of reasoning and a realm of discovery uninfluenced by values. For her, knowledge is always guided by interests and dependent on power relations.

Another argument against the separation of facts and values is Duhem's and Quine's *underdetermination thesis*. The underdetermination thesis states that there may be different theories that are equally well compatible with the empirical data and that no experiment can decide between them. Underdetermination opens a possibility space for different interpretations, so that in theory choice it is ultimately not empirical data and objective arguments that decide which theory should be preferred, but individual factors and subjective preferences (Kuhn 1977, p. 329; Harding 1995, p. 331 f.). If two theories are equally well confirmed empirically, one usually opts for the simpler and more elegant theory. Like Sandra Harding, Thomas Kuhn also points out that the decision in favor of a theory is not always justified by arguments and evidence alone (Kuhn 1977, p. 320).

Nevertheless, it does not follow that one must abandon the distinction between the context of justification and the context of discovery. Values, interests and feelings may be decisive in personal decisions between competing theories, but they do not enter into the *justification* of a theory because they have no argumentative force. Justification is a logical procedure in which a proposition is justified by deriving it from premises. If values played a role, they would have to enter the justification as normative premises. But since the propositions to be justified are descriptive propositions, they can in turn only be derived from descriptive premises. One may, as Peter Galison does in his book "Einstein's Clocks, Poincaré's Maps" (2003), point out historical, social and psychological influences that motivated Einstein to develop the special theory of relativity, but one will not be able to derive, for example, his formula for the mass increase of moving bodies from it.[9]

According to Gerhard Schurz (2014, p. 42), science-external values must not play any role in the context of justification: "A specific realm of scientific activity, namely their context of justification, should be free from fundamental science-external value assumptions." Schurz admits that values do have an influence on the discovery and exploitation context, e.g. in the choice of research topics and in the formulation of hypotheses. Which goals research should pursue, which research projects should be funded and which technical applications are intended are indeed subject to political influences and social values. Goals and values are set by politics or society. Science can only find out which means are suitable to achieve these goals: If a given end E is to be realized and if E can only be realized by means M, then the means M should also be realized (Schurz 2014, p. 39). For example: If we want to reduce the number of new infections in the COVID-19 pandemic, then we must take appropriate measures such as mandatory masks, distance bans, hygiene measures, and contact restrictions. Scientific experts can only make conditional recommendations, but they should not postulate values themselves.

Objectivity is sometimes identified with value freedom (Douglas 2004, p. 459 f.). "Objective means detached, disinterested, unbiased, impersonal, invested in no particular point of view (or not having a point of view)." (Lloyd 1995, p. 353) Against the fact-value dichotomy, the argument is put forward that concepts themselves can be value-laden (Risjord 2014, p. 28 f.). Words as such are value-neutral. Values are mental attitudes and attitudes of human individuals. They arise from our use of language and how we employ words. By using language we can express our feelings and attitudes towards people or events. Moral and political terms always have an emotional content. Terms such as freedom, racism, poverty, or unemployment are undoubtedly value-laden. Especially in the social and historical sciences, the demand for value freedom or value neutrality seems impossible to fulfill. A sentence such as "Thousands of people were murdered in Auschwitz" is a typical hybrid sentence that combines facts and values. We cannot simply take note of such a sentence without emotion. The question of how many people died in Auschwitz may be a question of fact. But in which cases it is a matter of murder or "merely" a matter of letting people die is a normative question. The accusation of lack of objectivity in the Auschwitz example is typically made by Holocaust deniers and relativizers, and is intended to distract from the actual facts. It is certainly possible to distinguish facts from normative conventions and evaluations. In the above example one simply has to define what "murdered" means. Valuations enter into definitions of terms, it depends, for example, on whether one defines a term narrowly or broadly and which things or events fall under the term. Once a definition has been chosen, it is always possible to decide whether murder has occurred or not.

---

[9] What disastrous consequences it can have when values instead of reasons are allowed to guide research show the examples of phrenology (Poskett 2019), Lyssenkoism (deJong-Lambert 2012), and race research (Sussman 2014).

The above sentence can therefore be justified in a value-neutral way by applying the legal definition of murder to the Auschwitz case and determining how many people were actually murdered in Auschwitz. This shows that the objectivity of scientific justifications cannot be disputed by referring to the value-ladenness of statements. If one were to abandon the ideal of objectivity, science would become biased. One could interpret facts in such a way that they fit into one's own value system or ignore inconvenient facts altogether. To abandon the claim to objectivity would be to abandon science. The goal of science is essentially to gain knowledge that is *independent* of subjective interests and attitudes. You can't make up the world to suit yourself. To describe facts we don't need values or feelings.

While Helen Longino identifies objectivity with intersubjectivity, Sandra Harding takes a different path: she replaces the traditional concept of objectivity with a different concept, which she calls "strong objectivity". For Harding, objectivity in the sense of value freedom, impartiality and disinterestedness does not exist. Instead, she urges us to become aware of the interests, values, and political influences that prevail in science and to critically question them. In doing so, she opposes a depoliticization of science – on the contrary, scientists should resolutely advocate such values as gender equity, diversity, and anti-racism (Harding 1995, p. 335; 2015, p. 35). Harding defends standpoint theory, according to which disadvantaged social groups are epistemically privileged because of their own experiences: "Standpoint theory claims that starting from women's lives is a way of gaining less false and distorted results of research." (Harding 1995, p. 346) Dominant social groups, she argues, are epistemically corrupted because of their inherent sexism and androcentrism. Therefore, Harding supports the values and perspectives of marginalized groups and calls for a "science from below" (Harding 2015, p. 46): "In any particular research situation, one is to start off research from the lives of those who have been disadvantaged by, excluded from the benefits of, the dominant conceptual frameworks." (Harding 1995, p. 344)

In a way, such an approach is paradoxical: objectivity is generally understood to be the opposite of subjectivity. Science is supposed to be group-blind, i.e. not favouring or disadvantaging any social group. Harding, on the other hand, wants to achieve objectivity by strengthening subjectivity and prioritizing particular group interests. Lorraine Code (2008, p. 726) takes a similar approach and demands that subjective views should be given more attention in science: "subjectivity has to be taken into account".

Noretta Koertge (2000, p. 54) criticizes Harding's approach and accuses her of an ideological stance: "There is an irony in the Emancipationist call to place ideological constraints on the content of science." Koertge (2000, p. 54) warns us that the sciences would thereby be politically instrumentalized and "lose not only its epistemic authority but also its rhetorical and political usefulness." Thus, she recommends, "We should make every attempt to keep politics and religion out of the laboratory." (Koertge 2000, p. 53)

It is legitimate and quite right that scientists represent values. However, these should be democratic and common social values and not group-specific values. What Harding propagates can be called a slave revolt of morality in science. The dominant values of the ruling class are to be replaced by the values of the oppressed class. But as Nietzsche already recognized, the power relations can also be reversed and the previously marginalized minorities can become the new privileged class: "These weaklings – in fact *they*, too, want to be the powerful one day, this is beyond doubt, one day *their* 'kingdom' will come too." (Nietzsche, GM I § 15, KSA 5, p. 283) Power imbalances cannot be eliminated in this way – on the contrary: the old power relations are just replaced by new power relations.

Like Harding, Rorty postulates a priority of the ethical over the epistemic and calls for solidarity rather than objectivity. In choosing between relativism and ethnocentrism Rorty prefers ethnocentrism: "We should say that we must, in practice, privilege our own group, even though there can be no noncircular justification for doing so." (Rorty 1991, p. 29) Objectivity for him – as for Longino – is "the desire for as much intersubjective agreement as possible" (Rorty 1991, p. 23) and true are those beliefs that we find good to believe (ibid., p. 24). Rorty thus provides a philosophical basis for post-factualism: a post-factualist believes only what he or his social group believes to be true. Truth is replaced by belief or mere opinion and is determined by group conformity.

2.7   Objectivity in Journalism

The work of a journalist can be compared to that of a scientist. Journalists are also in search of the truth. They want to convey a picture of events as objective as possible, interpret the world and provide knowledge. The empirical basis of journalistic research is given by news agency reports, documents, pictures, interviews and eyewitness accounts. In journalism similar criteria of objectivity apply as they do in science: a journalist should report in a neutral, unbiased, impartial and truthful manner. News should be factual and separated from commentary and personal opinion. The journalist must be able to verify reports and name his or her sources.

These high standards of objectivity have come under attack. The arguments of critique are the same as those in the critique of scientific objectivity. Brian Winston and Matthew Winston (2021, p. 7) believe that abstention from subjective opinions and influences is simply impossible: "the idea of a human being not being subjective is a contradiction in terms". Due to the theory-laden nature of perception, facts cannot simply be perceived, but have to be interpreted (Munoz-Torres 2012, p. 572). Moreover, facts and values cannot be strictly separated. The very selection of news and the assessment of their importance depend on values (Munoz-Torres 2012, p. 573 f.). Media in general describe only a specific fragment of reality and report from a particular perspective, whereby the selection of information and the type of reporting is determined by media gatekeepers. Media constructivism rejects the correspondence theory of truth. Siegfried Weischenberg and Armin Scholl (1995, p. 220 f.) justify this as follows:

First, journalists do not represent the world in their statements, but construct images of the world; they are observers (of second order) who present the results of distinctions they themselves have made. Media are not cameras; neither are photographers. Journalists establish, on the basis of these distinctions, relationships and thus, in the end, constructions they themselves have made. Second, it is ultimately the individual journalist who decides in what way what meaning is assigned to which events. This means that journalists cannot hide behind the term 'objectivity'.

This criticism is entirely justified, because journalists often do not have direct access to information and depend on reports from other people, e.g. insiders, whistleblowers and eyewitnesses, and have to trust the truth of their statements. Especially in war reporting, journalists do not have the possibility to compare statements of eyewitnesses with reality because being in war zones is very dangerous. In contrast to scientists who have their objects of observation directly in front of them in the laboratory, in journalism the information is transmitted by messengers. The truth content of a message that reaches the recipient depends on the credibility of the source and the trustworthiness of the messenger. As a consequence, journalistic truth criteria should include coherence and intersubjective agreement. If several independent sources report consistently on a fact, then the probability that the report is true is increased.

According to Christopher Meyers (2019, p. 228 ff.), the journalistic claim to objectivity is based on a naïve empiricism and does not take the filter function of the media into account (cf. Frost 2011, p. 76 ff.). The filters are conceptual schemes according to which perception and its interpretation are structured: "These include, among other factors, the observers' history, values, experience, politics, religion, and educational background." (Meyers 2019, p. 229) Media are therefore not passive mirrors of the world that depict events realistically; rather, they represent reality in a distorted way. Maras (2013, p. 66) and Meyers (2019, p. 234) speak of invisible ideological frames through which news is filtered. Events are not simply reported unmediated, but must be interpreted and contextualized by journalists: "all works of journalism are interpretations to some degree" (Ward 2011b, p. 224). Another argument, which speaks against the ideal of objectivity, is the political and social situatedness of the reporter or journalist, which leads to an inevitable subjectivity of reporting (Conway 2020, p. 96; Winston and Winston 2021, p. 160). Siegfried J. Schmidt (1994, p. 268 f.) therefore concludes: "Media do not provide an objective image of reality; rather, they are used to construct realities."

However, media constructivism can have a counterproductive effect, because most media users are realists: they do not want "constructed" realities, rather they expect an objective reporting. If media scholars openly admit that media are not objective, this can have the effect of disappointment and cause a turn to fake news media that promise their users the truth and nothing but the truth.

The journalistic standard of objectivity is sometimes understood as a demand for neutrality, according to which journalists should put aside their personal opinions and report in a balanced manner. In concrete terms, balance means that if there are two conflicting opinions on a politically controversial topic, both sides should have their say, their view should be heard, and the final evaluation should be left to the readers. In many cases, this leads to a noncommittal "he said, she said" journalism (Maras 2013, p. 64), where everyone is allowed to voice his or her opinion, but no discursive debate takes place. Does this mean, for instance, that the worldview of conspiracy theorists is allowed to be placed on equal footing and given equal weight against established scientific knowledge? If all perspectives are treated equally, this leads to relativism (Durham 1998, p. 124 ff.). Dentith (2017, p. 72) therefore fears that a misunderstood balancing opens a gateway for fake news: "*false* balance arguably allows fake news to flourish".

This criticism is conclusive, because balancing is based on a false understanding of objectivity. For if the obligation to journalistic objectivity is understood as the pursuit of truth, then true news and fake news cannot be juxtaposed as equal views. A journalist must take a clear stand against lies and can't let Trump's unsubstantiated claims about the allegedly rigged 2020 presidential election pass without comment. In fact, balancing and truth relativism are propagated especially by "alternative journalism" (Atton 2010, p. 172 f.) and postmodern media theories that reject the ideal of objectivity. Brian and Matthew Winston (2021, p. 11), for example, believe that there are no clear distinctions between truth and falsity in journalism; rather, a journalist constantly moves in a grey area between factuality and fictionality:

> There is, then, no meaningful true/false binary in journalism, and to ground a discussion of journalism's function in such terms is obfuscating. The issue of the 'truthfulness' of journalism is less a matter of black or white – honest or mendacious representation – than it is a matter of infinite shades of grey.

Against this view it must be objected that, if there are no clear criteria for distinguishing truth from falsehood, as Winston claims, then the journalist would be forced to permanently move in a post-factual twilight zone. The rejection of the ideal of truth and objectivity thus amounts to a "post-truth journalism" (Maras 2013, p. 76), which holds that the prevailing ideology determines what is true and real: "What counts as 'truth' in a given instance is determined by who has the power to define reality." (Allan 2010, p. 149).

Geoffrey Baym (2010, p. 379) goes even further and defends fake news as a resistance against the predominant point of view because it putatively reflects a broader diversity of opinion: "the fake news instead challenges the claims offered by those in power". And he praises it as the "way of the future": "fake news may indeed be 'the way of the future'" (Baym 2010, p. 382).

Objectivity critique is often connected with ideology critique. Ideology theory is based on social determinism, according to which being determines consciousness. Social conditions are held responsible for people's inability to recognize the truth. As a consequence, social structures, media and power structures shape our experience and distort our perception of reality: "In this approach, the news media are understood to reproduce the hegemonic or dominant ideologies of capitalist society, in the service of powerful commercial and state interests." (Calcutt and Hammond 2011, p. 105) Herbert Marcuse (2002) suspects the mass media of the capitalist world of a manipulation of needs and a new form of control that forces people to think in a "one-dimensional way". According to this view, there can be no objectivity: "there are only competing perspectives, none of them 'true'" (Calcutt, Hammond, ibid.). Objectivity is regarded as a political construct (Allan 1995, p. 135). Furthermore, political discourses and power structures are said to act as ideological frames that provide a deformed picture of reality: "frames distort or fail to measure up to a reality" (Maras 2013, p. 68). Objectivity norms are generally suspected of ideology, since they supposedly disseminate only the view of the dominant group and suppress dissenting opinions that are standing outside the social consensus (Raeijmaekers and Maeseele 2017, p. 649). In addition to that, Raeijmaekers and Maeseele (2017, p. 652) also view social consensus critically. They say: "every consensus is always at least partially the result of ideological domination and exclusion".

If reality is always socially constructed and ideologically distorted, then the "distortion thesis" makes no sense, because then there can be no undistorted reality behind the construction. Ideology critique cannot contribute to an unmasking of reality because it is itself also just one perspectival view among others and cannot provide an objective or at least a more objective view. False consciousness cannot be overcome by simply overturning the dominant perspective and replacing it with another perspective, since "there is no such thing as absolute truth" (Raeijmaekers and Maeseele 2017, p. 649).

The distortion thesis defies empirical testing. For it could only be verified by reference to social experiences or facts. But these experiences and facts are themselves ideologically shaped. Consequently, there is no theory-independent neutral authority that would be able to test the ideology thesis. The thesis is therefore self-confirming and cannot be falsified.

Ideology critique remains trapped in a binary true-false thinking despite all criticism of the correspondence theory of truth: On the one hand, there is the dominant group that, thanks to its hegemonic power in the media, provides a false picture of reality, and on the other hand, there are the marginalized and disadvantaged groups that, due to their enlightened social consciousness, debunk the false appearance and thus see the world correctly – or at least claim to see the world correctly. Chambers (2017, p. 179) formulates this intrinsic inconsistency as a question: "If our thoughts and practices are always shaped by ideology, how can we know what is right or wrong, good or bad?" However, the very fact that it is possible to expose false media reports shows that it is at least possible to come closer to a more objective view.

In order to unmask ethnocentric, racist or sexist prejudices, standpoint journalism gives preference to the perspective of discriminated minorities: "In other words, a critical examination of the journalist and the journalistic institution from the perspective of the most marginalized "object" of investigation would be at the core of every news story." (Durham 1998, p. 132) Durham suggests that the subjective perspective of marginalized groups should be included in reportage. This deliberately violates the requirement of neutrality. Journalism becomes partisan, the journalist becomes a social activist and supporter of identity politics and class struggle. But who belongs to the marginalized groups? Who determines which group can claim that status? (Ryan 2001, p. 15) Does it include, for example, Covid deniers or conspiracy theorists?

The traditional understanding of objectivity undoubtedly has its weaknesses. But when journalists abandon the pursuit of objective reporting and turn truth into an expression of subjective convictions or a class point of view, they give way to post-factualism. Truth thus becomes a game ball of opposing social groups and a mirror of political power relations. If there is a change of power, then the truth also changes. What was true before now becomes false and vice versa. Objectivity does not mean being neutral and accepting truth and fake news as equally valid opinions. A commitment to truth and objectivity is indispensable to journalistic work. Stephen Ward (2011a, p. 137 f.) writes:

> Without clear notions of truth and objectivity, media ethics lacks the resources to distinguish between good and bad journalism and lacks the authority to critique dubious practice. If journalists dismiss truth and objectivity as impossible, or as a cultural myth, they open the doors to subjective and misleading journalism. Who can criticize a biased journalist or critique subjective reporting if we doubt the ideal of truthful, objective journalism? On what basis do we critique journalism if we question the difference between truth and falsity, between subjectivity and objectivity? How can we complain about biased reporting if we no longer expect journalists to be objective? If everything is simply one's perspective, why bother constructing stories according to careful methods and demanding criteria?

Ward (2011a, p. 119) warns against a postmodern truth skepticism and recommends a pragmatic notion of objectivity that avoids the weaknesses of the traditional notion of objectivity, but still adheres to the concept of truth. Ward takes up a moderate position between a positivist understanding of objectivity and a social constructivist critique of objectivity. In his view, journalists do not depict reality one-to-one, they do not represent facts but interpret them. But interpretations cannot be arbitrary, they must be truth-adequate: "Interpretations must in some way agree with the way the world is." (Ward 2011a, p. 149). A journalist should therefore set aside his or her subjective opinion and exclude bias as much as possible. Reports must be coherent and empirically adequate. Ward adheres to the *coherence theory of truth:*

> Truth refers to (a) interpretations that fit well with the best available conceptual scheme on a topic, or (b) theories (as complex interpretations) that offer a more coherent account than rival systems. The idea of truth for coherence theory is holistic, involving the coherence of many beliefs. This stress on coherence fits very well pragmatic inquiry's idea of interpretations as the product of conceptualization and theorizing. (Ward 2011a, p. 146)

The question of what truth is is therefore not only relevant for journalism, it is the pivotal point in the debate on post-factualism. Is there such a thing as objective truth? How can it be defined and recognized? Is truth merely a social construct? In philosophy, there is no single definition of truth; rather, different competing theories of truth have been developed, such as the correspondence theory or the coherence theory. In the next chapter, I will present an overview of these different philosophical approaches and propose an epistemological model that is suitable to mediate between these opposing positions.

Facticity and Truth

3

Post-factualism rejects a metaphysical concept of truth, declares truth to be a social phenomenon and thus detaches it from reality. Even if post-factualism with its relativistic tendencies appears unacceptable, it nevertheless represents a challenge for philosophy and media theory, because it has some strong epistemological arguments that cannot be ignored: First, there is the context-dependence of meanings as well as the perspectivity and social origin of knowledge. Absolute truths and indisputable facts do not exist; rather, they are always theory-laden and in need of interpretation. We perceive the world from a particular perspective, which is historically, culturally and socially shaped. If there are no perspective-independent facts and if reality is cognitively inaccessible to us, how can we distinguish between truth and fake? If we want to save the concept of truth and not let it fall prey to relativism, we need an epistemology that does not make truth an arbitrarily negotiable, socially constructed agreement, but that ties it to reality. In this chapter I will give an overview of different theories of truth, discuss their strengths and weaknesses, and present the model of perspectival realism, which presents a compromise between perspectivism and realism.

3.1 The Correspondence Theory of Truth

The correspondence theory of truth states that a proposition is true if it corresponds to reality. In the twentieth century some thought-provoking objections have been raised against this theory. But despite this legitimate criticism, we have to remind ourselves that we use the correspondence theory successfully in everyday life, when we want to know whether a statement is true or not. Correspondence theory assumes realism and does not make truth an arbitrary discursive construction. This distinguishes it from other theories of truth and is its biggest asset. If someone claims that there is a robin sitting on the tree in

© The Author(s), under exclusive license to Springer Fachmedien Wiesbaden
GmbH, part of Springer Nature 2023
T. Zoglauer, *Constructed Truths*, https://doi.org/10.1007/978-3-658-39942-9_3

the garden, then the truth of this proposition can be easily verified by observation. We simply look if it is true by comparing the asserted fact with what we see. If the proposition and reality correspond, then the proposition is true; and if not, then it is false.

But it is not quite that simple. Let us consider the sentence "It is raining". Is the sentence true, if only a few drops fall? How many drops must fall per minute per square meter to confirm that it is raining? Our colloquial language is notoriously imprecise. Rain is a vague term whose range of extension has fuzzy boundaries. One can eliminate such vagueness by defining the term precisely, for example, by specifying truth conditions and defining what amount of precipitation must be measured that the sentence "It is raining" is true. Such definitions are arbitrary and are based on social conventions, but they establish uniqueness.

According to the correspondence theory, truth is conceived as a relation, namely as a correspondence between proposition and reality. A proposition is true if it corresponds to the facts. But what are facts and what is the correspondence relation? These critical questions have thrown the correspondence theory into a deep crisis. Many efforts have been made to answer these questions. Facts are things, events, or states of affairs in the world that can be described by true propositions. According to Wittgenstein, the whole world consists of facts: "The world is the totality of facts, not of things." (TLP 1.1)[1] Every true proposition corresponds to a fact. Here, however, the first problem arises, which I will explain using the sentence "Snow is white and grass is green" as an example (Marino 2006, p. 421). This sentence is undoubtedly true. It represents a conjunction of two single propositions, namely "snow is white" and "grass is green". Each of these propositions corresponds to a fact. One might therefore ask: Does the conjunction correspond to *one* fact, or are there *two* facts corresponding to it? One may regard the conjunction as a coexistence of two facts. Wittgenstein and Russell postulate the existence of complex facts. A fact consists of states of affairs in which objects are related to each other (TLP 2.01). When Wittgenstein says that the world consists of facts and not of things, he means that only facts and not things have an independent existence. We can also say that Wittgenstein advocates an ontology of facts and not an ontology of things. The proposition "Snow is white and grass is green" can be decomposed into two single propositions, whereby the individual propositions are so-called elementary propositions: "The simplest kind of proposition, an elementary proposition, asserts the existence of a state of affairs." (TLP 4.21) The individual states of affairs are independent of each other (TLP 2.061). Hence, we can say: the above conjunction describes two independent states of affairs, but only one fact.

Let us now consider the proposition A_1: "The Eiffel Tower is 300 m high." Again, we can say that the sentence is true because it describes a fact, let's call it T_1. Let's compare it with the proposition A_2: "The Eiffel Tower is taller than 200 m." This sentence is also true. The fact described here is more general than A_1, since it allows for more possibilities. We can imagine at will any other sentences that generalize the fact A_1, e.g.

---

[1] TLP = Tractatus logico-philosophicus.

A$_3$: "The Eiffel Tower is not 200 meters high."
A$_4$: "The Eiffel Tower is 300 meters high or it's raining in Paris."

They describe different facts. The mere fact that the Eiffel Tower is 300 m high makes all these propositions A$_2$, A$_3$ and A$_4$ true. David Armstrong refers to facts as *truthmakers* and understands them as parts of reality by which a proposition becomes true (Armstrong 2004, p. 5). The truthmaker theory provides an explanation for the Eiffel Tower example above. For truthmakers the *entailment principle* holds: if T is a truthmaker for proposition p and if proposition q follows from p, then T is also a truthmaker for q (Armstrong 2004, p. 10). In the Eiffel Tower example, the truthmaker of A$_1$ is also a truthmaker for the propositions A$_2$, A$_3$ and A$_4$, because the propositions A$_2$, A$_3$ and A$_4$ all follow from A$_1$.

Are there also negative facts? To answer that question, let us examine proposition B: "There are no unicorns" (Rasmussen 2014b, p. 29). The sentence is true. But what is the corresponding fact to this proposition? If there are no unicorns, then there is no part of reality that makes the proposition true. It seems as if negative existential judgments do not correspond to reality, even though they are true. Wittgenstein proposes a solution to that problem by postulating that a proposition and its negation correspond to the same reality (TLP 4.0621). In his "Notes on Logic" Wittgenstein writes: "There are *positive* and *negative facts* (…) but not true and false facts." (NB, p. 94) The sentence "This rose is not red" denotes a negative fact. The truthmaker of the sentence is a non-red rose. But are there non-existent unicorns? One would be inclined to say that statement B corresponds to the fact that there are no unicorns. One could list various things that are not unicorns and claim that all these things are truthmakers of statement B. Basically, all things in the universe are not unicorns. This would make the entire universe the truthmaker of proposition B.[2] The same is true of propositions such as "There are no winged horses," "There is no bald king of France," etc. All these sentences have the same truthmaker. This explanation of negative facts might save the correspondence theory, but at what cost? The contents of these propositions cannot be distinguished by referring to their truthmakers.

Another problem concerns the correspondence relation: What does it mean that a true proposition *corresponds* to a fact? What is the correspondence relation? Does it mean that a proposition is the same as a fact? In any case, such a coincidence of proposition and fact cannot be meant, for then proposition and fact could not be distinguished (Frege 1984, p. 353). Another possibility would be that the *idea* expressed in a proposition coincides with reality. But Frege rejects this possibility as well, because reality and ideas are categorically different and therefore there can be no exact correspondence of both. It would be like comparing apples with pears and looking for a correspondence. Between such things

---

[2] Armstrong speaks of a "huge general truth", which states the existence of all things. This general truth implies in particular all negative truths such as "There are no unicorns" or "There is no bald king of France". Therefore, the whole universe would be a truthmaker for all negative truths (Armstrong 2007).

one can indeed find similarities, but no correspondence. But we want truth, not half-truths, "for what is only half true is untrue" (Frege 1984, p. 353).

A fact is a part of material reality and thus something outside language. In order to compare two things, a *tertium comparationis* is needed, that is a property with respect to which a proposition and a fact can be compared. But what is this third kind beyond propositions and facts? Propositions and facts are ontologically distinct. Martin Heidegger (1998, p. 140) explains this difference using the example of the proposition "This coin is round": What are the proposition and the coin supposed to have in common? The coin is made of metal, the proposition is immaterial. The coin is round and occupies a certain volume. The proposition is neither round nor does it have any spatial shape. The coin can be used to buy something. A proposition has no monetary value. We can only compare things that belong to the same ontological category, that is, we can compare propositions with propositions, but not propositions with facts.

Correspondence is often defined as structural equality or isomorphism. True propositions are supposed to depict the relations between things. Wittgenstein explains this in his picture theory of language as follows: Language is a picture of reality. True propositions depict facts. That something can be depicted at all, there must be something identical in the picture and what it depicts (TLP 2.161). What picture and depicted have in common is what Wittgenstein calls the "logico-pictorial form" (TLP 2.2). Objects stand in relation to each other and this relation is represented in a proposition. True propositions and facts are therefore structurally isomorphic. The sentence "The Empire State Building is taller than the Eiffel Tower" expresses a comparison of height between the two buildings. This relation is linguistically represented by the expression "is taller than".

However, this explanation does not get us any further. In the example of the height comparison, this may still seem plausible. But logical connectives do not necessarily have a simple equivalent in reality. Let us take as an example a compound sentence that consists of a disjunction of two single propositions:

C: "In Berlin, the sun is shining or it's raining."

Here one might think that the corresponding fact is composed of sunshine and rain. But the disjunction is true even if only one of the two partial statements is true. Suppose that in Berlin the sun is shining, but it is not raining. Here we can no longer say that the corresponding complex fact contains both simple facts. Since it does not rain in Berlin, this fact does not occur in reality. The fact consists only of the sunshine in Berlin and does not represent the disjunction. Therefore, there is no structural isomorphism.

It is not clear what Wittgenstein means by "logical form". Jaakko and Merrill Hintikka (1983, p. 156) think that logical form is a modal concept and that only *possible* facts are represented in a sentence. In a diary entry of 29.9.1914 Wittgenstein (NB, p. 7e) writes: "In the proposition a world is as it were put together experimentally. (As when in the law-court in Paris a motor-car accident is represented by means of dolls, etc.)." Presumably the bracketed remark refers to the report of a trial in which a car accident was reconstructed in a miniature model, which Wittgenstein read about in a newspaper and which lead him to the idea of understanding language as a picture of reality (von Wright 2001, p. 8). Propositions represent possible states of affairs. Viewed in this way, a disjunction could be seen as a combination of two possible states of affairs, like in a model, namely that it is raining and that the sun is shining. The sentence C then does not represent reality, but *possible* realities. It leaves three possible states of affairs open:

1. In Berlin the sun is shining and it is raining.
2. In Berlin the sun is shining and it is not raining.
3. In Berlin the sun is not shining and it is raining.

The proposition C is true if and only if one of the three states of affairs is true. Wittgenstein would presumably speak here of a "configuration of objects" in a "logical space" (cf. TLP 2.0272 + 2.11). However, this still does not clarify which fact the proposition C depicts. A fact, after all, is supposed to be a part of reality and not something that exists in other possible worlds.

These considerations show that facts and truthmakers are very strange entities. For example, what is the corresponding fact of "2 + 2 = 4"? Or how can counterfactual truths such as "If Napoleon had conquered England, he would have abolished the English legal system" be explained? Leaving aside the problem of what ontological structure facts have, there is the very simple question: to what fact, for instance, should the statement that snow is white correspond? An obvious answer to this question would be: It is precisely the fact that snow is white. In describing the fact, the sentence is simply repeated. The fact is expressed in exactly the same words as the sentence itself. Despite this paradoxical formulation, this formula is continually repeated in philosophy: the proposition "snow is white" is true if and only if snow is white. It is not apparent what the difference is supposed to be between the proposition and the fact described in it. It is emphasized that a fact is a non-linguistic entity. Nevertheless, facts can only be described linguistically and can only be identified by propositions. If facts are not independent of their linguistic description, then a proposition is not confronted with reality, but only two linguistic descriptions are compared with each other (cf. Williams 2001, p. 140). Davidson (1990, p. 304) therefore concludes that correspondence theories "fail to provide entities to which truth vehicles (whether we take these to be statements, sentences, or utterances) can be said to correspond".

Robert Nozick raises the suspicion that the ontological categories by which we describe facts are projections of grammatical categories and that reality therefore has the same structure as its linguistic image. By describing things, facts and events linguistically, we project grammatical structures into the world and believe that the facts are structurally isomorphic to the sentences:

We do not yet know what the components of facts are. Are there ultimate components (absolute atoms)? There is a temptation to say that the components are things or objects, their properties and their relations. But this accords too well with grammatical categories, and so it raises the suspicion that linguistic units are being projected as ontological categories. (Nozick 2001, p. 73 f.)

Since linguistic descriptions of facts depend on conceptual schemes and categories, truth is also relative to these schemes. As a consequence, the truth of a proposition does not only depend on the fact it corresponds to, but also on the conceptual schemes and theories it is based on. C.I. Lewis (1956, p. 271) and William James (1959, p. 172) consider the possibility that there could be alternative conceptual schemes that organize and structure experience differently and therefore produce different truths.

The thesis of structural isomorphism of language and reality makes sense only if reality has a structure at all and if we can conceive this structure conceptually and describe it linguistically. But actually we project our own concepts onto the world and we pretend that they are real ontological categories. Concepts exist in our minds, not in reality. It remains a mystery how we can compare propositions with a non-conceptual reality. We can only compare propositions with propositions, but not propositions with facts. In order to compare the two elements of the truth relation, we would have to adopt a standpoint outside the world, a god's eye point of view, from which facts are immediately accessible to us. Since we cannot look at the world from outside with god's eyes, because we live *in* the world, we can only take an *internal* perspective and compare statements and theories with each other, that is, we can only compare things of the *same kind*.

Another problem with the correspondence theory is scientific progress. For example, if we want to know how far the earth is from the sun, how dangerous the Corona virus is, or whether there is man-made climate change, we ask scientists. Science seems to be the supreme authority when it comes to questions of truth. But science can only give provisional answers. When asked what the smallest constituents of matter are, elementary particle physicists would say: according to the standard model, there are only quarks, leptons, gauge bosons and Higgs particles. In the early twentieth century, the answer would have been different. In Rutherford's atomic model there were only electrons and atomic nuclei. And in 100 years, the answer could be different again: It could be superstrings or other exotic objects that make up matter. In other words: What is true today may be false tomorrow. Strictly speaking, there are no hypotheses in the natural sciences that are unalterably true. Scientific models represent simplifications and idealizations, and presuppose conditions that are not met in nature. The law of free fall, for example, considers bodies as point masses, neglects air resistance, pretends that free fall takes place in a vacuum and assumes that no forces other than gravity act on a falling body. Only under these assumptions, a metal ball and a feather fall at the same rate. Laws of nature do not describe facts, but are the result of idealizations. They are therefore not true – at least not in the correspondence-theoretic sense (cf. Gadenne 2015, p. 17; Zoglauer 1993, p. 222). In a sense, the laws of nature "lie," as the title of Nancy Cartwright's book (1983) suggests. But can't theories be at least *approximately* true?

3.2 **Approximate Truth**

In the research process, old theories are constantly replaced by new and better theories. A theory cannot be true if it can be discarded at any time and replaced by another, "truer" theory. For example, the laws of Newtonian mechanics cannot be said to be absolutely "true". For these laws turn out to be special cases of more general theories such as relativity or quantum theory. But also the laws of quantum mechanics cannot be true, if one does not want to give up hope for better and more general theories. We usually assume that truth has no degrees and that we therefore cannot speak of gradually "truer" theories. Popper (1962) introduced the notion of *verisimilitude*, meaning that theories become increasingly more truth-like as science progresses: they converge towards a true theory.

Popper sees the falsification of theories as a driver of progress, bringing them closer to the truth. Refutations contribute to progress by eliminating unsuccessful theories and replacing them with better theories. Thus, the goal of research is not truth per se, but growing truth proximity. The problem with this conception of progress is that it presupposes a measure of truth proximity, or criteria for deciding whether one theory is closer to the truth than another. This would be the only possibility how two competing theories can be compared in terms of their closeness to truth. According to Popper, the more easily a hypothesis can be falsified, the greater its empirical content. Put simply, a theory T_2 is better, i.e. more truth-like, than its predecessor theory T_1, if T_2 can explain and predict more facts than T_1 and passes more experimental tests successfully (Popper 1962, p. 232).

Boyd (1983), Leplin (1981), Newton-Smith (1983) and Aronson (1989) believe that the historical sequence of better and better theories *converges* towards a true theory. This is the reason why this approach is called "*convergent realism*". This theory introduces a teleological notion of progress, which assumes that the research process is goal-directed. The convergence thesis is based on the progress in making more precise measurements of fundamental constants of nature and the growing correspondence of theories with the measured data in many areas (Vollmer 1993, p. 172). Convergent realism claims, first, that there is such a thing as a final "theory of everything" towards which theories converge and, second, that convergence is not only qualitative in nature but can also be quantified. But what does convergence mean and how can it be quantified?

Rosenberg (1988) points out that the quantitative notion of convergence presupposes a measure of the "distance" of a theory from the final "true theory". But until we know the final theory, we cannot determine the convergence of theories T_n. A possible way out is offered by Cauchy's notion of convergence, which requires that the distance between any two theories T_m and T_n in the historical sequence tends to zero: $d(T_m, T_n) \to 0$. But again, the problem of how we can measure the "distance" between two theories remains unsolved. Quite apart from this, it is not clear why this sequence should converge at all (Rosenberg 1988, p. 173).

The convergence thesis also has the paradoxical consequence that generally accepted common-sense truths are less truthful than our latest scientific theories. For newer theories are closer to the truth than older theories. But why should the proposition "This tomato is red", even if it can be directly confirmed by perception, be further from the truth than the proposition "The light reflected from the tomato has a wavelength of 710 nm"?

To avoid these problems, Psillos proposes to abandon the notion of convergence and to speak instead of an *approximate fittingness* of theories to experience: "According to these intuitions, a theory is approximately true if the entities of the general kind postulated to play a central causal role in the theory exist, and if the basic mechanisms and laws postulated by the theory approximate those holding in the world, under specific conditions of approximation". (Psillos 1999, p. 267) Psillos explains this with the example of celestial mechanics. Planetary observation provides a lot of measurement data, for example, about the positions of Mars. A good theory should be able to establish an accurate model of the Mars orbit and to calculate the planetary positions exactly. The smaller the deviation between the theoretically determined positions and the observed positions, the better the theory fits reality and the more likely it is that the theory is approximately true. Psillos is aware that we will never obtain an exact match, this is why convergence is unrealistic. The reason is because the theory makes idealizing assumptions that are not satisfied in reality. For example, Newton's model treats the orbit of Mars as a two-body problem, considers only the gravitational effects of the Sun and Mars, and neglects the gravitational forces of other planets. In contrast to Popper's theory of verisimilitude, truth is here no longer understood as correspondence to reality, but only as a relative adjustment of a theory to experience.

The predictive and retrodictive success of a theory is of prime importance, i.e. how well the theory can reproduce measured data and how well it can predict data. The inference goes from the success of the theory to its truth. This connection between success and truth is regarded as the pivotal argument for scientific realism. It is said that only realism could satisfactorily explain why our theories can make correct empirical predictions, why this success increases over time, and why there is any scientific progress at all (Almeder 1989; Leplin 1981). If theories could not describe reality at least approximately correctly, their apparent success would be a miracle, as Smart (1963) and Putnam (1975) emphasize. Hilary Putnam (1975, p. 73) has expressed this *"no-miracle argument"* very succinctly:

> The positive argument for realism is that it is the only philosophy that doesn't make the success of science a miracle. That terms in mature scientific theories typically refer (this formulation is due to Richard Boyd), that the theories accepted in a mature science are typically approximately true, that the same term can refer to the same thing even when it occurs in different theories – these statements are viewed by the scientific realist not as necessary truths but as part of the only scientific explanation of the success of science, and hence as part of any adequate scientific description of science and its relations to its objects.

The no-miracle argument can be reconstructed as follows:

1. Science is successful.

2. The best explanation for the success of science is to assume that successful scientific theories are approximately true.
3. If successful theories were not approximately true, their success would be a miracle.
4. Therefore, successful scientific theories must be at least approximately true.

The argument infers the approximate truth of a theory from its success, using an *inference to the best explanation*. The inference to the best explanation is not a compelling logical argument, because it offers only *one* possible explanation for the success of a theory and leaves open whether there are other possible explanations. It merely asserts that among all possible explanations for the success of a theory, approximate truth is the *best* explanation. Such conclusions are valid only with a certain probability (Harman 1965).

Scientific models can be successful even if they are not an exact replica of reality. Peter Lipton (2005) compares a theory with a map: Suppose we want to travel from location A to location B, we use a map for orientation. The map does not represent all the topographical features of the area around A and B. If the map is a road map, no mountains or valleys are drawn. Geology and vegetation will usually not be of interest for a motorist. To successfully get from A to B, a motorist only needs to know which roads connect the two places. The map must show the roads, the motorway access and exit roads, as well as service stations and petrol stations. Most other details can be omitted because they are not important for the motorist. That is, a map depicts only those features of the world that are pragmatically relevant. A map is not a one-to-one representation of reality. The map of the London Underground (London Tube Map) shows only the network of lines and stops; the map depicts connections but not real-world distance relationships. Other maps show territories and country borders, i.e. conventional entities that do not exist in nature. World maps that depict the whole earth are always distorted in perspective, depending on which projection method is used. They are either true to angle or true to area, but cannot be both at the same time. A map can therefore never depict the world in a structurally isomorphic way, but can only show certain features and provide a user-oriented perspective. Different maps provide different perspectives on the world, and users choose the perspective that is most useful for their purposes. A satellite photo from Google Earth may depict reality more accurately than a road map. However, road maps are more useful to a car driver than Google Earth.

The same is true for scientific theories. Truth or approximate truth in the sense of structural correspondence is not necessary for their success. False theories can also be successful. Larry Laudan (1981) listed many historical examples of theories that were all very successful in their time, but which are regarded false today because they postulate the existence of objects that do not exist in reality, such as epicycles in ancient and medieval astronomy, the phlogiston in eighteenth-century chemistry, vital forces in physiology, or the ether in nineteenth-century physics. Conversely, approximately true theories that refer to real objects need not necessarily be successful. Laudan therefore concludes:

The fact that a theory's central terms refer does not entail that it will be successful, and a theory's success is no warrant for the claim that all or most of its central terms refer. The notion of approximate truth is presently too vague to permit one to judge whether a theory consisting entirely of approximately true laws would be empirically successful. What is clear is that a theory may be empirically successful even if it is not approximately true. (Laudan 1981, p. 47)

From the success of a theory we can conclude its empirical adequacy in the sense of Psillos, namely that it matches the observational and measured data. Hence Bas van Fraassen makes the following statement:

[T]he aim of science is not truth as such but only *empirical adequacy,* that is, truth with respect to the observable phenomena. Acceptance of a theory involves as belief only that the theory is empirically adequate (but acceptance involves more than belief). (…) the criterion of success is not truth in every respect, but only truth with respect to what is actual and observable. (Fraassen 1989, p. 192 f.)

Despite all the criticisms of scientific realism and the correspondence theory of truth that underlies it, we can claim: Our best available scientific theories are very successful. If we look at the history of science, we can see that our theories are better and better adapted to empirical data and that their empirical adequacy therefore increases. We cannot know whether a theory is true in the metaphysical sense. We can only judge whether a theory is successful in the sense of empirical adequacy. Therefore, it makes sense to define truth in terms of success. In doing so we replace the metaphysical concept of truth with a pragmatic one. We will examine in the next chapter whether a pragmatic theory of truth is better suited than a correspondence theory to explain truth.

3.3   The Pragmatic Theory of Truth

Pragmatism is a philosophical movement that was founded at the end of the nineteenth and beginning of the twentieth century by Ch. S. Peirce, William James and John Dewey and has had a lasting influence on American philosophy up to the present day. William James became one of its most famous protagonists with his book "Pragmatism" (1959), first published in 1907, in which he attacks the correspondence theory and introduces a pragmatic concept of truth. He takes up an idea of Immanuel Kant, according to which our mind makes use of certain forms of intuition and categories to bring order into the confusing manifold of sensory impressions. James reinterprets Kant's transcendental philosophy pragmatically and regards concepts as useful tools to cope with reality. Conceptual systems serve a practical purpose. Substance and causality are not innate concepts, they do not denote anything real, but are free constructions of the human mind that are highly useful to us and help us to understand the world and make it intelligible. Science introduces hypothetical objects like the ether, electric fields, and virtual particles and deals with them *as if* they exist. In reality, however, they are merely useful fictions and tools to explain natural phenomena.

James presents several definitions of truth. First, truth is equated with usefulness (James 1959, p. 203), then truth is explained as that "which gives us the maximum possible sum of satisfactions" (ibid., p. 217) and "the expedient in the way of our thinking" (ibid., p. 222) and at another time truth means nothing else than verifiability (ibid., p. 220). James claims that if an idea is successful, then it is true. Against this identification of truth with success Russell mockingly objected: "if Germany had been victorious [in World War 2], pragmatists would have had to hail the Nazi creed as pragmatically 'true'." (Russell 1975, p. 132). A functionalization and purpose-orientation of the concept of truth must indeed be viewed critically. For even a lie can be useful and successful, providing satisfaction to the liar. As Laudan has shown, false theories can also be successful, and assumptions that later turn out to be correct can fail the practical test. Fatally, for James it isn't so important whether an opinion is really useful, what matters to him is that it conveys just the *feeling* to be useful. A belief must provide satisfaction. Hence James speaks of "satisfaction" as a criterion of truth: "The matter of the true is thus absolutely identical with the matter of the satisfactory." (James 1909, p. 159 f.)

Russell suspects that James's main concern with his pragmatic definition of truth was "to find some way of asserting that the statement 'God exists' is true without involving himself in metaphysics" (Russell 1975, p. 134). Belief in God has proven to be beneficial. Religion strengthens social cohesion, creates a common spirit, admonishes people to behave morally, and helps them to cope with contingency. But can we conclude from the usefulness of religious belief the existence of God? If all that matters is a feeling of satisfaction, then, as Russell notes, two people can hold opposing views and still both feel satisfaction in doing so (Russell 1975, p. 134). Does it follow that both are right? If so, then two contradicting statements could both be true and the law of non-contradiction would not hold. Such a consequence would be deeply counterintuitive.

From the perspective of pragmatism, even such obvious falsehoods as Trump's claim that the 2020 presidential election was rigged can pass for truth. The idea that he actually won the election gives Trump a personal satisfaction and flatters his narcissism. If his supporters are also convinced of this, they will support him with donations in his hopeless legal battle to declare the election results null and void, which benefits him politically and financially. Trump can therefore say with full pragmatic conviction: what I say is true.

What is useful and what is not depends on one's personal perspective. We have to ask ourselves *for whom* and *for what* something is supposed to be useful. Theories about neutrinos, Higgs bosons and black holes may be extremely useful for a physicist, but hardly for ordinary people, for whom it is more important to plug the black holes in their household budgets.

The criterion of verifiability does not get us anywhere either. For how can we as outsiders be able to verify the assertion of another person who says: "I have a headache"? After all, we can't see inside another person's mind. And some scientific hypotheses, such as that there is life on other planets, can probably never be verified, even if they are true. As we know from the history of science, the methods and means of verification can change over time. What was in principle unverifiable before can be empirically verified later. As a consequence, truths would also change.

James believes in realism and regards the existence of things as a prerequisite for their usefulness to us (James 1909, p. 207). But he does not explain the relation between realism and pragmatism. Is usefulness a criterion of reality? Does Santa Claus exist, if believing in him makes us happy? The pragmatist wants to liberate the concept of truth from its metaphysical baggage and anchor it in the reality of human life. In rejecting the correspondence theory, James cuts the bond that connects propositions to reality. Truth becomes a social construction. In this view, truth is not discovered, but made.

Richard Rorty, a modern representative of American pragmatism, is much more consistent than James and advocates a radical anti-realism. He rejects the realist notion of "world" and is happy with the "world well lost" (Rorty 1972). He believes that we can well do without a concept of truth:

> The intuitive realist thinks that there is such a thing as philosophical truth because he thinks that, deep down beneath all the texts, there is something which is not just one more text but that to which various texts are trying to be 'adequate'. The pragmatist does not think that there is anything like that. He does not even think that there is anything isolable as "the purposes which we construct vocabularies and cultures to fulfill" against which to test vocabularies and cultures. (Rorty 1982, p. xxxvii)

Rorty separates language from the world and makes truth a purely language-immanent phenomenon (Rorty 1989, p. 5). Truth, for him, does not exist independently of language. Truth is not "out there," it is part of a language game: "The world does not speak. Only we do." (Rorty 1989, p. 6) A proposition is true not because it corresponds to reality, but because it is believed to be true. True is "what is good in the way of belief" (Rorty 1982, p. 162). Truth is identified with justifiability. A proposition is true if it can be justified: "There is simply the process of justifying beliefs to audiences." (Rorty 1999, p. 36) If the audience accepts the justification, then the proposition is true. Rorty views justification as a social phenomenon "rather than a transaction between 'the knowing subject' and 'reality'" (Rorty 1979, p. 9).

As an example, consider the successful prediction of a solar eclipse. What makes the prediction true? Is it the mere fact that the scientific audience applauds because the prediction came true? Is it true because it is part of an academic language game or because the scientist has calculated correctly? Isn't it rather the case that the prediction turned out to be true because of the way the *world* is: because the earth, the sun, and the moon were in such a position relative to each other at the predicted time that the moon's total shadow obscured the area where the eclipse is observed?

Simon Blackburn (2005, p. 157 ff.), in his critique of Rorty, takes up Lipton's (2005) map example to defend the realist interpretation of true statements. Suppose a pilgrim wants to visit a chapel and picks up a map to find it. If he reaches his destination by using the map, we would say that the map correctly depicts the landscape. The success of the pilgrim is not based solely on technical map conventions, e.g. by which symbol the chapel is represented, or on social practices of map makers and map users, but at least partially on the correct representation of reality: "That is why, once a set of conventions has been put in place, a map can be correct or incorrect. In other words, it can represent the landscape as it is, or represent the landscape as it is not." (Blackburn 2005, p. 157) The pilgrim, having arrived at his destination, may feel a sense of satisfaction, he may praise the usefulness of the map, and other travellers may verify the correct representation: all these things are not causes but effects of correct representation. What makes a proposition true is not the social practice of people, but it is reality itself.

3.4   The Deflationary Theory of Truth

One argument against the correspondence theory of truth implies that facts can only be described linguistically, and that truth is thus an intra-linguistic phenomenon. Rorty considers the concept of truth to be superfluous, metaphysically overloaded, and philosophically overrated. Basically, he contends that the use of the word "true" merely fulfills a pragmatic function in order to affirm statements. With this claim Rorty places himself in the tradition of the deflationary theory of truth, which was advocated in different versions by Ramsey, Ayer, Belnap and Horwich in the twentieth century and which pursued the goal of demystifying the concept of truth and reducing it to its colloquial use. Truth, according to this view, is not a mysterious property that belongs to propositions, but merely a rhetorical device of assertion. When one says that a proposition p is true, the expression "true" is actually superfluous, because the mere assertion of p already implies its truth. "Snow is white" is true if and only if snow is white. The affirmation "… is true" adds no new information to the statement and can therefore be omitted. According to this view, the concept of truth is redundant. For Paul Horwich, truth is not further analysable: "truth is not susceptible to conceptual analysis and has no underlying nature" (Horwich 2004, p. 71). However, the deflationary theory of truth says nothing about how to verify the truth of a proposition. It does not provide truth criteria.

The deflationary theory of truth reduces the concept of truth to the simple Tarski scheme (T):

"p" is true if and only if p.

The elimination of the truth term is done by disquotation, by omitting the quotation marks in which the phrase "p" is bracketed. The Tarski formula represents a logical equivalence that can be read from left to right as well as from the right to the left side. It eliminates the truth term by referring to the corresponding object-language term p. Conversely, one can also add the affirmation "p is true" to any statement p without changing anything about the content of the statement. If I say "It is raining", I want to express that I believe the proposition to be true and that I believe that it is indeed raining. I want the hearer to believe me and to be convinced of the truth of my assertion. As Habermas quite rightly states, asser-toric speech acts automatically involve truth claims (Habermas 1995, p. 137 ff.).

Despite this consideration, we shall not forget that it still makes a difference whether I merely assume something or whether I am convinced of the truth of my assertion. Gottlob Frege, who is regarded as one of the founders of the deflationary theory of truth, agrees that the content of the propositions "p" and "p is true" is the same, but he qualifies his statement in saying that truth expresses more than a mere assumption:

> It is also worth noting that the sentence "I smell the scent of violets" has just the same content as the sentence "It is true that I smell the scent of violets". So it seems, then, that nothing is added to the thought by my ascribing to it the property of truth. And yet is it not a great result when the scientist after much hesitation and laborious researches can finally say "My conjec-ture is true"? (Frege 1984, p. 354)

A truth assertion involves being able to give reasons and evidence for the truth of a propo-sition, rather than merely assuming it. Speech acts can also be used in non-assertive ways. A statement p can be meant as an exaggeration, a compliment, an insult, or just ironically. It therefore makes a big difference whether one merely believes that something is true or whether the statement corresponds to reality. This difference is not expressed in the Tarski formula (T). If I say: "It is raining", then I don't just want to evoke intersubjective agree-ment or express that it is useful to believe in it, but I want to say something about the world.

Paul Horwich (2004, p. 32 ff.) denies that there is a connection between truth and real-ism. In the deflationary theory of truth, truth is not grounded in the world. Language is isolated from the world and truth is locked in the contextual network of language. This also means that there is no longer a criterion for distinguishing between truth and untruth. The mere assertion p makes it true, since "p" and "p is true" are logically equivalent.

Willard v. O. Quine is considered as one of the main representatives of a deflationary theory of truth. For him, truth is always relative to a language or to a theory: "Truth, for me, is immanent. Factuality, or matterhood of fact, is likewise immanent." (Quine 1998, p. 367) Truth, for him, consists in disquotation: "Truth is disquotation." (Quine 1987, p. 213) Nevertheless, he does not seem very comfortable with this conception of truth. On the one hand, he affirms that truth is immanent in language, but on the other hand he also says that it is not sentences that are true, but reality that makes them true:

> Truth hinges on reality; but to object, on this score, to calling sentences true, is a confusion. Where the truth predicate has its utility is in just those places where, though still concerned with reality, we are impelled by certain technical complications to mention sentences. Here the truth predicate serves, as it were, to point through the sentence to the reality; it serves as a reminder that though sentences are mentioned, reality is still the whole point. (Quine 1986, p. 11)

Language is a tool to describe the world. The truth predicate is a mediator between lan-guage and the world: "What is true is the sentence, but its truth consists in the world's being as the sentence says." (Quine 1992, p. 81) In this statement, Quine sympathizes with a correspondence theory of truth. Therefore, Davidson (2005, p. 85) doubts that Quine can be called a deflationist.

Quine traces the origin of truth back to observation sentences. Observation sentences are those sentences that are in direct contact with experience, such as "Snow is white," "It is raining," or "The cat is lying on the mat." An observation sentence is true if all members of a speech community would agree with it (Quine 1974, p. 39; 2013; p. 39, 2019, p. 38). Quine avoids speaking of correspondence. Instead, he attributes the truth of observation sentences to intersubjective assent. But this criterion of truth does not solve the problem. For the speech community can agree to an observation sentence even if it is false, e.g., if the community falls prey to a collective deception or if it simply wants to believe it. Trump claimed that there were more people at his inauguration than at Obama's oath ceremony. Trump's supporters agreed with this claim, despite clear evidence of its falsity. A mere assertion or agreement by the speech community does not make a proposition true.

Nevertheless, it would be premature to criticize Quine on this point. What he describes in his book "Word and Object" (2013) is the ontogeny of language acquisition that is very much influenced by behaviorist learning theory. According to this theory, sensory stimuli cause immediate reactions in observers that lead them to utter certain observation sentences and believe them to be true. We have to remind ourselves that the truth of observation sentences is always provisional because they merely mark the starting point of the cognitive process, but not its result. Observation sentences are verification instances for theories, but they are also theory-laden (Quine 1992, p. 7), revisable and fallible. Observations can fall prey to deception, the observer can make biased judgments, the observational and measurement instruments can be flawed, or a well-confirmed theory can show that there is a systematic measurement error. Quine compares observation and theory with two antagonistic forces, where sometimes one side prevails, other times the other: "Normally, observation is the tug that tows the ship of theory; but in an extreme case the theory pulls so hard that observation yields." (Quine and Ullian 1978, p. 29).

In Quine's holistic theory model, "our statements about the external world face the tribunal of sensory experience not individually but only as a corporate body" (Quine 1963, p. 41). When theory and experience contradict each other, either the observation sentences or the theory must be revised. The crucial point here is to make the sentences fit each other in such a way that the theory is consistent with the observational data. In this context Quine refers to the coherence theory of truth, which has always been in competition with the correspondence theory. For Quine, coherence and correspondence are not competing concepts, but complement each other:

> Coherence and correspondence, properly considered, are not rival theories of truth, but complementary aspects. The coherence aspect has to do with how to arrive at truth, by the best of our lights. The correspondence aspect has to do with the relation of truths to what they say about. (Quine 1987, p. 214)

Quine sees a close connection between truth and the assumption of an external reality (Quine 1995, p. 67). Accordingly, coherence is a necessary condition for the whole theory to be consistent with reality. However, this leaves two questions unanswered: What is coherence and why is coherence an indicator of truth? We will see in the next chapter whether coherence theory can answer these questions.

3.5   The Coherence Theory of Truth

Coherence theory has its roots in the idealistic philosophy of F.H. Bradley, Harold Joachim, and Brand Blanshard. The British idealists conceive reality as a unified, coherent whole and truth as an expression of this holistic unity. Bradley (1909, p. 492) writes:

> Truth is an ideal expression of the Universe at once coherent and comprehensive. It must not conflict with itself and there must be no suggestion which fails to fall inside it. Perfect truth in short must realise the idea of a systematic whole.

In order to grasp truth, we would have to attain a complete knowledge of the world. This is only possible by approximation, which is why truth has different shades and allows for gradations. The more comprehensive and complete the system of knowledge, the truer it is. Therefore, truth is not a property of individual isolated propositions. Only a complete coherent system of propositions can be true. Joachim justifies this with the contextuality of propositions and explains this with the example of the sentence "Caesar crossed the Rubicon in the year 49 BC" (Joachim 1906, p. 104). In order to understand the sentence, one must know who Caesar was, what the Rubicon is, and why Caesar crossed the Rubicon. The singular event is connected to a whole chain of other historical events. Only on the background of this historical knowledge, in the context of Caesar's biography and his political ambitions, does the sentence make sense. You have to know the whole story to understand the sentence. "The true is the whole," as Hegel (2018, p. 13) says. Truth, for Joachim, is "systematic coherence."

For Joachim, coherence is more than logical consistency (Joachim 1906, § 25). Blanshard characterizes a coherent system of knowledge by a high degree of inferential interconnectedness. All propositions support each other and do not contradict each other: "Fully coherent knowledge would be knowledge in which every judgment entailed, and was entailed by, the rest of the system." (Blanshard 1964, p. 264) Since complete knowledge, if we ever attain it, reflects the whole universe, there can only be *one* complete truth.

Coherence theory was taken up again in the 1930s by Otto Neurath, who was critical, or even hostile, to idealism. His main concern was to free philosophy and science from any metaphysical assumptions and to admit only empirically meaningful propositions. Neurath defended an uncompromising physicalism: a scientific theory should consist only of those propositions that can be reduced to verifiable physical propositions. The basis is formed by *protocol sentences,* the function of which is to check other empirical sentences for validity. Protocol sentences are phrased in the third person singular and contain information about the person, time, place, and content of an observation or measurement. For example, "Otto sees a white swan swimming on the lake at 3:13 pm". By observing white swans, the hypothesis "All swans are white" can be confirmed. The observation of a black swan, on the other hand, would disprove the hypothesis.

However, Neurath doesn't think that propositions are always evident and irrefutably true. A proposition can also turn out to be false if it is based on an error or a deception. Therefore, for Neurath, it is not possible to finally falsify universal propositions by observations. The proposition "Otto sees a black swan" stands in contradiction to the hypothesis "All swans are white". Nevertheless, the incompatibility of the two propositions does not necessarily imply the falsity of the universal proposition. Otto could, after all, have been mistaken. This is the reason why a proposition cannot simply be compared with "reality". A proposition can only be compared to other propositions. If a proposition can be integrated into a system of existing propositions and can be made consistent with it, then it is true. If integration without contradiction is not possible, then either the statement must be rejected as false or the existing system of statements must be modified so that it can coexist with the new statement. The aim of research is to bring the propositions of natural science into agreement with as many protocol sentences as possible (Neurath 1983, p. 109).

> If a statement is made, it is to be confronted with the totality of existing statements. If it agrees with them, it is joined to them; if it does not agree, it is called 'untrue' and rejected; or the existing complex of statements of science is modified so that the new statement can be incorporated; the latter decision is mostly taken with hesitation. *There can be no other concept of 'truth' for science.* (Neurath 1983, p. 53)

Interestingly, Neurath does not use the term coherence, presumably to distance himself from idealistic theories of coherence. Basically, for Neurath, if he were to use the term, coherence means nothing else than consistency. Unlike the British idealists, Neurath (1983, p. 105) abandons the idea that there can be only *one* consistent system of hypotheses. Which of the competing systems of propositions we choose is for him a matter of convention. In this way, Neurath anticipates the thesis of the empirical underdetermination of theories, which was later made famous by Quine: scientific theories cannot be built on a firm empirical foundation. Rather, theories are free-floating entities that need only be brought into agreement with experience. Neurath compares a theory to a ship that never comes into contact with solid ground and must be held together by repeated rebuilding: "We are like sailors who have to rebuild their ship on the open sea, without ever being able to dismantle it in dry-dock and reconstruct it from the best components." (Neurath 1983, p. 92).

Like Neurath, Nicholas Rescher also advocates coherentism, according to which knowledge does not rest on a firm foundation and cannot be traced back to indubitable basic propositions. Rescher (1973, p. 319) explains the difference to fundamentalism as follows:

In a way, the coherentist approach is exactly the inverse of the foundationalist. The foundationalist begins his epistemological work with a very small initial collection of absolutely certain truths from which he proceeds to work *outwards* by suitably *additive* procedures to arrive at a wider domain of truth; by contrast, the coherentist begins with a very large initial collection of insecure pretenders to truth from which he proceeds to work *inwards* by suitably *eliminative* procedures to arrive at a narrower domain of truth.

Rescher compares research with a jigsaw puzzle in which one tries to fit together as many pieces as possible and thus obtains, piece by piece, a more comprehensive and coherent picture of the world (Rescher 1973, p. 41). For Rescher, in contrast to Neurath, the starting point of the cognitive process are not protocol sentences. Rather, the knowledge system resembles an interconnected network in which all nodes of the network are of equal importance and no sentence can claim epistemic priority over others (Rescher 1974, p. 700). One starts with individual propositions, called *data* by Rescher, which are assumed to be true but whose truth is not certain. Data can be observations, reports, hypotheses, or conjectures. The initial system of propositions may be inconsistent. Individual elements of this system may contradict each other. The sentences are then tested to see if they fit together. A sentence is accepted as (provisionally) true if it coheres with all other sentences. If not, individual sentences can be modified or removed from the knowledge system. Or auxiliary hypotheses can be introduced to adapt a theory to the empirical data. In addition to theoretical coherence, Rescher introduces the criterion of pragmatic efficacy: the system of knowledge must not only be coherent at the theoretical level, but must also be successful at the practical level (Rescher 1992, p. 175).

It can be objected that the concept of coherence remains vague and unspecific in Rescher's work. It is not clear what coherence is supposed to be more than consistency. It is therefore necessary to specify the concept of coherence. Laurence Bonjour (1985, pp. 95–99) lists five coherence criteria that a knowledge system must meet:

1. A system of beliefs is coherent only if it is logically consistent.
2. A system of beliefs is coherent in proportion to its degree of probabilistic consistency.
3. The coherence of a system of beliefs is increased by the presence of inferential connections between its component beliefs and increased in proportion to the number and strength of such connections.
4. The coherence of a system of beliefs is diminished to the extent to which it is divided into subsystems of beliefs which are relatively unconnected to each other by inferential connections.
5. The coherence of a system of beliefs is decreased in proportion to the presence of unexplained anomalies in the believed content of the system.

Conspiracy theories are highly incoherent according to these criteria: they are probabilistically inconsistent because they are based on improbable assumptions. They consist of a hodgepodge of ad hoc hypotheses and belief postulates with few inferential connections.

Conflicting evidence is simply ignored or neutralized by the addition of more conspiracy hypotheses. As Kuhn (1970) has shown, anomalies can occur in even the best scientific theories and cause a crisis. In contrast to conspiracy theories, crises are taken seriously in science and lead to a reconstruction of the theoretical system that can culminate in a scientific revolution. Such paradigm shifts are prevented in the case of conspiracy theories, since they try to protect their incoherent worldview under all circumstances and immunize themselves against any criticism.

Two main objections have been raised against the coherence theory: First, false theories can also exhibit a high degree of systematic coherence and thus be regarded as true *(fairy tale objection)*, and second, there can also be more than *one* comprehensive coherent theory *(underdetermination objection)*. It is therefore by no means certain that coherence is a reliable indicator of truth. The fairy tale objection was raised by Moritz Schlick, among others.[3] He writes:

> Anyone who takes coherence seriously as the sole criterion of truth must consider any fabricated tale to be no less true than a historical report or the propositions in a chemistry textbook, so long as the tale is well enough fashioned to harbour no contradictions anywhere. (Schlick 1979, p. 376)

Russell objects to the coherence theory that there can be multiple, equally coherent belief systems:

> It may be that, with sufficient imagination, a novelist might invent a past for the world that would perfectly fit on to what we know, and yet be quite different from the real past. (Russell 2001, p. 71)

The coherence theory, so the objection, cannot convincingly explain why there can be only *one* coherent overall system. It could be possible that there are several equally coherent belief systems. The decisive question is therefore whether increasing coherence automatically leads to truth in the sense of correspondence and what the connection is between coherence and correspondence.

Coherence is an internal relation between propositions of a belief system. If a system is only *internally* tested for coherence and never *externally* confronted with reality, it is claimed, coherentism would become a kind of unrealistic idealism and anti-realism. It seem as if our cognitive system is epistemically closed and that there is no input. So the question arises: How can coherentism be reconciled with realism?

Rescher's response to this is that the goal should not be internal coherence, but "coherence with our experience" (Rescher 1992, p. 174). In this link to empiricism, Rescher's

---

[3] Like Schlick, C.I. Lewis points out that also a pack of lies can be coherent and consistent: "A sufficiently magnificent liar, however, or one who was given time and patiently followed a few simple rules of logic, could eventually present us with any number of systems, as comprehensive as you please, and all of them including falsehoods". (Lewis 1946, p. 340)

and Neurath's coherentism differs from idealistic theories of coherence. Rescher regards the assumption of an external reality as a basic prerequisite for the possibility of knowledge (Rescher 1992, p. 270). For him, truth and realism are closely connected:

> We need the notion of reality to operate the conception of truth. A factual statement on the order of "There are pi-mesons" is true if and only if the world is such that pi-mesons exist within it. By virtue of their very nature as truths, true statements must state facts: they state what really is so, which is exactly what it is to characterize reality. (Rescher 1992, p. 260)

Rescher therefore endorses a correspondence theory of truth. The contact to reality is established by the practical success of a theory. And Bonjour, too, sees no contradiction in combining a coherence theory with a correspondence theory of truth (Bonjour 1985, p. 88). It has to be shown that increasing coherence of knowledge leads to an increasing correspondence between theory and reality. To solve this problem, Bonjour constructs a "metajustificatory argument" for the coherence theory to connect coherence and correspondence, justification and truth. It is to show that beliefs that are justified in terms of the coherence theory are true, or at least tend to be true, in terms of the correspondence theory. The realist must convince the skeptic "that someone with a (more or less) coherent set of beliefs has a reason to suppose his beliefs are not mistaken in the main," as Davidson (2001, p. 146) puts it. Bonjour is convinced that coherent theories converge towards a true description of the world (Bonjour 1985, p. 170). But why should coherent systems of beliefs evolve toward truth? It may be quite possible that they lead away from truth, or that they move in circles (Christlieb 1986, p. 401).

To close this explanatory gap, Bonjour introduces the principle of *metajustification*. It states that a system of beliefs that remains coherent and stable over the long run and that receives constant empirical input is increasingly likely to correspond to reality (Bonjour 1985, p. 171). Davidson argues along the same lines as Bonjour. Like Bonjour, Davidson concludes from coherence to the truth of a theory, because a high degree of coherence enhances the probability that "many of our beliefs are true." (Davidson 2001, p. 137). The connection between coherence and truth is a probabilistic one: if our beliefs are coherent, then they are *likely* to be true:

> The presumption increases the larger and more significant the body of beliefs with which a belief coheres and, there being no such thing as an isolated belief, there is no belief without a presumption in its favor. (Davidson 2001, p. 153)

Bonjour's metaprinciple does not give us any *certainty* that our best coherent theories are true or at least truth-like, it only states that coherent theories, if they remain coherent in the long run, are *likely* to be true. Conversely, it follows that false belief systems are incoherent.

The principle of metajustification is also of media-epistemological relevance. Coherence is suitable as a journalistic criterion of truth when information is not directly verifiable but merely based on testimony. In this case, the rule applies that a report is more likely to be true the more independent sources report on it concurrently. For the same reason it would be highly improbable if several independent sources happened to report exactly the same story. Also in the case of testimony, lies and falsehoods are most likely to be exposed because of contradictions and discrepancies in the accounts. It is indeed difficult to keep a large body of lies consistent. Liars inevitably become entangled in contradictions at some point and their web of lies collapses. Coherence checks are therefore an important tool in fact checking to distinguish truth from fake. Fake news is likely to be embellished or exaggerated and, when being retold, it is often varied and altered. Serious news agencies that obey criteria of journalistic objectivity transmit news as truthfully as possible.

Quine has a surprising answer to the fairy tale objection and the underdetermination objection: both objections are justified, but they do not have a negative effect on science. In Quine's view, scientific theories differ only in degree from fairy tales and fictions; they are merely better adapted to experience: "Epistemologically these are myths on the same footing with physical objects and gods, neither better nor worse except for differences in the degree to which they expedite our dealings with sense experiences." (Quine 1963, p. 45) Also the argument that coherent theories are underdetermined doesn't affect Quine, because according to him theories are underdetermined by experience, with the consequence that there can be different theories that agree equally well with experience (Quine 1963, p. 47). That is, based on the data we have no reason to prefer any of the theories. The theories can equally well explain the phenomena.

The underdetermination thesis follows from Quine's holistic theory model. Quine compares the knowledge system to a "man-made fabric which impinges on experience only along the edges" (Quine 1963, p. 42 f.). Within a theory there are propositions that are closer to the periphery, such as the observation sentences, and propositions that are theoretical in nature and more distant from the periphery. The theory network responds flexibly to new data. New experiences can be assimilated if they can be coherently integrated into the system. If, on the other hand, an anomaly occurs, i.e. a contradiction between theory and empirical data, the theory can be saved from contradiction by the introduction of auxiliary hypotheses. Only if the anomalies become more numerous and serious, then fundamental modifications must be made that affect the theory core. Such modifications may create new theories or different versions of a theory that agree equally well with the empirical data. This coherence model can explain equally well both the structure and the dynamics of scientific theories (cf. Zoglauer 1993, ch. 4).

Nevertheless, some questions still remain. Rescher and Bonjour define truth as correspondence and consider coherence merely as a criterion of truth. Coherence provides a test "for judging that objective truth conditions are satisfied" (Davidson 2001, p. 137). Coherence is used to infer truth, "for we have reason to believe many of our beliefs cohere with many others, and in that case we have reason to believe many of our beliefs are true." (Davidson 2001, ibid.) This still leaves one problem: The correspondence theory is based on a metaphysical notion of reality that is not conceptually explainable. It is therefore important to clarify the relationship between truth and reality.

3.6   Perspectival Realism

We have yet not come any closer to answering the question of what truth is. From what has been said so far, it should have become clear that the concept of truth is closely related to the concept of reality. A purely discourse-immanent definition of truth, in which different discourses of truth are equally valid, would lead to post-factualism. A speech community cannot simply stipulate truth by convention or consensus, because objective truths are supposed to hold independently of human beings. In contrast, correspondence theory and approximation theory presuppose a metaphysical concept of truth, namely, a truth that is completely detached from the human subject. Accordingly, all our theories are, strictly speaking, false, because they are constantly being improved and thereby coming closer to the truth. We are thus faced with the dilemma of defining truth either internally, i.e. in terms of language and theory, or externally, i.e. in terms of reality.

Before we can clarify the concept of truth, we have to understand first what we mean by "reality", since different concepts of reality circulate in philosophical discourses and it is often claimed that reality is socially constructed. Let us consider an example. Arthur Stanley Eddington, in the introduction to his book "The Nature of the Physical World" (1929), describes how he is sitting on a chair in front of his desk, picking up paper and pen to write the introduction to his book. He surprises the reader by claiming that there is a duplicate of every object. There are two tables, two chairs, and two pens. The table he sits in front of has a spatial extent, it has a color, a smooth surface, and it feels hard and impenetrable. As a physicist, however, he can describe the table in another way: The second table consists of protons, neutrons, and electrons, and besides that empty space. The thingness and substantiality of the first table disappear and turn out to be an illusion. The electrons orbiting the atomic nucleus do not possess the properties we know from ordinary bodies: They are colorless, indistinguishable, and cannot be precisely located in space. Strictly speaking, they are not particles, but quantum fields. One may therefore ask: which of the two tables is real? Should we trust quantum mechanics more than our sense perception? Is the world of appearance just an illusion? Or do our common-sense experience and physics provide two equally valid descriptions of reality?

Obviously, for the everyday person and for the physicist, reality is something different. When we talk colloquially about the world, we use ordinary language. Scientists of different disciplines, on the other hand, use their own specialist language, in which not only observation terms but also theoretical terms occur, which may have a different meaning than observation terms in ordinary language (cf. Zoglauer 1993). In ordinary language, the concept of reality has a clearly defined meaning: something is real if we can perceive it without error. Everyday objects like tables, chairs, flowers or trees are real because we can see, feel and touch them. But I can still ask the question: Does the tree exist if I do not perceive it? And what about objects that are beyond my visual horizon, things I have never seen? In this case the objects are cognitively constructed by our mind. I can usually rely on the testimony of my friends, as well as media and scientific evidence, to be sure that a particular object exists. For example, I have never seen Rio de Janeiro's Sugarloaf Mountain with my own eyes, but I know it exists because I have seen pictures, reports, and movies of it. I also know that Mars has two moons, Deimos and Phobos, because I've read that in astronomy books. Sugarloaf and the moons of Mars are therefore real to me, even though I have never seen them. Reality is the result of a cognitive construction from the knowledge I have.

A physicist, on the other hand, has to deal with electrons, gravitational waves and black holes, which are not so easy to observe, but which are nevertheless assumed to exist. Physicists use different criteria than in everyday life to decide whether something exists. A physicist cannot observe electrons and other elementary particles directly, but only indirectly with the help of complex devices and measuring instruments. She uses other terms and categories to describe reality. For her, an electron is both a particle and a wave – Eddington (1929, p. 201) speaks of a "wavicle", a mixture of "wave" and "particle". In an electron cloud, an electron does not occupy a precisely determined location; rather, only the probability to find the electron in a particular region of space can be specified. Science constructs a symbolic world, which Eddington calls a "shadow world". The apparent substantiality of things dissolves and is replaced by abstract, shadowy objects such as electron clouds, which can only be described accurately in the language of mathematics. Reality is constructed theoretically in physics, albeit not arbitrarily, but in such a way that it corresponds to empirical data.

We have to take into account that there are different views among physicists about what is real. For example, are electric fields real or are they just useful theoretical tools to describe electrical phenomena? For Albert Einstein, a physical quantity has a counterpart in reality if it is possible to predict its value with certainty without disturbing the system (Einstein et al. 1935). Niels Bohr (1929), on the other hand, objects that with every measurement the object to be measured is influenced, which is why a deterministic description of the object is impossible. Accordingly, a physical quantity can be regarded as real only if it has been measured. Werner Heisenberg (1958, p. 54 f.) justifies this with the thesis that a quantum mechanical system is only in the mode of possibility and changes into the state of reality after a measurement. Other scientists believe they can get by without reference to real entities. *Instrumentalism* assumes that unobservable objects such as electrons, quarks or neutrinos are merely useful fictions postulated in order to better understand and explain the world.

In the everyday world there are colors, but for the physicist they are electromagnetic waves with different wavelengths. For us, the table seems to be continuously filled with matter. Physically, it consists of 99.99% empty space. Yet, we believe that both descriptions are useful because they capture different aspects of the same reality. The two worlds are not independent, they overlap and there are transitions between the two modes of description. Consequently, the common-sense perspective and the physical perspective are not incommensurable. Niels Bohr (1929) considers the classical and quantum mechanical approaches as complementary to each other. The quantum mechanical formalism describes the behavior of a system without the influence of an observing and measuring subject.

Only when a measurement is made an interaction between subject and object occurs. By performing a measurement, quantum mechanical phenomena are transferred into the observable world and become describable in terms of classical physics.

Eddington's example shows: We can describe what reality is only within a conceptual system. Nevertheless, in using different linguistic and theoretical means we still believe that we are describing the same world. As a consequence, we are not perceiving *two* different tables, but only *one* table that can be viewed from two different epistemic perspectives. The perspectives just show an *apparent* world, behind which a mind-independent reality is hidden, which itself remains unknowable. Every appearance is an appearance of something, and Kant calls this something the thing in itself:

> In fact, if we view the objects of the senses as mere appearances, as is fitting, then we thereby admit at the very same time that a thing in itself underlies them, although we are not acquainted with this thing as it may be constituted in itself, but only with its appearance, i.e., with the way in which our senses are affected by this unknown something. (Kant 2004, p. 66)

The concept of reality is confusing and contradictory. When we say "this tree is real", we are using linguistic means to refer to an object of our sense perception. Yet, by using the term "tree" we are referring to something that is *outside* of language. "Reality" is therefore on the one hand language-dependent, because it can only be described by linguistic means, but on the other hand it points beyond language and transcends the world of appearances. To avoid such confusion, it makes sense to use two different terms and to distinguish between "reality" and "REALITY": Reality exists only within a language or conceptual scheme. In contrast, REALITY, Kant's thing in itself, is independent of any language and cannot be grasped conceptually. REALITY is thus something that simply exists and is not socially constructed. If REALITY did not exist, we would live in a world of illusion and appearance and would not be real ourselves.

Rudolf Carnap (1950) distinguished between internal and external questions. For Carnap, it is an external question whether there exists a mind-independent REALITY, whereas natural science can only answer internal questions about the existence of concrete objects. For example, if we want to know whether black holes exist, we are talking about objects of physics and are using a scientific language. We can describe black holes within the framework of general relativity. The question of the existence of black holes can be answered empirically. There are verification criteria that we use to decide whether a particular everyday object, such as a tree, exists. The thing world is described in a thing language, just as the physical world is described in a physical language. But the question of the REALITY of the thing-world is not an internal question; it cannot be answered within the thing language; it is an external question because it transcends any language framework and cannot be answered by empirical means. External questions are metaphysical questions, such as "Do uncountable sets exist?" or "Why is there anything at all and not rather nothing?". In order to answer them, one would have to adopt a God standpoint, which is impossible. Statements about the REALITY of the external world have no truth values, because there are no verification criteria for their truth.

Carnap advocates a deflationary metaphysics, according to which metaphysical problems are merely pseudoproblems that cannot be decided empirically or a priori.[4] Nevertheless, ontologies have an orientational function and thus a practical utility. Which ontology and conceptual framework we prefer depends on practical considerations. In the lifeworld context, an ontology of ordinary substantial objects turns out to be convenient, whereas quantum mechanical phenomena can be better explained within a field ontology. Quine (1963, p. 19) therefore argues for tolerance and openness in the choice of an appropriate ontology, and is willing to include abstract objects such as classes in his ontology besides physical objects.

Occasionally it is claimed that a mind-independent REALITY is a self-contradictory concept. For by thinking a REALITY, it is no longer thought-independent. The very claim that a mind-independent REALITY exists makes use of the ontological notion of existence. Marcus Willaschek (2015, p. 14) draws attention to the problem of "giving the notion of mind-independent existence any intelligible content." The question is: how can we speak in language about something that lies beyond language and cannot be grasped conceptually? Wittgenstein says, "The limits of my language mean the limits of my world." (TLP 5.6) For Wittgenstein there are things about which we cannot speak, which point beyond language, and which merely "make themselves manifest" (TLP 6.522).

In a sense, it is a semantic problem. When we talk about the everyday world, we use colloquial language. And when a physicist talks about electrons, quarks, and quantum fields, he is operating within the theoretical framework of quantum theory or quantum field theory. Again, it makes sense to say that "electrons are real". But in physics, "reality" has a different meaning than in colloquial language. Reality is therefore always relative to a conceptual system or epistemic perspective. The concept of *REALITY* is different. We cannot describe REALITY because we lack a suitable conceptual framework and language for doing so. Nor can we recognize REALITY. And even if we could recognize it, we would not know it because we cannot compare our conception of REALITY with REALITY itself and determine whether it corresponds to it or not.

Nevertheless, I think that the philosophical concept of REALITY makes sense. Since the semantics of ordinary language and physical language cannot be used to talk about REALITY, we have to introduce another semantics. The solution to the problem could be provided by a fictionalist semantics (Predelli 2020). In fictional discourse we talk about fictional things that do not exist or that we do not know whether they exist. We pretend *as if* they exist. Hans Vaihinger (2021) considers Kant's thing in itself as a fiction. He accuses Kant of unjustifiably applying the categories of thing, property, and causality to the thing in itself in order to establish a connection between the real external world and our world of appearances. On the other hand, we cannot help but designate something that exists

---

[4] Besides Rudolf Carnap, also Hans Vaihinger, William James, W.v.O. Quine and Hilary Putnam can be mentioned as representatives of a deflationary metaphysics.

independently of us with a category, "for otherwise it is not only unthinkable but even inexpressible" (Vaihinger 2021, p. 69). We *must* assume the existence of things in themselves "as if they influenced us and thus gave rise to our idea of the world" (Vaihinger, ibid.). The existence of a mind-independent REALITY is a philosophical fiction, but a meaningful and indispensable fiction, without which the world would seem completely incomprehensible to us.

If there were not a REALITY beyond our world of experience independent of our perception, the reality of a tree would consist only in its being perceived and the world would be an illusion. And the same holds in physics: if beyond theory and measurement won't be a REALITY independent of theory, the reality of an electron would consist only in the measurement of its physical properties. The two tables described by Eddington would indeed be different, they would be *two* tables, if there were not a REALITY independent of these epistemic perspectives, so that common-sense and physics refer to the *same* object and we can speak of *one* table. We can therefore say: there are different realities, but only *one* REALITY.

Just as there are two realities in the case of Eddington's two tables, there are also two truths: a truth in ordinary language and a physical truth. The sentence "The table has brown color" is true in ordinary language because the truth of the sentence can be confirmed by perception. Physically, however, the atoms and molecules of the table are colorless, so the sentence is scientifically false. Strictly speaking, there is no such thing as a table, only a table-like arrangement of atoms. Truth is always relative to an epistemic perspective or conceptual scheme. This conflict between different truths would be problematic only if all possible perspectives and thus also the truths associated with them were equally valid, or if they were epistemically incommensurable. The consequence of such truth relativism would be post-factualism. But as we have already seen, we cannot accept that all perspectives are equally valid. Besides the common-sense perspective and the scientific perspective, there are also less credible worldviews, such as pseudoscience, esotericism, and conspiracy theories. If we had to choose between science and pseudoscience, we would certainly prefer science. We will choose the epistemic perspective that has the greatest explanatory content, is most consistent with experiential data, has the highest degree of coherence, and which expands our knowledge. If we want to explore the nature of things and want to know, for example, what this table is made of, we cannot stop at the level of sense perception and everyday experience, but must examine the table scientifically.

I will propose perspectivism based on scientific realism as a solution to these problems. In philosophy this approach is known as *perspectival realism*, which was founded by Ronald Giere and Michela Massimi. Ronald Giere (2006, p. 81) argues that truth is always relative to a perspective. Michela Massimi (2018b, p. 347) emphasizes the perspectival character of scientific knowledge: "Knowledge claims in science are dependent on a given historically and/or intellectually situated scientific perspective." Massimi (2018a, p. 170 f.) summarizes the central theses of perspectival realism (PR) as follows:

1. PR endorses the realist *metaphysical* tenet about a mind-independent (and perspective-independent) world.
2. PR endorses the realist *semantic* tenet about a literal construal of the language of science.
3. Finally, PR endorses the realist *epistemic* tenet in thinking that acceptance of a theory implies the belief that the theory is true (and even shares the realist intuition that truth has to be cashed out in terms of correspondence rather than coherence, warranted assertibility and so forth).

It is not clear how these theses are supposed to be compatible with each other. On the one hand, Massimi, like Giere, postulates a pluralism of perspectives and says that there is no "God's eye view" and that knowledge is always historically and culturally relative. On the other hand, she advocates a correspondence theory of truth and claims that there are facts and truths independent of perspectives: "There are facts about water and its properties that are independent of scientific perspectives." (Massimi 2018a, p. 171) Massimi justifies this as follows: Truth claims are always perspective-dependent, but truth itself is perspective-independent. Perspectives merely provide context-dependent truth conditions, which can be translated from one perspective to another by using transformation rules. Due to scientific progress, later theories are better able to explain phenomena and assess hypotheses. Massimi therefore recommends more epistemic modesty: our current scientific theories may not be true, but from our current perspective they are the best theories available (Massimi 2018a, p. 173). We have to agree with Massimi on this point: If there is any access to truth at all, then only science can provide it.

However, Massimi's perspectival realism struggles with the same problems as the correspondence theory of truth. What can it mean that there is a perspective-independent truth? What are the corresponding counterparts of true statements in reality? What are the truth-makers? If there is no "God's eye point of view" and if truth conditions are always historically contingent and only valid within a perspective, as Massimi repeatedly emphasizes, how can there be a perspective-independent truth at all?

Perspectival realism is therefore faced with the dilemma to decide between one of the following alternatives: Truth is either perspective-dependent or perspective-independent. A solution might be found in a compromise: Truth is context-dependent and perspective-immanent, but it also has a perspective-independent reference to REALITY. Scientific theories construct different realities that are grounded in a theory-independent REALITY. Without this reference to REALITY, our best scientific theories would be dangling in the air disconnected from the ground and would be mere fantasy. Without "the world out there" there would be no error-correcting authority which could falsify our hypotheses and theories.

My version of perspectival realism differs from Massimi's version in the following point: I reject the correspondence theory and the associated metaphysical concept of truth. Whether a statement is true or false can only be determined within a conceptual system. Any truth is only provisionally valid, since with the progress of knowledge our network of theories and concepts is adapted to new experiences and thus the truth values of statements can change. With new knowledge we gain new truths and can refute old truths.

The perspectival realism presented here has much in common with Hilary Putnam's *internal realism*. Reality, for Putnam, can only be a reality within a conceptual system. Different theories are based on different ontologies with their own criteria of reality. Each ontology with its corresponding conception of reality has its legitimacy. Objects are thus always theory-dependent: "In my picture, objects are theory-dependent in the sense that theories with incompatible ontologies can both be right." (Putnam 1992, p. 40) Elsewhere, Putnam (2016) refers to Eddington's example of the two tables and sees no contradiction between common-sense realism and scientific realism: both tables are equally real. A table can be described as hard, brown, and impenetrable as well as a quantum mechanical object consisting of particles and fields (see also Putnam 1983, p. 230).

However, my conception of realism differs from Putnam's internal realism. Putnam refers to Peirce's concept of truth and defines truth as ideal rational acceptability (Putnam 1981, p. 55). For him, a statement is true if it can be justified under "epistemically ideal conditions". Unfortunately, Putnam cannot explain what he means by ideal conditions: "Epistemically ideal conditions, of course, are like 'frictionless planes': we cannot really attain epistemically ideal conditions, or even be absolutely certain that we have come sufficiently close to them." (Putnam 1981, p. 55) Peirce (1955, p. 38) defines truth as "the opinion which is fated to be ultimately agreed to by all who investigate." Like Peirce, Putnam (1987, p. 54) also believes that if scientists would only think long enough, they would finally arrive at a view that would withstand any criticism and which would then have to be accepted as true. In this context, Putnam mentions Karl-Otto Apel and Jürgen Habermas, who also refer to Peirce and have arrived at the same conception of truth. Apel (2002, p. 133) summarizes Peirce's argument as follows:

> *Truth* (with regard to *reality* in general) is that consensus which *would* finally *be* reached in an infinite research community, if the research process could be continued under ideal communicative (i.e., related to intersubjective understanding) and epistemic (i.e., related to the respectively given truth criteria) conditions, that means *potentially infinitely*.

Habermas (1998a, p. 367) defines truth as follows: "A proposition is true if it withstands all attempts to refute it under the demanding conditions of rational discourse." These definitions of truth presuppose a long list of idealizing conditions: the discourse community is a "community of inquirers of potentially infinite size" (Putnam 1987, p. 54), which must have "sufficient experience of the kind that it is actually possible for beings with our nature" (Putnam 1981, p. 64), meaning as much as that it must have sufficient background knowledge and expertise. In the words of Apel (1988, p. 429), it must be an "ideal communication community". Discourse must be "free of domination" and take place in an "ideal speech situation" (Habermas 1971, p. 136 ff.) and participants must have unlimited time at their disposal so that consensus is finally reached. It should be obvious that these ideal conditions can never be fulfilled in the real world. Truth thus remains an unattainable distant goal. In this way a metaphysical concept of truth enters the theory through the back door, because it represents a fictitious ideal. The truth so defined would not be falsifiable and would be absolutely valid.

There is another reason why we cannot free ourselves from the perspectivity of our conceptual schemes by performing an infinite discourse: The human capacity for cognition is limited in principle. Putnam repeatedly reminds us that our knowledge depends on underlying conceptual schemes, which we cannot take off. Even if our theories converge towards a final truth, that truth will still be a truth within a conceptual scheme. Even asking the simple question "How many objects really exist?" makes no sense independent of a given conceptual scheme (Putnam 1987, p. 20). Other conceptual schemes lead to other truths.

Unlike Putnam, I stick to a perspective-dependent concept of truth: there can only be provisional truths that can be refuted at any time and replaced by better truths, where "better" is to be understood in the sense of higher empirical adequacy. Like Putnam, I believe in scientific progress. But it does not necessarily follow that there is a convergence towards an infallible absolutely true theory. There are good reasons to believe that science will never reach an end and that there are insurmountable limits of knowledge (Rescher 1992, 1999). Science is a fundamentally unfinished and unfinishable endeavor. For every question we can answer, at least ten new questions arise that await an answer. Rescher distinguishes between "our concept of reality and reality as it really is" (Rescher 1999, p. 163). I call the former "reality," the latter "REALITY." Since science is always fallible, it can never fully or even partially represent REALITY adequately.[5] It can only describe a model-like, theoretically constructed reality. As Rescher (1999, p. 165) puts it, "Within a setting of vast complexity, reality outruns our cognitive reach; there is more to this complex world of ours than lies – now or ever – within our ken."

Conceptual relativism shows that truth is always relative to an epistemic perspective. Nevertheless, not all perspectives are equivalent. Perspectival realism grants scientific theories a special status because we believe science is most capable to yield objective knowledge which enables us to orientate ourselves in the world. However, a skeptic might question the preference of scientific theories over alternative epistemic perspectives: Why should only scientific theories have a connection to reality and not religious belief systems, myths, or indigenous worldviews? Doesn't perspectival realism amount to *scientism*, that means, science's exclusive claim to truth? The term scientism is often used pejoratively to criticize a too narrow understanding of rationality. In the positivism dispute, representatives of the Frankfurt School in particular have repeatedly accused empirical-analytical philosophy to support scientism. Jürgen Habermas defines scientism as "science's belief in itself: that is, the conviction that we can no longer understand

---

[5] If REALITY were knowable, this would amount to idealism. Vittorio Hösle (2015, p. 40) explains the basic idea of objective idealism as follows: "Being must be conceived essentially intelligibly." If this were so, there would no longer be an epistemic and ontological distance between mind and world; rather, the world itself would be spiritual in nature.

science as one form of possible knowledge, but rather must identify knowledge with science" and accuses it of being "regressed behind the level of reflection represented by Kant's philosophy" (Habermas 1972, p. 4 f.). And Adorno (1976, p. 22) takes the same line: "Since scientistic truth desires to be the whole truth it is not the whole truth."

Recently, the scientism controversy has flared up again, as various publications show (Boudry and Pigliucci 2017; de Ridder et al. 2018; Peels 2017a). Van Woudenberg et al. (2018, p. 2) understand scientism as "the view that only science can provide us with knowledge or rational belief, that only science can tell us what exists, and that only science can effectively address our moral and existential questions". Rik Peels (2017b, p. 168) defines scientism by the thesis: "Only natural science delivers knowledge." In these definitions it is claimed that the natural sciences have sole ownership of truth and knowledge. In the same move, other forms of knowledge, such as common-sense knowledge, are discredited and their truth denied. Non-scientific sources of knowledge are considered unreliable. But why should a sentence such as "This table is brown" be false? Just because color is a subjective quality and not a physical property? Common-sense knowledge can certainly provide us with useful and sometimes even vital guidance. Religious beliefs such as "God exists", although not scientifically justifiable, can also give many people support and comfort in difficult existential situations and help to cope with the contingencies of life. Conflicts can arise, however, when "religious truths", as they are maintained for example by the "Young Earth Creationists", contradict scientific truths.[6] Questions of fact have to be answered by science.

A preference for scientific forms of knowledge does not mean the delegitimization of other epistemic perspectives. Instead, there can be a prioritization or gradation of different perspectives whose value is judged according to their ability to generate knowledge. The evidence-based scientific method is distinguished by its capacity for error correction and openness to criticism. In this ability science is superior to other epistemic perspectives, as demonstrated by scientific and technological progress. Perspectival realism is not committed to any particular ontology, such as reductionism, materialism, or physicalism, especially since physical theories also make use of quite different ontologies, for example the particle ontology of Newtonian mechanics, the field ontology of quantum field theory, or substantivalist and relationist space-time ontologies. There are scientists and philosophers for whom mathematical structures are as real as rocks, stars, or black holes (Barrow 1992; Penrose 1989; Tegmark 2015). Rik Peels (2017b) remarks that the natural sciences rely on non-scientific sources of belief such as introspection, memory, intuition, and metaphysical principles to produce knowledge. Perspectival realism is therefore not committed to scientism, because we can advocate a pluralism of perspectives and partly admit non-scientific sources of knowledge and still grant science a privileged epistemic status.

Our best available scientific theories form a reference system on the basis of which truth claims can be decided. Science provides a picture of the universe, albeit incomplete,

---

[6]Young Earth Creationists take the Bible literally and believe that the earth is no more than 10,000 years old and that humans and dinosaurs lived together before the Flood.

but one that is constantly expanding and improving. Different disciplines such as physics, biology, chemistry, and psychology contribute different, mutually complementary aspects to the overall picture. In this way a view of reality emerges, which, although changeable in perspective and history, nevertheless provides a successful and indispensable frame of reference for our thoughts and actions. But this *reality* is not *REALITY*, rather it is a theoretically constructed ersatz REALITY that we deal with *as if* it were real. The earth, moon, and sun are real to us. When astronomers assure us that the earth revolves around the sun, that proposition is true for us. We establish the truth of this proposition by comparing it with empirical data. The empirical data are, to use Quine's term, part of the periphery of our network of theories with which we describe the world. The data are independent of us because we cannot influence them. But they are described in a conceptual framework provided by the theory, in this case an astronomical theory. A part of reality, namely that which we passively experience without being able to actively influence it, exists independently of us, while the theoretical framework is the result of a construction process. From the axioms of Newtonian mechanics and Kepler's laws it follows that the planets move in elliptical orbits around the Sun: This is the truth for us. Truths, however, can change. In the Aristotelian-Ptolemaic worldview, the Earth stood immovably in the center and the Sun orbited the Earth in a perfect circular path. Today we know that this is false.

As already said, science provides only an incomplete picture of the world. Many scientific questions, such as whether there is life on other planets or whether the universe is finite or infinite, cannot be answered according to the current state of research. We do not know whether the sentence "There is extraterrestrial life" is true or false. At best, we can say that for all we know, it is very *likely* that extraterrestrial life exists somewhere in the universe. In our scientific worldview, therefore, there are *"truth value gaps"*: propositions whose truth value cannot (yet) be determined. Even if we do not know the truth value of such propositions, we at least know the truth criteria. When it comes to the question of the existence of extraterrestrial life, we know what life is and how to detect the presence of life. Whether or not there is life anywhere outside of Earth is fixed independently of us. It is part of REALITY. In the context of our biological theory, therefore, the above proposition has a definite truth value that we merely do not know. Truth-value gaps are therefore epistemic, not ontological.

Unlike truth value gaps, there can be no *"reality gaps"*. The visible universe may be limited, but we assume that there are galaxies, stars and planets beyond the horizon of observation. Although the epistemically accessible reality may be incomplete, REALITY definitely is not. Gaps in reality are filled ontologically and reality is thus completed. In this way a truth-value definiteness can be guaranteed. Truths are discovered, not invented. What is invented or constructed are our theories and conceptual schemes. But within this theoretical framework, truths are fixed independently of us.

Michael Dummett has elaborated a *verification theory of truth,* or a "justificationist theory of meaning" as he calls it. In his view, a statement can only be called true if we can show that it is true, that is, if the claim has been verified. And it is false if it has been falsified. But if we do not know whether it is true or false, then it has no truth value. Therefore, according to Dummett, the proposition "There is life on Mars" is neither true nor false because we have not yet discovered life on Mars, on the other hand we cannot rule it out either. This theory of truth has drastic consequences. First, it rejects the law of the excluded middle: "A justificationist theory of meaning (…) cannot admit the principle of bivalence: for a statement we have no effective means of deciding, we have no guarantee that we shall arrive at a justification either of it or of its negation." (Dummett 2010, p. 136) And second, this leads to the existence of reality gaps: "The resulting metaphysics is one that allows the existence of gaps in reality." (Dummett 2010, ibid.) According to Dummett, the limits of our knowledge are the limits of our world: the world literally vanishes there. The world of the anti-realist is thus much smaller than the world of the realist. Therefore, it is better to remain a realist.

Social constructivism is right in one respect: Our theories and perspectives are socially constructed. Our image of reality is the result of a historical, social and cultural construction process. But it does not follow from this that all these perspectives are equally valid. Perspectival realism does not lead to truth relativism. For among the many different perspectives there are better and worse ones. Some can explain the world better than others. Among all perspectives, scientific theories have proven to be superior. We owe the scientific-technological revolution the overwhelming success of science, which helped to enforce enlightenment against superstition. If we abandon the scientific path to truth, or believe that there are multiple truths from which we can choose at will, if we trust demagogues and post-truthers more than experts, then we are following a dangerous path that leads finally to a post-truth society.

Information and Knowledge

4

4.1 Information Ecology

Let us return to the initial question I posed at the beginning of Chap 1: How can we orientate ourselves in a world in which we are permanently surrounded by information of all kinds and how can we distinguish between true and false information? We have to select and evaluate information, separate the important from the unimportant, truth from fake. How can we gain knowledge from information?

Due to the digitization of the everyday world, we are constantly exposed to a flood of information that we have to channel. Information overload can cause stress and make decision-making more difficult (Tessier 2020). More information also means: more false, unreliable and misleading information, fake news and bullshit. Since we don't always have the time to check information for its truthfulness and sources of information for their reliability, misinformation may break through our cognitive firewall and take root in our memory.

I will use the term *information ecology* to refer to the relationship of humans to their information environment. Luciano Floridi (2013, p. 6) refers to the human information environment as the "*infosphere*". This chapter will focus on distinguishing different types of information, which are present in the infosphere, and asking for their informational and truth value. We have to remind ourselves that an uncritical reception of information can lead to misinformation and a distorted view of reality with dangerous social and political consequences. Floridi compares the world created by the infosphere with the "Matrix" from the Hollywood movie of the same name. This is because the subjective reality is cognitively constructed from the information that is assimilated and processed by our brain. The informational construction of the world begins with sensory perception. In the sense organs, physical stimuli are converted into nerve impulses and transmitted to the brain, which interprets these signals. According to Heinz von Foerster (2003) and Gerhard

T. Zoglauer, *Constructed Truths*, https://doi.org/10.1007/978-3-658-39942-9_4

Roth (1987), our nervous system uses the "principle of undifferentiated encoding": "The response of a nerve cell does not encode the physical nature of the agents that caused its response. Encoded is only "how much" at this point on my body, but not "what."" (Foerster 2003, p. 215)

This means "that the brain, instead of being open to the world, is a cognitively closed system that interprets and evaluates neural signals according to internal criteria. About the true origin and meaning of these signals it knows (absolutely) nothing" (Roth 1987, p. 235). Gerhard Roth puts it succinctly: "the sensually perceived world is nothing but a construct of our brain" (ibid.). Radical constructivism concludes from this that at the level of sensory stimuli there is "no representation of the world", but only a "mosaic of elementary states of stimuli" (Roth 1992b, p. 290). The actual information about the nature of the stimulus can only be reconstructed at a higher cognitive level, through the accounting and processing of *all* neural signals, although it is not clear whether an already existing information is *reconstructed* in the process or whether the information is thereby generated in the first place. According to Humberto Maturana and Francisco Varela (1992, p. 164), the human cognitive system is operationally and thus also informationally closed. Whatever one may think of this constructivist thesis, it must in any case be admitted that sensory information at the neural level is not atomistically distributed, but has a holistic quality: only the totality of all neural stimuli provides us with information about the external world. The neural system is not endowed with a semantics. Neurons cannot understand anything, instead the information is *generated* by our brain.

What was started on the neural level continues on the social and communicative level. More and more digital media are interposed between us and the world, giving us access to the world through which we communicate, receive information and maintain social relationships. This represents an enormous expansion of our perception of the world: Through the Internet we are connected to the world at all times and can, in principle, access any information we want. The whole world is digitized and delivered to our homes.

The digitization of the everyday world is not only reflected in the use of digital information and communication media, but also in the transformation of the concept of information: "*informatio*" (Latin) originally meant an idea or the meaning of a word, but also instruction and teaching about its content. This colloquial meaning was replaced in the twentieth century by a technical concept of information. Nowadays, information is mainly present in digital form. Through digitization, information is decontextualized, translated into a sequence of zeros and ones, and transported from the sender to the receiver. It is only at the receiver that the message is decoded. Digitization is therefore accompanied by a *destruction of meaning*. Warren Weaver, besides Claude Shannon one of the pioneers of modern information theory, puts it this way: "In fact, two messages, one of which is heavily loaded with meaning and the other of which is pure nonsense, can be exactly equivalent, from the present viewpoint, as regards information." (Shannon and Weaver 1963, p. 8) That is, you cannot tell from a digital message whether it is true or false information or just plain nonsense.

Information has become a commodity and a power factor. However, information has first to be obtained. The knack consists in finding the desired information among the flood of data. *Data mining* uses special algorithms and statistical methods to analyze large amounts of data and to extract information. It is occasionally said that data is the oil of the twenty-first century, the raw material from which knowledge is gained. Robert Laughlin (2008, p. 4) supports the thesis that in the information age, "access to understanding has become more important, in many instances, than access to physical means." By interpreting data we gain information and from true information we gain knowledge. When talking about data, information and knowledge, these terms are rarely defined precisely. Often the terms "data" and "information" are used interchangeably. The confusion stems from the fact that the terms are based on different intuitions. It is therefore important to distinguish and differentiate between these terms.

Data are symbols that stand for things, events, persons or their properties. They are something like the smallest units of information, the "atoms of information", so to say (Nerurkar and Gärtner 2020, p. 196). That can be instrumental readings, health data or information about age, gender, income and political attitudes of citizens. The data itself, the so-called "raw data", are just numbers and symbols – itself meaningless unless they can be assigned to persons or things and thus be interpreted. Thomas Bächle (2016, p. 111) insists to take into account that data is not something given, but something made. From the standpoint of semiotics, data are signs that stand for something and were created by someone for a specific purpose. Only if one knows to which objects the data refer and in which context they stand, then they acquire meaning and only then they become *information.*

4.2   Semantic Information

The concept of information is omnipresent and has become a basic concept of the digital age. Nevertheless, the term remains mysterious and surrounded by legends (Janich 2018). Even in the scientific literature, there is no unique definition to be found and everyone understands something different by information depending on the disciplinary context: in computer science, Shannon and Weaver's (1963) technical concept of information is used, while in biology, a functional concept of information is more common (see Zoglauer 1996). Philosophers prefer to speak of "semantic information", this theory was founded by Rudolf Carnap and Yehoshua Bar-Hillel (1964) and further developed by Luciano Floridi (2011).

According to a widespread view, information is a subject-independent entity. For example, the American philosopher Fred Dretske (1981, p. vii) describes information "as an objective commodity, something whose generation, transmission and reception do not require or in any way presuppose interpretative processes". The English physicist Tom Stonier goes even further and regards information as a basic ontological structure of the universe:

Information exists. It does not need to be *perceived* to exist. It does not need to be understood to exist. It requires no intelligence to interpret it. It does not have to have meaning to exist. It exists. (Stonier 1990, p. 21)

According to Stonier, a book would still contain information even if no human being read it, and even if all humans who could understand the book had died out.[1] Carl Friedrich von Weizsäcker, who has contributed more than almost anyone else to the clarification of the concept of information, also occasionally falls back into a naturalistic way of speaking when he writes in "The Structure of Physics" (2006, p. 213): "The chips in a computer, DNA in a chromosome contain their information objectively, independently of what a human being knows about it." The physicist Anton Zeilinger (2005, p. 217) speaks of information as a "primordial substance of the universe" and equates it with reality: "Reality and information are the same" (ibid., p. 229). In opposition to this metaphoric idealization, Peter Janich (2018) attests information theory a kind of of mysticism and a removal from our colloquial understanding of information. The reason is that the technical concept of information pursues a different knowledge interest than the information-seeking citizens, who just want to "inform" themselves.

Claude Shannon was concerned with the problem of noiseless signal transmission: How can a message be decoded if there are distortions and interferences in the communication channel and the signal has to be filtered out from the background noise? For a given noise level, how much of the transmitted information reaches the receiver? To address these questions, Shannon first had to define the concept of information with mathematical precision. For an engineer it is not important to decode the *meaning* of a message; what is crucial for him is to recognize a signal as such in the first place and to distinguish it from statistical noise. As Shannon and Weaver (1963, p. 31) remark: "Those semantic aspects of communication are irrelevant to the engineering problem." So the crucial question is: is it a signal or not? The more signals, i.e. data, are transmitted and arrive at the receiver, the more information the message contains. The elementary information unit, 1 bit, corresponds to a yes-no answer or a binary alternative. Therefore, the technical notion of information is not concerned with what meaning a message has, but rather with the problem of whether or not a signal can carry any meaning at all. A sequence of zeros and ones may have no meaning for us, but it *can* have a meaning and, for example, control a computer program as a machine language. Hans Christian von Baeyer (2005, p. 43 f.) explains Shannon's concept of information as follows: "To find the information content of a message, first translate this message into the binary code of the computer and count the number of digits in this sequence of zeros and ones."

---

[1] The philosopher Fred Dretske (1985, p. 174) expresses himself in a similar way. For him, information exists objectively and independently of human beings: "Information, as defined above, is an objective commodity, the sort of thing that can be delivered to, processed by, and transmitted from instruments, gauges, computers, and neurons. (…) It is something that was in this world before we got here."

However, Shannon's definition does not correspond to our common-sense understanding of information. For us, only a meaningful message can have information value. The sentence "the sun is shining" contains information because it represents a fact, whereas the string "het nus si gishinn", which was created by a simple transposition of the letters from the first sentence, contains no information for us because it is meaningless and has no representational content. Nevertheless, according to Shannon and Weaver, both sentences contain the same information value.

In order to remove the deficits of Shannon's concept of information and to restore our ordinary understanding of information, Carnap and Bar-Hillel (1964) introduced the concept of *semantic information* (cf. Zoglauer 1995, 1996). Put simply, it is a measure of the meaning content of a message. While Shannon and Weaver ascribe an information value also to single signs, Carnap and Bar-Hillel allow only meaningful statements as information carriers. The more a sentence tells, the more information it contains. For example, the sentence "Today the sun is shining *and* it is raining" contains more information than the sentence "Today it is raining" and the latter in turn contains more information than the sentence "Today the sun is shining *or* it is raining". And the sentence "All men are mortal" has a higher information value than the sentence "Mr. Smith is mortal", because the second sentence is a conclusion from the first.

The semantic information theory of Carnap and Bar-Hillel, however, has a paradoxical consequence: tautologies like the law of non-contradiction say nothing about reality and thus contain no information. And what is perhaps even more perplexing: contradictions, i.e. propositions of the form "p and not-p", have the highest information value. This is called the *Bar-Hillel-Carnap paradox*. To rule out this paradoxical consequence, Floridi (2011) modified the semantic notion of information. According to Floridi, an information-containing sentence must not only be meaningful, but also true. This requirement is called "*veridicality thesis*". False information would therefore not be semantic information according to Floridi. For him, the formula is: Information = Data + Meaning + Truth. Information is what a sentence tells about the world. Floridi bases his theory of semantic information on Wittgenstein's picture theory of language: true sentences are images of reality (TLP 2.222, 2.223). But since only those sentences contain information that tell something about reality, only true sentences can be informative. False propositions say nothing about reality. Dretske (2008, p. 276) takes a similar view: "Not only must information be about something, what it says about what it is about must be true for it to count as information. If it isn't true, it isn't information."

Unfortunately, this view does not take into account the pragmatic dimension of language. Information is always context-dependent and is constituted by the recipient's interpretation of the data. Information is thus not a natural object that can be transported from sender to receiver. Information does not exist in the world, it cannot be naturalized, but requires consciousness in order to be interpreted (Zoglauer 1996). I would like to illustrate this with an example. When a mother says to her eight-year-old son, "Daniel, clean up your room!" a lot of information is communicated by this sentence, namely that the room is untidy, that the mother wants her son to clean up the room, that Daniel is neglecting his duties, and that his negligence will have educational consequences. Daniel will know from the tone of his mother's admonition that she is very upset and will conclude that he will be confined in his room if he does not clean up. Even a silence can carry information, as Romele (2020, p. 29) demonstrates with an example: if a man asks his wife a question and the wife does not respond, this can mean that she did not hear the question or that she is upset and refuses to answer. All this information can be inferred from the specific context of action in which the utterance is made.

Just as texts can contain a hidden message, a *subtext,* also information can contain *sub-information.* When Donald Trump told his supporters to march to the Capitol on January 6, 2021, to express their displeasure about the allegedly rigged presidential election, they took this, in the context of the heated atmosphere, as an encouragement to storm the Capitol and turn violent. These examples show that questions, commands, and even a silence can contain semantic information even though they have no descriptive content. The informative content can vary depending on the situation and the articulation of the speech act. The manner of an utterance, even if false, can provide information about the speaker. For example, Trump's numerous lies reveal a great deal about his state of mind. Lies thus also have informational value. Floridi's veridicality thesis is therefore untenable.

Suppose a thief breaks into a jewelry store, is caught by the store owner, and as a result, the burglar shoots the manager. Hoping to get off with a lighter sentence, he admits to the burglary in court but denies murder. He says, "I broke into the store, but I didn't shoot the store manager." According to the correspondence theory, this statement is false, because he has already been convicted of murder. Therefore, under Floridi's theory, the statement contains no information. Nevertheless, the defendant provides an important piece of information: namely, he admits that he committed the burglary. Formally, the statement represents a conjunction of a true and a false proposition. If one conjunct is false, the whole sentence becomes false. Therefore, one cannot conclude from the falsity of the statement that it does not contain a true proposition and thus information.

Some sentences, which were once believed to be true, may later turn out to be false. In the past, people believed that the earth was flat. For many people, this represented an important information about the shape of the earth. Today we know that the sentence is false. But for us contemporaries it also contains information about the worldview of ancient times. Lundgren (2019, p. 2893) cites Newtonian mechanics as another example that contradicts the veridicality thesis:

> Proponents of the veridicality thesis would have to say that Einstein showed that Newton's mechanics is not semantic information. But it is much more reasonable to think that we can classify Newton's mechanics as semantic information *and* add that it is false.

Weather forecasts are another example (Lundgren, ibid.). Weather forecasts have a probabilistic character. For example, it is said that the probability of rain tomorrow will be 90%. This information causes many people to take their umbrellas with them the next day. Semantic information evokes an effect in the recipient: it may be a change in behavior, as in the weather forecast example, or simply the fact that the listener gains a conviction or believes something. And even if it doesn't rain tomorrow, that doesn't erase the information or make it worthless. Probabilities say something about possibilities or tendencies, but nothing about reality. According to Floridi, they should therefore contain no information, which seems counterintuitive. As we have seen, statements about possibilities or tendencies do indeed have an information value.

Dretske (2008, p. 280) believes that information can be sent like a letter: "Write down what you mean, put it (what you've written) in a stamped envelope, deposit it in the mailbox, and – bingo! – meaning gets from Chicago to Vienna in a few short days." Dretske speaks of an "information flow," as the title of his book (1981) indicates, because he thinks that information can "flow" from sender to receiver. According to this view, the meaning of the message is coded in its material carrier: "meaning goes with the ink marks" (Dretske 2008, ibid.). This does not take into account that meaning only exists if there is an interpreter who can read and understand the message. Without interpreters, the information would be lost and the letter would only contain ink blots without meaning. A transmission of information only succeeds if the sender and receiver interpret the data in the same way. The following example shows how such a transmission can go wrong: Suppose Barbara wants to do some workout. Therefore she calls a fitness center and says, "I want to hire a coach." Unfortunately, she dials the wrong phone number and ends up with a bus rental service. The information is transmitted correctly, but misunderstood by the recipient. As a result, Barbara can now enhance her fitness by bus driving.

In order for an information to "flow" from A to B, the transmission of information must be *transitive*, i.e. it must be possible to copy it repeatedly. Dretske (1985, p. 173) calls this the "*xerox principle*": If A contains information B and B contains information C, then A also contains information C. Dretske explains this with an example:

> If the acoustic pattern reaching my ears carries the information that the doorbell is ringing, and the ringing of the bell carries the information that the doorbell button is being pressed, then the acoustic pattern also carries the information that the doorbell button is being pressed (xerox principle). (Dretske 1985, p. 175)

The transitivity of information transfer can be easily refuted by a counterexample. Suppose someone claims:

1. Everything in this book is wrong.
   The sentence (1) is in this book. Therefore it contains the information
2. The sentence (1) is wrong.
   If sentence (1) is false, then it follows from (2):
3. Not everything in this book is wrong.

(1) and (3) contradict each other, so the sentence (1) cannot contain the information (3). Therefore, the xerox principle is wrong.

The notion of information transfer from sender to receiver is, as Jakob Krebs (2014) shows, misleading. Information has a relational character and is not a substance that can be transported from A to B. If the context changes, the information also changes.

4.3   Misinformation and Disinformation

Of the millions of bits of information that reach us every day, most of it turns out to be unimportant or useless. We receive spam, are bombarded with advertising on all channels, and we hear and read all kinds of rumors, gossip, and tittle-tattle. The Internet invites people to spread false information in order to manipulate others. One can speak of a downright "information pollution". Stanislaw Lem therefore considers it extremely important to recognize and evaluate the informational value of incoming stimuli: "A necessary prerequisite for not "drowning" in the swelling flood of information is to recognize the quality of the information, not to take note of unimportant information, advertising, trivialities, and nullities." (Lem 2002, p. 275 f.) It is important to distinguish true from false news and to correctly assess the reliability, credibility, accuracy, relevance and objectivity of information. Information quality depends on the trustworthiness of the source, the type of information, but also on the information channel. This is because the quality can decrease on the way from the sender to the receiver due to incorrect forwarding. One might think of the game "Chinese whispers", popular among children, in which a message arrives at the recipient garbled, disfigured, and distorted after a long chain of transmission.

If one assumes, as Floridi and Dretske do, that information is always true, there should actually be no misinformation or disinformation (Floridi 2011, p. 93 ff.; Dretske 2008, p. 276 ff.). *Misinformation* is information that is false. There is a whole continuum of intermediate values between truth and falsity, which makes it difficult to clearly distinguish true information from false information. For example, are exaggerations, embellishments, or compliments misrepresentations? Is bullshit or inaccurate representation a form of misinformation? Bullshit in the sense of prattle, waffle, or drivel (Dietz 2017, p. 51) is not necessarily false. Rather, it is information without informational value. The expectation of accuracy of a statement depends on the context and purpose of the information. If the physics teacher asks a student what the speed of light is, she will be satisfied with the answer "300,000 km/s". But for astronomical calculations, a more precise number is needed: 299,792.45 km/s. Therefore, it is important to distinguish information not only in terms of its truth content, but also in terms of its *information quality*.

When false information is disseminated with the intent to deceive, it is called *disinformation*. Don Fallis (2014, p. 137; 2016, p. 333) defines disinformation as intentionally misleading information. Fake news therefore represents a special form of disinformation because it has the characteristics of misleading and intent to deceive. In contrast, Zimmermann and Kohring (2020) do not regard the intention to deceive as a necessary criterion for disinformation. They justify this with the examples of clickbaiting and misinformation intentionally incorporated into Wikipedia articles to test whether these errors are noticed and corrected. Clickbaiting is the use of sensational headlines in Internet articles to attract attention and curiosity, thus driving up traffic and advertising revenue. However, the examples mentioned by Zimmermann and Kohring are not convincing, as the clickbaits are set with the intention of creating false expectations in the reader. It is irrelevant whether the information is believed by the readers or not. The intentional misleading as such implies an intent to deceive because the readers are not getting what they expect. Similarly, in the case of intentionally manipulated Wikipedia articles, it is irrelevant whether the misinformation is believed by Wikipedians or not. They are pretending something that is not true. Thus, there is an intent to deceive.

As we have seen, information is neither true nor false in itself, but is *interpreted* as true or false. If it is misinterpreted, it is *misinformation*. Conspiracy theorists in particular tend to misinterpret information. Let me illustrate this with an example. When Neil Armstrong became the first man to walk on the moon on July 21, 1969, the event could be seen live on television screens around the world. The blurry black and white images were of poor quality compared to today's high definition television images. From a technical point of view, the images had little information value. You could see Armstrong as a black shadow descending the barely discernible ladder of the lunar module and setting his foot on a bright surface that must have been the "Mare Tranquillitatis." In the context of news reporting, a particular interpretation of the images is given: Neil Armstrong makes the first step on the lunar surface. Conspiracy theorists, however, interpret the images differently: an actor descends the model of a lunar module in a Hollywood studio and touches the studio floor covered with sand and stones with his foot. The information content of the images allows for both interpretations. How one interprets the television images – whether as a live broadcast from the moon or as a Hollywood production – depends on the framing. A conspiracy theorist believes that the USA has always been involved in plots and conspiracies and thinks that the government and the media deceive the citizens also in the case of the moon landing. For conspiracy believers, the media reports are part of a gigantic disinformation campaign.

We can consider the television image of the first step of a man on the moon as an ambiguous figure: If you trust the media, it is a document of the first moon landing. If, on the other hand, one assumes a conspiracy, it is a fake. Only by contextualizing the perceived image in one's own worldview and in the background context the information becomes a proposition that can be true or false. If one does not confine oneself to the shadowy television images, but also takes into account the films, photographs, and rock samples that the astronauts brought from the moon to earth, as well as the testimonies of NASA engineers and the scientists who examined the moon rocks, one must conclude that the television images were authentic and that the moon landing actually took place. Information then becomes knowledge.

4.4   Knowledge in Context

The difference between true and false information is so important because we can gain *knowledge* only from true information. Keith Hossack (2007, p. 7; 2011, p. 71) defines knowledge as a relation between mind and world: I know that p if and only if p is a fact. According to this view, knowledge has a representational character: it represents the world or a part of the world in my mind. I stand in an epistemic relation to the world when I know something. This conception of knowledge, however, assumes a naive realism and presupposes a correspondence theory of truth (see Sect. 3.1). We do not know what the world is like in itself, but can only construct a model of the world and build a coherent system of knowledge on the basis of it. Wittgenstein (OC, § 410) writes: "Our knowledge forms an enormous system. And only within this system has a particular bit the value we give it." Accordingly, a proposition p can count as knowledge only if p is part of this comprehensive belief system. When we know something, we connect it with other knowledge: "we are placing it in the logical space of reasons, of justifying and being able to justify what one says" (Sellars 1997, p. 76). This knowledge system includes not only empirical knowledge, but also logical and mathematical knowledge. Knowledge always has the form "S knows that p", where S is a human subject and p is the propositional content of knowledge.[2]

Knowledge always has a subjective and an objective component. The subjective component represents the attitude of the subject towards the propositional object of knowledge: I can *believe* that p is true, I can be *convinced* that p is true, or I can be *certain* that p is true. The objective component is the content of the belief, that is, the proposition p itself. The proposition can be true or false. Whether it is true or false does not depend on the subject, but is objectively fixed.

To know something, I must be able to give *reasons* for the truth of the proposition p. I must be able to justify p. With this requirement an accidentally true belief is ruled out. For example, I can guess in a dice game that I will roll a six next. As it happens, a six does indeed appear. But I can't claim that I *knew* it, because I had no grounds for my belief. Consider another case: "I know that a total solar eclipse occurred in Germany on August 11, 1999." I can justify this knowledge either by my perception, because I was an eyewitness to this event, or I can retrodict the event by using the laws of celestial mechanics and calculating when the solar eclipse did happen, or I can refer to testimonies and television reports and other media accounts documenting the event. Once I have come to the reasonable conclusion that proposition p is true, I can add it to my corpus of knowledge.

Knowledge involves three things: a belief, a justification, and the truth of the proposition. It is these three elements that make up the classical definition of knowledge: Knowledge is a true justified belief. S knows that p if and only if (i) p is true, (ii) S believes that p, and (iii) S is justified in believing that p. This definition contains all the important

---

[2] In addition to propositional "knowing-that", there is also a "knowing-how" or implicit knowledge that describes practical skills. However, such non-propositional forms of knowledge will not be examined here.

aspects of knowledge. However, Edmund Gettier (1963) raised objections to this definition, which led to a long-lasting controversy about the necessary and sufficient conditions of knowledge. His counterexamples satisfy all three requirements for knowledge – truth, belief, and justification – but cannot be called knowledge. The examples are constructed in such a way that someone has a true, justified belief that p, but p just *happens* to be true. Let me illustrate this with an example that doesn't go back to Gettier, but was devised by Alvin Goldman (1976).

Henry makes a car ride with his son and they come to an area where there are barns on the left and right side of the road. His son points to one of the barns, which stands out because of its striking red color, and asks, "Dad, what's that?" His father replies, "That's a barn." Let's assume that Henry is right. Because the object does indeed look like a barn, he is justified in his belief. What Henry and his son don't know, is that they are currently driving through a Potemkin village where sets have been built for a film production. All the barns, except one, are dummies. Coincidentally, his son pointed to the only real barn. So Henry had a true, justified belief. Still, we wouldn't call this knowledge. Henry was just lucky with his guess.

The trick of such Gettier-type examples is that two different perspectives on an issue are presented: Henry doesn't know that most of the barns are fakes. In his perspective, seeing only the seemingly real facades, he is perfectly justified in identifying the object shown by his son as a barn. Readers of the story, however, get an important additional information that Henry does not have: We know that these facades are fake barns and that only the red barn is real. This additional information exposes Henry's knowledge as pseudoknowledge: Henry is not, for all *we* know, justified in calling it a barn. The barn example, therefore, in no way refutes the classical model of knowledge. It merely shows that whether there is knowledge depends on the context and background knowledge.[3]

Common-sense knowledge and scientific knowledge are judged by different standards. To use Eddington's table example: I know that the table I am sitting in front of is brown, although at the same time I know that the atoms that make up the table have no color. The two statements seem to contradict each other: Either the table has a color or it has no color, but it cannot be both the case. The contradiction resolves when we consider that we are speaking of the table in different contexts. In the first case I consider the table as an everyday object and use colloquial language, while in the second case I speak of the table as a physical object in a scientific context. A layperson and an expert may well come to different conclusions. We can either claim that these are two different concepts of knowledge or that there are different degrees of knowledge and that expert knowledge is an extension of common-sense knowledge. Physical knowledge is founded on common-sense knowledge and refines it. Therefore, epistemic *contextualism* does not lead to relativism. Everyday life and science merely apply different standards or requirements to knowledge. Peter Baumann (2015, p. 79) takes it for granted that the standards for knowledge in one context can be lower or higher than in another context: "Thus, one has to know the context in order

---

[3] On epistemic contextualism, see: Baumann (2016), Ichikawa (2017).

to judge whether a person knows that this or that is the case or not. Knowledge varies with and depends on context." As Michael Blome-Tillmann (2019, p. 177) puts it, "Epistemic contextualism is, as a consequence, a linguistic or semantic view – namely, the view that the truth-values of 'knowledge'-ascriptions – sentences of the form 'x knows p' – may vary with the context of utterance."

4.5   Degrees of Knowledge

Fake news and conspiracy theories are regarded as categorically different from scientific knowledge. However, it is not taken into account that there are different degrees of knowledge and that fluid transitions from established knowledge to mere conjecture and ignorance are possible. For the reception of information it is therefore important to distinguish between different qualities of information and knowledge.

In epistemology, it is generally assumed that knowledge does not admit of degrees. We may be *convinced* of something to a higher or lower degree, but we would not normally claim "that someone knows something to a higher (or lower) degree than another", as Elke Brendel (2013, p. 121) writes. In contrast to this orthodox view, I want to argue for a *knowledge gradualism* according to which there are degrees of knowledge and it makes a difference whether someone knows something for *sure* or whether it is merely a well-grounded guess.

The orthodox view is based on the law of the excluded middle, according to which a proposition is either true or false, but there are no other truth values between true and false. If knowledge is defined as "true justified belief", a belief can be either true or false, and hence there can only be knowledge or non-knowledge, but nothing in between. This does not take into account that justifications may well admit degrees: An opinion can be well or badly justified, well or badly empirically confirmed, and therefore we can know something more or less.

Norman Malcolm (1963) was one of the first to distinguish between knowledge in the strong sense and knowledge in the weak sense. Knowledge in the strong sense is when I am *sure* that I know something. If I am not sure, if I know something only in the weak sense, then I check it and make further investigations in order to be completely sure:

> When I use "know" in the weak sense I am prepared to let an investigation (demonstration, calculation) determine whether the something that I claim to know is true or false. When I use "know" in the strong sense I am not prepared to look upon anything as an *investigation;* I do not concede that anything whatsoever could prove me mistaken; I do not regard the matter as open to any *question;* I do not admit that my proposition could turn out to be false, that any future investigation *could* refute it or cast doubt on it. (Malcolm 1963, p. 64)

Malcolm explains this with an example (ibid., p. 62 ff.): Suppose I want to calculate 92 × 16 and arrive at the result 1472. If I am asked, "Are you sure?", I reply, "I am pretty sure. But since I'm not that good at mental arithmetic, I want to do the math again." So I know it only in a weak sense. On the other hand, when I'm asked, "How much is 2 + 2?", I say, "4" without hesitation, and I can spare myself the recalculation, because I am absolutely sure that the result is correct. In this case, I know it in the strong sense.

Now, one could object to Malcolm that his distinction and his examples only concern the *degree* of a belief, but not the *content* of a belief. Gerhard Ernst (2010, p. 61 f.) distinguishes two dimensions of a belief: its strength and its content. In Malcolm's example, the proposition "92 × 16 = 1472" is the content or object of the belief. The belief may be strong or weak, certain or uncertain; in any case, it characterizes the subjective attitude of the knower toward the proposition. The content of the belief, on the other hand, admits of no degrees. The law of the excluded middle asserts: either 92 × 16 = 1472 or 92 × 16 ≠ 1472. If the calculation is correct, then the result is objectively correct, whether one is convinced of it or not. Therefore, if one wants to defend knowledge gradualism, one has to show that not only the strength of one's belief but also its content allows for quantitative differences. And indeed, one can know more or less, one can have a rich detailed knowledge or possess only a superficial knowledge.

Stephen Hetherington (2005, 2011) differentiates between different degrees of knowledge or depth of knowledge and explains this with an example (Hetherington 2011, p. 170): Suppose I see a bird sitting in my garden and realize that it is a goldfinch. I recognize it by its black, white, and red head and its call, which sounds like "didlit." By these characteristics I can distinguish it from other species of birds. I can therefore confidently claim, "I know that this is a goldfinch," even though I am not a bird expert. An ornithologist knows birds better than I do and will additionally be able to identify the goldfinch (carduelis carduelis) by its wings, flight, breeding behavior, and feeding habits, and therefore be able to assert with greater certainty that it is a goldfinch. A molecular biologist can identify the bird according to its genetic code and can derive the phylogenetic tree of this species from it. That means, the more characteristics or typical aspects of an object I know, the more I know about that object. It is not just subjective belief, but the larger background and contextual knowledge that leads to a deepening of knowledge. I can be mistaken as a layperson and mistake the goldfinch for a chaffinch, but an expert knows more about birds than I do and can judge more accurately.

Assertions can be more or less credible, well or less confirmed, hypothetical or speculative. The quality of knowledge depends, among other things, on the *degree of confirmation*. The better a hypothesis is empirically confirmed, the more convincing it is. Consider, for example, the proposition "All swans are white". The more white swans I have observed, the better the hypothesis is confirmed. However, it can also happen that I observe a black swan and my hypothesis is thereby falsified. My knowledge about swans thus turns out to be wrong. But one can also say: My knowledge about swans is expanded. I learn that there are different species of swans, of which mute swans (cygnus olor) have white plumage, while black swans (cygnus atratus) are black. I therefore modify my original hypothesis and know now that "All swans of the species cygnus olor are white" and "All swans of the species cygnus atratus are black". In this way my knowledge is refined and deepened.

We hold knowledge to be absolute because we believe that a true proposition is a faithful representation of reality. But as we have seen, knowledge always represents only a perspectival model of the world and can never represent the world as it is in itself. A model can be more or less adequate, which is why truth also admits of gradations and degrees. The degree of truth is an inner-theoretical criterion of the reliability of an assertion or a model, but it cannot indicate how "close" it is to reality. Just as there is a continuum between truth and falsity, there are also degrees of knowing and not knowing, ranging from established scientific theories to pseudoscience and conspiracy theories.

4.6   Second-Hand Knowledge

People who believe in fake news or conspiracy theories or doubt accepted scientific theories, get their knowledge second-hand, e.g. from dubious internet sources. They use social media and believe rumors or trust what their friends and like-minded people say. Information p is transmitted from a source A to a receiver B according to the principle: A believes that p, B trusts A and therefore also believes that p. There is no independent verification of the truth of p. Such information transfer can go well if p is true, A has good reasons for p, and thus B also acquires a knowledge of p. But a knowledge transfer can also fail, e.g. if B falls victim to a mistaken belief. In the following we will investigate under which conditions a knowledge transmission can succeed and the receiver B actually acquires a knowledge of p.

Knowledge from hearsay is indirect knowledge and is therefore more prone to error than direct knowledge. We acquire direct knowledge through perception, or the truth of an assertion, e.g. a mathematical theorem, is immediately obvious or provable a priori. Perceptual knowledge is non-inferential knowledge because it is given directly and does not have to be inferred from other knowledge. Inferences can be deductive or inductive, that is, information-preserving or information-expanding. Inductive inferences are therefore more prone to error because they are based on presumptive knowledge. Leaving aside the a priori truths of logic and mathematics, we can gain direct empirical knowledge only by perceiving our immediate environment and drawing conclusions from it. Everything else we learn from the reports of others or infer it inductively. Children learn from their parents or acquire their knowledge from teachers. We obtain much of our knowledge from the media: books, newspapers, radio, television, the Internet. All this knowledge is second-hand knowledge.

David Hume regards such indirect knowledge with suspicion and attributes to people a credulity towards the reports of others. He notes "a remarkable propensity to believe whatever is reported, even concerning apparitions, enchantments, and prodigies, however contrary to daily experience and observation" (Hume 1978, p. 113). In this way, he is addressing a phenomenon known today as "fake news" that spread in the eighteenth century in the form of superstition and belief in miracles. The question therefore arises: How trustworthy and reliable is second-hand knowledge?

The optimists among the epistemologists tend to grant a high degree of trust in the reports of others. Thomas Reid (1818, p. 353 f.) refers to God and believes that he has endowed people with a love of truth and trust in the testimony of others, so that we may believe their reports. Tyler Burge assumes, similar to Reid, that we may accept other people's accounts as true unless there are opposing reasons not to do so. Burge (2013, pp. 237, 265) calls this the *acceptance principle:* "A person is entitled to accept as true something that is presented as true and that is intelligible to him, unless there are stronger reasons not to do so." Burge justifies this by saying that in social interaction with other people we have to regard them as rational beings, because this is for him a necessary presupposition of communication. And he adds that rationality implies truthfulness. Therefore we can trust other people.

I think this view is naive. It means that we have to accept fake news and conspiracy theories as true, as long as there are no opposing reasons. Fake news spreads so quickly and unstoppably precisely because many people adhere to the acceptance principle and trust the reports of others without question. In the worldview of Trump supporters, there is no reason to distrust his tweets because they all *seem* true. Those who believe that the results of the 2020 presidential election were rigged don't think that there is any need for proof of that. Rather, it would be up to Biden supporters to make sure that there was no fraud. The acceptance principle basically calls for a reversal of the burden of proof: it is not the conspiracy theorists who would have to justify their claims, but rather one is allowed to believe in them as long as there are no reasons *against* the existence of a conspiracy. But conspiracies, unfortunately, cannot be falsified.

In order for the recipients of a message to know something, stronger criteria than Burge's acceptance condition must be met. A reasonable conjecture seems to be the following *transmission principle:*

(A) If A knows that p and A tells B that p, then B also knows that p.

Let's consider the following example: Albert knows that Christine is in New York. Christine has sent him selfies with the Statue of Liberty in the background. Albert therefore has good reasons to believe that Christine is in New York. Albert tells Bennie that Christine is in New York and Bennie will believe him. Albert and Bennie are good friends. Albert has never lied to Bennie. Therefore, Bennie trusts his friend. Trust is obviously an important prerequisite for successful knowledge transfer. John Hardwig (1991) considers trust to be a more fundamental source of knowledge than empirical data or logical arguments. Therefore, we can modify the transmission principle (A) as follows:

(B) If A knows that p and A tells B that p, and B trusts A, then B knows that p.

What is the basis of Bennie's trust that Albert is telling the truth? Albert has not shown Bennie the photos of Christine. The trust is based solely on Albert's testimony and his behavior in the past: so far, Albert has always told the truth. From this, Bennie concludes that Albert has a trustworthy character. Trust thus becomes a matter of character. Hardwig (1991, p. 702) regards this to be the basis of the knowledge we receive from others: "I have claimed that trust in the testimony of others is necessary to ground much of our knowledge, and that this trust involves trust in the character of the testifier." However, Hardwig here confuses trust with justification: in order to obtain knowledge, a belief must be *justified*. Justification requires good reasons. Trust in the character of others is not sufficient for this. Trust is a subjective psychological attitude, whereas reasons have the form of objective rational arguments.

Bennie's trust that Albert is telling the truth is based on his knowledge of Albert's character and past behavior. Trust thus presupposes a knowledge, namely a *meta-knowledge* about another person's knowledge. Consider another example: Barbara is very interested in mathematics. Although she has never studied mathematics, she enjoys solving mathematical puzzles and reading popular science books on mathematical topics. Her friend Andrew is a famous mathematician and tells her that he has just proved Fermat's conjecture, which states that the equation $x^n + y^n = z^n$ has no positive integer solutions if n is a natural number greater than 2.[4] Andrew tells her he is sure that Fermat's conjecture is true. Let p be the Fermat conjecture. Andrew knows that p is true because he knows the proof. Andrew tells Barbara how he found the proof. Unfortunately, she doesn't have enough expertise to understand Andrew's proof. But Barbara trusts Andrew. Thus, the conditions for using the transmission principle (B) are met. Does Barbara know that p is true? Are the reasons Barbara has for the truth of p sufficient to call it knowledge?

As we have already seen, there are different degrees of knowledge. If Barbara has read about Fermat's theorem on the Internet, this is a form of knowledge. But Barbara is not an expert in the field of number theory. Mathematicians know more about that. Not every mathematician is able to follow the complicated proof of p in all its details. Few experts have a complete overview of all the steps in the proof. Andrew undoubtedly has a complete knowledge of p. Barbara's knowledge is limited. She does not know all the reasons Andrew has for p. But she does possess a *meta-knowledge* about Andrew: she knows that Andrew is a recognized expert in the field of mathematics, that his proof has been thoroughly peer-reviewed by other experts, has appeared in a prestigious journal, and has become widely accepted. Because of this meta-knowledge, she can trust Andrew. We can therefore modify the transmission principle as follows:

(C) If A knows that p and A tells B that p and B has meta-knowledge about A that justifies B's trust in A, then B also knows that p.

The example of Andrew and Barbara shows how knowledge is weakened as it is transferred from A to B. The attenuation can have the following reasons: B does not possess a complete background knowledge of A; B does not know all the reasons why A is convinced of p; B lacks the necessary understanding of p; or B does not trust A, or B does not have complete meta-knowledge of A. The loss of knowledge is especially noticeable when

---

[4] Fermat's conjecture was proved in 1994 by Andrew Wiles in collaboration with Richard Taylor. The proof is 98 pages long.

knowledge is transferred through a long chain of many people. In this case not only the knowledge about p, but also the meta-knowledge of A must be transferred from the messengers to the subsequent recipients. If this meta-knowledge is missing, the knowledge source is not trustworthy.

We have found that the quality of knowledge deteriorates through transmission. I would like to call this the *principle of diminishing knowledge:* If no new information or new reasons or evidence are added along the transmission path, then the quality of knowledge deteriorates. But can transmission also *generate* new knowledge? Jennifer Lackey (1999, p. 473) claims that the receiver B can gain knowledge of p even if the sender has no knowledge of p. She states: "I shall claim that there are some plausible ways in which a hearer can acquire knowledge that p via a speaker's testimony that p despite the fact that even the first speaker in the chain in question fails to know that p." Lackey justifies her thesis with the following example (Lackey 1999, p. 477): Mrs. Smith is a biology teacher who teaches at a Catholic school. The curriculum includes Darwin's theory of evolution. However, Mrs. Smith is a devout creationist and does not believe in evolutionary theory. Nevertheless, she must teach her students what is required by the curriculum. Therefore, she goes to the library, reads books about the theory of evolution, and teaches her students the necessary knowledge. She doesn't show that she thinks Darwin's teaching is blasphemous nonsense, but diligently follows the textbooks she has read. The students now know all about the theory of evolution. But Mrs. Smith has no knowledge of evolutionary theory because she does not believe in it, and belief is in fact a necessary condition for knowledge. How can a knowledge be transmitted if the sender (Mrs. Smith) does not possess the knowledge? Doesn't this contradict the principle of diminishing knowledge?

Let's consider where the students' knowledge comes from. Mrs. Smith is ruled out as a source of knowledge. Let us analyze the case from the viewpoint of information transmission. The students receive the information about the theory of evolution from Mrs. Smith. Mrs. Smith obtained the information from textbooks and passed it on to her students unchanged. The information from the textbooks came from other scientific sources and ultimately go back to Charles Darwin, the founder of the theory of evolution. Of Darwin we can rightly say: he possessed a sound knowledge of the theory of evolution, he was convinced of it, and he had good reasons and empirical evidence for its correctness. Darwin is thus the real source of the students' knowledge, the "first speaker" in the transmission chain, so to say. Mrs. Smith merely acts as a transmitter of information. She could have taught the subject by simply reading it to her students word by word from a textbook. Mrs. Smith could have been replaced with a robot that read the material just as she did. Or the students could have extracted their knowledge from the Internet. Mrs. Smith is just a passive messenger – like a mailwoman or like a phone line. Let us assume for a moment that the lesson is only intended to impart knowledge of the history of science, and that the students are instructed to know what Darwin wrote in his book "On the Origin of Species," then this knowledge is transmitted from Darwin to the students via many intermediate steps and Mrs. Smith is one link in this transmission chain. No new knowledge is added along the way. On the contrary, the students cannot know everything that Darwin knew. Therefore, the principle of diminishing knowledge holds here as well.

One can doubt that in the case of Mrs. Smith the students really acquire a knowledge from her. This is because the students do not have a complete meta-knowledge of their teacher. If the students knew that she was a staunch creationist, they would not trust her. Consequently, the conditions for the transmission principle (C) are not met and the students do not possess a reliable knowledge of evolutionary theory. This consideration shows the importance of background knowledge and context in assessing the quality of knowledge. The students believe they have a solid knowledge of evolutionary theory. However, Lackey's story provides a different view: Mrs. Smith is in fact not a reliable and unbiased teacher. If she rejects the theory of evolution outside of class, she cannot simply put her beliefs aside in class and appear as a convinced Darwinist. The students' knowledge is thus compromised and impaired. The problem also has a political dimension: should devout creationists be allowed to teach biology in schools? Or can we trust doctors who have appeared as Covid deniers or who are active in the anti-vaccination movement?

Edward Craig (1993) adds the notion of a "good informant" to the classical definition of knowledge as true justified belief: Knowledge must come from a reliable source of information about which we know, or at least can assume with a high degree of probability, that it is not lying to us. Craig tightens his requirement with the additional condition that the good informant not only has to tell the truth factually, but also tell the truth in other possible worlds similar to our world and the factual situation (Craig 1993, p. 69). Consider again the example of Mrs. Smith and her students. Mrs. Smith tells her students the truth about the theory of evolution. She seems to be a good informant. But now let's change the initial situation a bit and suppose that Mrs. Smith is annoyed about the headmaster, who thinks that she is an untrustworthy teacher because she polemicizes on blogs and social media against evolutionary theory and defends creationism. In her anger, she drops her restraint and openly tells the students that she thinks the theory of evolution is wrong because it contradicts the creation story. In this case, she is not a good informant. But since this hypothetical case is similar to the situation Lackey describes and could occur at any time, Mrs. Smith cannot be considered trustworthy even if she strictly adheres to the curriculum. To put it in other words: Mrs. Smith is a weak link in the chain of knowledge transmission. The students' biology books are good informants, as are the textbooks Mrs. Smith has read in preparation for her classes. But she remains trapped in her religious worldview and offers no guarantee for reliably conveying the subject to her students in an unbiased manner. Mrs. Smith is therefore not trustworthy.

Peter Graham (2006) takes Lackey's example and modifies it a little. This time the teacher is called Mr. Jones, who is supposed to teach his students the theory of evolution. Like Mrs. Smith, he is also a staunch creationist and does not believe in evolutionary theory. He just pretends to accepts the theory to fulfill his duties as a teacher. He gets his information from textbooks and passes it on to his students. In this respect, the starting point is the same as in the case of Mrs. Smith. In Graham's case, however, the story takes an unexpected turn. Jones makes a discovery one day: he finds the fossil of an extinct animal that he believes should not actually exist. That's because it's at least one million years old, making it much older than the world according to the creation story. But Jones does not show his astonishment and his doubts and slips again into the role of the convinced evolution theorist. He shows the fossil to his students, keeps his opinion to himself, and explains the fossil as Darwin would have done. The students now know that the fossil is older than one million years. Jones does not believe this. Graham argues that this gives the students a *new* knowledge. This is because nobody knew about the fossil before Jones discovered it. Therefore, no one could have known before that it was older than one million years. Graham (2006, p. 113) concludes: "Testimony sometimes generates knowledge."

Where does this knowledge come from? It obviously did not come from Jones, since he does not believe what he tells his students. Darwin also did not know how old the fossil is, because he did not know the fossil at all. Jones merely uses a conclusion: if the theory of evolution is true, then the fossil is at least one million years old. To make this inference, he does not have to believe in evolutionary theory, since the antecedent of the implication is just assumed hypothetically. Formally, the conclusion has the form: If p, then q. p denotes the theory of evolution, q the age of the fossil. Therefore, the proposition q does not actually represent new knowledge, but is a logical consequence of evolutionary theory. The chain of transmission looks like this: Darwin knew that the theory of evolution was true (= p). And Darwin also knew: If the fossil of an extinct animal should ever be found, it would have to be older than one million years. Students know everything they need to know about Darwin's theory and can infer the knowledge about the age of the fossil from that.[5] The knowledge of the premise goes back to Darwin. With the discovery of the fossil, new information is added, but no new knowledge is created. The supposed new knowledge about its age arises as a conclusion from the theory of evolution and the fossil discovery. Graham's conclusion is therefore not justified and the principle of diminishing knowledge not disproved.

Peter Baumann defends the view that knowledge is social in nature and that knowledge from hearsay is not reducible to other forms of knowledge. According to this view, the receiver can trust the sender and need not verify the truth of the message himself. Baumann (2015, p. 279 ff.) substantiates his thesis with an example: Maria goes for a walk, taking longer than planned, and wants to look at her watch. Now she notices that she has forgotten her watch and hasn't taken her smartphone with her. Therefore, she asks a pedestrian for the time. The pedestrian looks at his watch and gives the desired information: "It is now a quarter past 3." Does Maria thereby acquire knowledge? Does she now know what time it is? Maria does not know the pedestrian, so she has no meta-knowledge about him and cannot assess whether he is telling the truth or just trying to mislead her. On what basis can she trust him? She could draw on her experience: In the past, when she wanted to know something from someone else, she always got the right answer. Maria can now inductively conclude from her experience that the pedestrian is also telling the truth. Baumann, however, considers this approach unrealistic and remote from life. Usually, no

---

[5] The conclusion makes use of the *closure principle,* which states that "if a person S knows that p, and if S also knows that q follows from p, then S also knows that q." (Ernst 2010, p. 117) The closure principle is a theorem of epistemic logic (Ditmarsch et al. 2008, p. 27).

one keeps record of how often other people tell the truth and, apart from that, we would have to check the truthfulness of their statements and for that reason we have to consult other sources of knowledge. If this knowledge again comes from second-hand sources, an infinite regress results. Baumann draws from this the conclusion that we have to rely on the information of other people. "Hearsay cannot be reduced to other, non-social sources of knowledge – such as perception and inference – but constitutes an independent source of knowledge on a par with other sources." (Baumann 2015, p. 281) Baumann justifies this with the social nature of language acquisition: even children have to rely on the assumption that their parents teach them the truth.

This brings us back to the problem of trust: Can we trust other people? Do we perhaps even have to trust them, because otherwise, apart from first-hand knowledge, we would not be able to gain any new knowledge? This would be risky. If we had to rely on the principle of trust, then Trump supporters would also be justified in believing their idol's Twitter messages. We must therefore think carefully about *whom* we want to trust. That children can trust their parents is undeniable. Whether randomly chosen pedestrians tell the truth when being asked depends, among other things, on what you want to know from them. If you just ask them what time it is, they usually have no reason to lie. On the other hand, if you ask a Trump supporter who got the most votes in the 2020 presidential election, you can expect to get a false answer. Virologists and anti-vaxxers will make different statements about the dangerousness of the Corona virus. Scientists make judgments based on the current state of research. A science denier, on the other hand, does not care about facts, but trusts his gut feeling: if he believes that the Corona virus is not dangerous, then this is the truth for him. The difference consists in how experts and laypeople arrive at their findings. We should therefore primarily not trust persons, but trust in those methods of knowledge acquisition that are reliable and scientifically sound. If a pedestrian determines the time according to a reliable method and shares his knowledge with us, we can rely on it.

These considerations show that second-hand knowledge should always be treated with caution. We take the easy way if we accept something as true unchecked just because other people assert it. We can only trust those sources of knowledge which we know well, which use reliable methods of knowledge acquisition, and about which we possess meta-knowledge in order to assess them as good informants. This applies especially to internet sources, as I will explain in the case of Google and Wikipedia.

4.7   Internet Knowledge: Is Google a Good Informant?

When we want to know something, we ask Google or look it up on Wikipedia. It makes us think that knowledge can simply be downloaded from the Internet. But do Wikipedia and Google really deliver knowledge? In fact, research shows that Wikipedia articles are in most cases as reliable as Encyclopedia Britannica articles (Fallis 2011; Frost-Arnold 2019). Nevertheless, we should be cautious. Because of the anonymity of the authors, we do not know whether the articles are written by experts or laypeople, what scientific qualifications and expertise the authors have, or whether the author is a troll intentionally spreading misinformation or simply writing nonsense. How are we supposed to trust a source about which we know nothing? We have no meta-knowledge about the authors. Moreover, Wikipedia is vulnerable to epistemic vandalism perpetrated under the protection of anonymity: "Wikipedia maintains an openness that makes it vulnerable to those with harmful motives" (Frost-Arnold 2019, p. 33).[6]

A similar case is Google. Google provides a vast amount of information. Whether it is knowledge we can trust depends on the sources. A search engine only provides links that refer to other websites. Thus, Google is nothing more than a transmitter of information, but it is not unbiased and neutral. Rather, Google's PageRank algorithm selects and prioritizes information. Not all Google links refer to reliable sources. Therefore, one has no guarantee to get only true information. In this respect, Google is not a good informant. In a way, Google is like Mrs. Smith: even when a Google source tells the truth, the information can be biased and provide an ideologically distorted picture of reality.

It is not only up to the sender, but also up to the receiver whether he or she gains knowledge from the information provided by Google. Many Google users consume the information without reflection and blindly trust the source. In order to gain knowledge, one must be able to understand the information and place it in a context. It is not enough just to gather facts. One must also know how these facts are related. One must be able to *interpret* them (cf. Lynch 2017, p. 164 ff.; Zoglauer 2020, p. 80 f.). I will illustrate this with an example.[7]

John is a guest at a dinner party where he has a very animated conversation with the other guests. The conversation turns to religion. One guest remarks that Karl Marx once said: "God is dead". A lady objects that the quote is not from Marx, but from Dostoyevsky. Next to her is an older gentleman who disagrees: "No, I'm quite sure I read it in Heidegger." John has not read the works of Marx, Dostoyevsky, or Heidegger and fears he has nothing to contribute to the intellectual discourse. He would like to say something, too. When nobody watches him, he reaches for his smartphone, types "God is dead" into Google, and eventually lands on a Wikipedia page about Friedrich Nietzsche, where he gets the desired information. What he reads there is new to him. All he knew about Nietzsche until now was that he wrote a book called "Thus Spoke Zarathustra." Now he can finally impress his interlocutors by pretending the great Nietzsche expert, saying, "The quote is from Friedrich Nietzsche's "Gay Science", Aphorism 125, where Nietzsche is talking about the madman." The other guests are flabbergasted. Instinctively, John hopes that they don't want to know more about Nietzsche and quickly change the subject.

Basically, John has just picked up a piece of information, a grain of knowledge which is useless for him. He can't say anything about Nietzsche's philosophy, nor does he know who the "madman" is or what is meant by "God is dead". What he has found on Wikipedia

---

[6] Wikipedians point out that authors have to earn their trust through their contributions and active participation in the wiki community (Jemielniak 2014, p. 118).

[7] My story is a modified version of an example by Carter and Gordon (2017).

is a puzzle piece that he cannot assemble into a complete picture. He possesses a dead body of knowledge that he can't bring to life. But like John, many internet users feel the same way. You look something up quickly, get the information off the net, don't care if the source is trustworthy and reliable, and thus think you know something. At best, it is a fragmentary "Google knowledge" that lacks a deeper understanding. Knowledge requires active and critical engagement with the content. Moreover, Google does not distinguish between true and false information. Secondary knowledge cannot replace primary knowledge. Google is a good source of information. But only an enlightened user can gain knowledge from it.

In 1909, the English author E. M. Forster wrote a science fiction story called "The Machine Stops" (2009), which reads like a parable of today's Internet society. People live in underground cells where they lack all contact with the outside world and where a machine cares for them. In their smart home, they can use video communication to contact friends who also live in their honeycombs underground. The communication network described in the story is very close to the Internet known today. There are no books any more, people receive all information from the "Machine". Since the inhabitants cannot enter the earth's surface, they do not know what it looks like there. The Machine tells them that the world there is uninhabitable. But they cannot verify what the Machine tells them. All their knowledge is second-hand. First-hand knowledge does not exist and is despised as inauthentic. The information that the Machine gives them about the past refers to other sources in which texts interpret other texts and in which the outside world exists only as an imaginary world (see Zoglauer 2018, p. 38 ff.). The texts and messages that the Machine produces do not refer to facts, but only to other texts and signs within the Machine's infosphere:

> First-hand ideas do not really exist. They are but the physical impressions produced by live and fear, and on this gross foundation who could erect a philosophy? Let our ideas be second-hand, and if possible tenth-hand, for then they will be far removed from that disturbing element – direct observation. Do not learn anything about this subject of mine – the French Revolution. Learn instead what I think that Enicharmon thought Urizen thought Gutch thought Ho-Young thought Chi-Bo-Sing thought Lafcadio Hearn thought Carlyle thought Mirabeau said about the French Revolution. (Forster 2009, p. 29)

What Forster describes here is the dystopia of a post-truth society. The facts have faded and disappeared long before or are inaccessible. It no longer matters whether the information which the Machine supplies is true or false. The world is "delivered to people's homes" by the Machine and has become "phantom and matrix" without contact to reality (Anders 1994, p. 97 ff.). The Machine is not a good informant. The people do not know who programmed the Machine or whether it is telling the truth about the world on the surface of the earth. But the Machine is the only source of information they have. The only way to gain a first-hand knowledge is to escape from the cave and climb to the Earth's surface to check with one's own eyes what the world looks like up there. Kuno, one of the inhabitants of the underground city, finds a way to the surface. He realizes that the world on the surface is very different from the one described by the Machine: It is a world where the sun shines and the stars twinkle at night, and the air is not as stuffy as the artificial air produced by the Machine. But the Machine is stronger than Kuno. Its tentacles seize the fugitive and drag him back into the cave world.

Forster's story shows that second-hand knowledge cannot replace authentic first-hand knowledge. Assertions must be tested against reality. To do that, you have to break out of the echo chamber. If we want real knowledge, we can't rely on the Internet. This is why Michael Lynch (2017, p. 19) advises us that "real knowledge – knowledge of what is the case as opposed to what we just happen to think is the case – is possible only by escaping the machine and getting to the world 'outside'".

4.8   The End of Enlightenment?

David Hume's critique of the belief in miracles provides an explanation for why so many people are deluded by mistaken beliefs and trust false authorities. Tales of ghosts, angels, demons, witchcraft, magic, and clairvoyance were widespread during Hume's lifetime and were, so to speak, the fake news of the day. Everyone had heard of such wondrous occurrences, but few had supposedly witnessed them themselves. Knowledge was based entirely on hearsay. Hume observed, to his surprise, that the more fantastic the miracle tales were, the more readily they were received. The stories were imaginatively embellished, skillfully presented rhetorically, and eagerly absorbed by a gullible audience: "Eloquence, when at its highest pitch, leaves little room for reason or reflection; but addressing itself entirely to the fancy or the affections, captivates the willing hearers, and subdues their understanding." (Hume 2007, p. 85) Listeners are moved, feeling chosen to be allowed to share this knowledge and to be heralds and messengers to announce the sensation to others: "The pleasure of telling a piece of news so interesting, of propagating it, and of being the first reporters of it, spreads the intelligence." (ibid.)

With this discourse analysis of miracle communication, Hume wants to show how dangerous it is to rely solely on second-hand reports without critically questioning them or asking for evidence. The psychological mechanisms for spreading fake news are the same today as they were in the past. Only the narratives and the technical means to spread them have changed. Samuel Fleischacker (2013, p. 180 f.) laments a widespread hostility to science and denial of empirical facts in the US, concluding that people are unwilling to use their own minds. Lee McIntyre (2015) speaks of "willful ignorance", when people adhere to a false belief, shield themselves from criticism and ignore facts. Such a dogmatic attitude is not only irrational, it contradicts the method of critical examination, which according to Hans Albert (1991, p. 42 ff.) is a basic principle of the search for truth. Hume recommends sticking to facts and evidence. He leaves no doubt that for him science and the empirical method are the only authorities that people can trust: "It is experience only, which gives authority to human testimony." (Hume 2007, p. 92) For McIntyre (2015, p. 120), the best method for gaining knowledge is the scientific method because it critically examines its own findings and is able to correct errors. Fleischacker (2013, p. 181) suggests that critical thinking and the empirical scientific method should be included more extensively in school curricula.

What we need is a new Enlightenment. The Enlightenment is a critical project. It wants to critically question alleged certainties and, as Kant explains in his "Critique of Pure Reason", reason also has constantly to reassure itself of its own foundations. Unfortunately, the Enlightenment, for which Hume and Kant stand exemplary, has recently fallen into disrepute. Postmodern thinkers identify the Enlightenment "with a hegemonic form of moral and political universalism, a blind faith in abstract reason, and a reductive and isolating focus on the individual" (Rasmussen 2014a, p. 1). Enlightenment philosophy is blamed for colonialism, racism, imperialism, arrogant Eurocentric ways of thinking, and the oppression of women (Allen 2016, p. 16; Rasmussen 2018, p. 44): "Enlightenment ideals are entangled with relations of colonial domination and epistemic violence." (Allen 2016, p. 204) Undoubtedly, there is a temporal connection between the Enlightenment and hegemonic politics. But to make a causal connection out of it and to blame philosophy for all the evils of the time would be a fallacy. If one wants to uncover the genealogical roots of hegemonic thinking, one has to dig deeper. For colonialism, racism, imperialism, and discrimination against women existed already in antiquity. As Dennis Rasmussen (2014a) shows, the "enlightenment bashing" is based on a distorted image of the Enlightenment and a misinterpretation of its ideals.

Post-factualism is a form of counter-enlightenment. The Enlightenment thinkers regarded truth as the adversary of power and wanted to attack with their philosophy the church's claim to sole representation of truth. Post-factualism, on the other hand, restores the once separate connection between truth and power. The postmodern doctrine holds that truth is produced by power: "the constructivist idea is that the power relations that generate and define discourses produce truths." (Prado 2006, p. 84) Therefore, according to this theory, there are no truths and no facts independent of discursive practices (Prado 2006, p. 126). If truth is discourse-relative, then such post-factual discourses can no longer be criticized, since each discourse generates its own truths. There is the truth of science deniers, the truth of the conspiracy theorists, and the truth of the Trump supporters. If one wanted to criticize such discourses, one would have to criticize the exercise of power on which the discursive production of truth is based. One would have to distinguish between legitimate and illegitimate forms of exercising power and take a moral stand in this dispute. This presupposes, first, a primacy of ethics over truth, and second, one has to acknowledge that this moral discourse produces its own criteria of truth and is itself based on power relations. Those who see themselves morally on the right side and subordinate truth to morality no longer need to worry about facts and can safely ignore them. Such indifference to truth is dangerous and sets us back behind the Enlightenment.

Stanley Fish (2016) indignantly rejects the charge that postmodern philosophy is responsible for Donald Trump's post-factual politics. This accusation is indeed false. Nonetheless, Fish claims that there is no independent standard by which we can distinguish truth from falsehood: "there is no impartial benchmark that can independently sort out the true facts from what is mere opinion or error." Fish is not entirely wrong on this point either. For facts are always dependent on an epistemic perspective, and other perspectives can lead to other truths. However, Fish insists that facts are discourse-relative:

> there are no facts that stand to the side of argument and can settle arguments; there are only facts that emerge in the course of argument, facts to which at least some people have been persuaded, although given what persuasion is, its effects are unlikely to last; persuasion can't be done once and for all. (Fish 2016)

According to this view, facts are not immovably fixed, but are discursively negotiable. But how are facts negotiated? Is it done by referring to facts that are established by our best scientific theories, or by asserting something until the hearer believes it? Since there is no discourse-independent standard for truth, according to Fish, the latter is more likely the case: assertions of fact are just rhetorical tools that can be used to push a particular opinion. In this view, an opinion is true if you can get away with it. It is precisely this conception of truth that Donald Trump has made the guiding principle of his post-factual politics and that ultimately helped him to triumph: you only have to sell something as truth until it is accepted, then it is true. Thus, Fish's strategy of distancing himself from post-factualism fails. Without wanting to, he implicitly legitimizes Trump's truth claim.

Are we living in a post-factual age? Immanuel Kant answered to the question of whether he was living in an enlightened age with a definite no. He regarded the Enlightenment as a process that had just begun during his lifetime and was not yet finished. Therefore, he could say that he lived in an "age of enlightenment." Just as in Kant's day, it is doubtful that people today are enlightened and use "their own understanding (…) without another's guidance" (Kant 1996, p. 21). In this respect, we are living in an age that is not yet post-factual, but very much in danger of becoming post-factual.

References

Adorno ThW (1976) Introduction. In: Adorno ThW et al (eds) The positivist dispute in German sociology. Heineman, London, pp 1–67

Albert H (1991) Traktat über kritische Vernunft. Mohr, Tübingen

Alcoff LM (2005) Reclaiming truth. In: Medina J, Wood D (eds) Truth. Blackwell, Malden, pp 336–349

Allan S (1995) News, truth and postmodernity: unravelling the will to facticity. In: Adam B, Allan S (eds) Theorizing culture. UCL Press, London, pp 129–144

Allan S (2010) News culture, 3rd edn. Open University Press, Maidenhead

Allen A (2016) The end of progress. Columbia University Press, New York

Almeder R (1989) Scientific realism and explanation. Am Philos Q 26:173–185

American Anthropological Association (1947) Statement on human rights. Am Anthropol 49:539–543

Anders G (1994) Die Antiquiertheit des Menschen, vol 1, 7th edn. Beck, München

Apel K-O (1988) Transformation der Philosophie, vol 2, 4th edn. Suhrkamp, Frankfurt a. M

Apel K-O (2002) Pragmatismus als sinnkritischer Realismus auf der Basis regulativer Ideen. In: Raters M-L, Willaschek M (eds) Hilary Putnam und die Tradition des Pragmatismus. Suhrkamp, Frankfurt a. M., pp 117–147

Arendt H (1968) Between past and future. Eight exercises in political thought. Viking Press, New York

Armstrong DM (2004) Truth and truthmakers. Cambridge University Press, Cambridge

Armstrong DM (2007) Truthmakers for negative truths, and for truths of mere possibility. In: Monnoyer J-M (ed) Metaphysics and truthmakers. Ontos, Heusenstamm, pp 99–104

Aronson J (1989) Testing for convergent realism. British J Philos Sci 40:255–259

Ashton N (2019) Rethinking epistemic relativism. Metaphilosophy 50:587–607

Ashton N (2020a) Scientific perspectives, feminist standpoints, and non-silly relativism. In: Cretu A, Massimi M (eds) Knowledge from a human point of view. Springer, Cham, pp 71–85

Ashton N (2020b) Relativising epistemic advantage. In: Kusch M (ed) The Routledge handbook of philosophy of relativism. Routledge, London, pp 329–338

Ashton N, McKenna R (2020) Situating feminist epistemology. Episteme 17:28–47

Atton C (2010) Alternative journalism: ideology and practice. In: Allan S (ed) The Routledge companion to news and journalism. Routledge, London, pp 169–178

Bächle TC (2016) Digitales Wissen, Daten und Überwachung zur Einführung. Junius, Hamburg

Bacon F (2000) The new organon. Cambridge University Press, Cambridge

Baghramian M, Coliva A (2020) Relativism. Routledge, London

T. Zoglauer, *Constructed Truths*, https://doi.org/10.1007/978-3-658-39942-9

Barbrook R, Cameron A (2001) Californian ideology. In: Ludlow P (ed) Crypto anarchy, cyberstates, and pirate utopias. MIT-Press, Cambridge, pp 363–387

Barlow JP (2001) A declaration of the independence of cyberspace. In: Ludlow P (ed) Crypto anarchy, cyberstates, and pirate utopias. MIT-Press, Cambridge, pp 27–30

Barnes B (1974) Scientific knowledge and sociological theory. Routledge, London

Barnes E (2017) Realism and social structure. Philos Stud 174:2417–2433

Barnes B, Bloor D, Henry J (1996) Scientific knowledge. Athlone Press, London

Barrow J (1992) Pi in the sky. Oxford University Press, New York

Baumann P (2015) Erkenntnistheorie, 3rd edn. Metzler, Stuttgart

Baumann P (2016) Epistemic contextualism. A defense. Oxford University Press, Oxford

Baym G (2010) Real news/fake news: beyond the news/entertainment divide. In: Allan A (ed) The Routledge companion to news and journalism. Routledge, London, pp 374–383

Berger P, Luckmann T (1991) The social construction of reality. Penguin, London

Bernal P (2018) The internet, warts and all. Cambridge University Press, Cambridge

Blackburn S (2005) Truth. A guide for the perplexed. Allen Lane, London

Blanshard B (1964) The nature of truth, vol 2. Allen & Unwin, London

Blome-Tillmann M (2019) Knowledge as contextual. In: Hetherington S, Valaris M (eds) Knowledge in contemporary philosophy. Bloomsbury, London, pp 175–193

Bloor D (1991) Knowledge and social imagery, 2nd edn. University of Chicago Press, Chicago

Bloor D (1997) Wittgenstein, rules and institutions. Routledge, London

Boghossian P (2006) Fear of knowledge. Against relativism and constructivism. Clarendon Press, Oxford

Bohr N (1929) Wirkungsquantum und Naturbeschreibung. Naturwissenschaften 17:483–486

Bonjour L (1985) The structure of empirical knowledge. Harvard University Press, Cambridge

Boudry M, Pigliucci M (eds) (2017) Science unlimited? University of Chicago Press, Chicago

Boyd R (1983) On the current status of the issue of scientific realism. Erkenntnis 19:45–90

Bradley FH (1909) Coherence and contradiction. Mind 18:489–508

Brandom R (1994) Making it explicit. Harvard University Press, Cambridge

Brendel E (2013) Wissen. de Gruyter, Berlin

Brin D (2001) Getting our priorities straight. In: Ludlow P (ed) Crypto anarchy, cyberstates, and pirate utopias. MIT-Press, Cambridge, pp 31–38

Bronner G (2016) Belief and misbelief asymmetry on the internet. ISTE, London

Brown JR (2001) Who rules in science? Harvard University Press, Cambridge

Bufacchi V (2021) Truth, lies and tweets: a consensus theory of post-truth. Philos Soc Criticism 47:347–361

Burge T (2013) Cognition through understanding. Oxford University Press, Oxford

Burr V (2015) Social constructionism, 3rd edn. Routledge, London

Calcutt A, Hammond P (2011) Journalism studies. Routledge, London

Carnap R (1950) Empiricism, semantics, and ontology. Rev Int Philos 4(11):20–40

Carnap R, Bar-Hillel Y (1964) On the outline of a theory of information. In: Bar-Hillel Y (ed) Language and information. Addison-Wesley, Reading, pp 221–274

Carter JA, Gordon E (2017) Googled assertion. Philos Psychol 30:490–501

Cartwright N (1983) How the laws of physics lie. Clarendon Press, Oxford

Cassam Q (2016) Vice epistemology. Monist 99:159–180

Chambers C (2017) Ideology and normativity. Aristotelian Soc Suppl 91:175–195

Chaos Computer Club (2020) Hacker ethics. https://www.ccc.de/en/hackerethics. Accessed 12 Aug 2020

Child W (2011) Wittgenstein. Routledge, London

Christlieb T (1986) Coherence and truth: Bonjour's metajustification. South J Philos 24:397–413

Clark M (1990) Nietzsche on truth and philosophy. Cambridge University Press, Cambridge

Coady D (2011) An epistemic defence of the blogosphere. J Appl Philos 28:277–294

Coady D (2012) What to believe now. Wiley, Malden

Coady D (2019) The trouble with 'fake news'. Soc Epistemol Rev Reply Collectiv 8(10):40–52

Coddington M (2019) Aggregating the news. Columbia University Press, New York

Code L (2008) Taking subjectivity into account. In: Bailey A, Cuomo C (eds) The feminist philosophy reader. McGraw-Hill, New York, pp 718–741

Conway K (2020) The art of communication in a polarized world. AU Press, Edmonton

Cook J (2017) Understanding and countering climate science denial. J Proc R Soc New South Wales 150(2):207–219

Cosentino G (2020) Social media and the post-truth world order. Palgrave Macmillan, Cham

Craig E (1993) Was wir wissen können. Suhrkamp, Frankfurt a. M

Crasnow S (2014) Feminist standpoint theory. In: Cartwright N, Montuschi E (eds) Philosophy of social science. Oxford University Press, Oxford, pp 145–161

Curran J (2012) Reinterpreting the internet. In: Curran J, Fenton N, Freedman D (eds) Misunderstanding the internet. Routledge, London, pp 3–33

D'Ancona M (2017) Post truth. Ebury, London

Daston L, Galison P (2007) Objectivity. Zone Books, New York

Davidson D (1984) Inquiries into truth and interpretation. Clarendon Press, Oxford

Davidson D (1990) The structure and content of truth. J Philos 87:279–328

Davidson D (2001) Subjective, intersubjective, objective. Clarendon Press, Oxford

Davidson D (2005) Truth, language, and history. Clarendon Press, Oxford

de Ridder J, Peels R, Woudenberg R (eds) (2018) Scientism. Oxford University Press, New York

deJong-Lambert W (2012) The cold war politics of genetic research. Springer, Dordrecht

Del Real J (2021) Battles over truth itself will outlast Trump, scholars say. Washington Post, 19 January, p A6

Dentith MRX (2017) The problem of fake news. Public Reason 8:65–79

Dentith MRX (2019) Conspiracy theories on the basis of the evidence. Synthese 196:2243–2261

Dietz S (2017) Die Kunst des Lügens. Reclam, Stuttgart

Ditmarsch H, van der Hoek W, Kooi B (2008) Dynamic epistemic logic. Springer, Dordrecht

Douglas H (2004) The irreducible complexity of objectivity. Synthese 138:453–473

Dretske F (1981) Knowledge and the flow of information. MIT-Press, Cambridge

Dretske F (1985) Précis of knowledge and the flow of information. In: Kornblith H (ed) Naturalizing epistemology. MIT-Press, Cambridge, pp 169–187

Dretske F (2008) The metaphysics of information. In: Pichler A, Hrachovec H (eds) Wittgenstein and the philosophy of information. Ontos, Heusenstamm, pp 273–283

Dummett M (2010) The nature and future of philosophy. Columbia University Press, New York

Durham MG (1998) On the relevance of standpoint epistemology to the praxis of journalism: the case for "strong objectivity". Commun Theory 8:117–140

Eddington AS (1929) The nature of the physical world. Cambridge University Press, Cambridge

Einstein A (1905) Zur Elektrodynamik bewegter Körper. Ann Phys 17:891–921

Einstein A, Podolsky B, Rosen N (1935) Can quantum-mechanical description of physical reality be considered complete? Phys Rev 47:777–780

Entman R (1993) Framing: toward clarification of a fractured paradigm. J Commun 43:51–58

Epstein R, Robertson R (2015) The search engine manipulation effect (SEME) and its possible impact on the outcome of elections. PNAS 112:E4512–E4521

Ernst G (2010) Einführung in die Erkenntnistheorie, 2nd edn. Wissenschaftliche Buchgesellschaft, Darmstadt

Eversberg T (2013) Hollywood im Weltall. Springer Spektrum, Heidelberg

Faber K-G (1975) Objektivität in der Geschichtswissenschaft. In: Rüsen J (ed) Historische Objektivität. Vandenhoeck & Ruprecht, Göttingen, pp 9–32

Fallis D (2011) Wikipistemology. In: Goldman A, Whitcomb D (eds) Social epistemology. Essential readings. Oxford University Press, Oxford, pp 297–313

Fallis D (2014) The varieties of disinformation. In: Floridi L, Illari P (eds) The philosophy of information quality. Springer, Cham, pp 135–161

Fallis D (2016) Mis- and disinformation. In: Floridi L (ed) The Routledge handbook of philosophy of information. Routledge, London, pp 332–346

Fallon K (2019) Where truth lies. University of California Press, Oakland

Farkas J, Schou J (2020) Post-truth, fake news and democracy. Routledge, New York

Farmer GT, Cook J (2013) Climate change science: a modern synthesis, vol 1. Springer, Dordrecht

Feyerabend P (1976) Wider den Methodenzwang. Suhrkamp, Frankfurt a. M

Feyerabend P (1978) Science in a free society. New Left Books, London

Fish S (2016) Don't blame Nietzsche for Donald Trump. https://foreignpolicy.com/2016/08/09/dont-blame-nietzsche-for-donald-trump/. Accessed 12 Aug 2020

Flaxman S, Goel S, Rao J (2016) Filter bubbles, echo chambers, and online news consumption. Public Opin Q 80:298–320

Fleck L (1979) Genesis and development of a scientific fact. University of Chicago Press, Chicago

Fleischacker S (2013) What is enlightenment? Routledge, London

Floridi L (2011) The philosophy of information. Oxford University Press, Oxford

Floridi L (2013) The ethics of information. Oxford University Press, Oxford

Fogelin R (2003) Walking the tightrope of reason. Oxford University Press, Oxford

Forster EM (2009) The machine stops. In: Johnson D, Whetmore J (eds) Technology and society. MIT-Press, Cambridge, pp 13–36

Foucault M (1980) Power/Knowledge. Pantheon Books, New York

Frank J (2018a) Trump on the coach. Avery, New York

Frank R (2018b) Fake news vs. "foke" news. A brief, personal, recent history. J Am Folk 131:379–387

Frankfurt H (2005) On bullshit. Princeton University Press, Princeton

Frege G (1984) Collected papers on mathematics, logic, and philosophy. Blackwell, Oxford

Frost CH (2011) Journalism ethics and regulation, 3rd edn. Pearson, Harlow

Frost-Arnold K (2019) Wikipedia. In: Coady D, Chase J (eds) The Routledge handbook of applied epistemology. Routledge, London, pp 28–40

Fukuyama F (2018) Against identity politics. Foreign Aff 97(5):90–114

Fuller S (2018) Post-truth. Knowledge as a power game. Anthem Press, London

Funtowicz S, Ravetz J (1993) The emergence of post-normal science. In: Schomberg R (ed) Science, politics and morality. Kluwer, Dordrecht, pp 85–123

Gadenne V (2015) Wahrheit oder Problemlösung? Welchen Stellenwert hat Wahrheit in der Wissenschaft? In: Kautek W, Neck R, Schmidinger H (eds) Wahrheit in den Wissenschaften. Böhlau, Wien, pp 11–29

Galison P (2003) Einstein's clocks, Poincaré's maps. Norton, New York

Gelfert A (2018) Fake news: a definition. Informal Logic 38:84–117

Gergen K (2015) An invitation to social construction, 3rd edn. Sage, London

Gettier E (1963) Is justified true belief knowledge? Analysis 23:121–123

Giere R (2006) Scientific perspectivism. University of Chicago Press, Chicago

Glock H-J (1996) A Wittgenstein dictionary. Blackwell, Oxford

Goldman A (1976) Discrimination and perceptual knowledge. J Philos 73:771–791

Goldman A (2002) Pathways to knowledge. Oxford University Press, Oxford

Goldman A (2008) The social epistemology of blogging. In: van den Hoven J, Weckert J (eds) Information technology and moral philosophy. Cambridge University Press, Cambridge, pp 111–122

Goodin R, Spiekermann K (2018) An epistemic theory of democracy. Oxford University Press, Oxford

Google (2020) Find fact checks in search results. https://support.google.com/websearch/answer/7315336. Accessed 3 June 2020

Gorbach J (2018) Not your grandpa's hoax: a comparative history of fake news. Am J 35:236–249

Götz-Votteler K, Hespers S (2019) Alternative Wirklichkeiten? Transcript, Bielefeld

Graham P (2006) Can testimony generate knowledge? Philosophica 78:105–127

Haack S (2019) Post "post-truth": are we there yet? Theoria 85:258–275

Habermas J (1965) Erkenntnis und Interesse. Merkur 19:1139–1153

Habermas J (1971) Vorbereitende Bemerkungen zu einer Theorie der kommunikativen Kompetenz. In: Habermas J, Luhmann N (eds) Theorie der Gesellschaft oder Sozialtechnologie – Was leistet die Systemforschung? Suhrkamp, Frankfurt a. M., pp 101–141

Habermas J (1972) Knowledge and human interests. Beacon Press, Boston

Habermas J (1984) The theory of communicative action, vol 1. Beacon Press, Boston

Habermas J (1990) Moral consciousness and communicative action. MIT-Press, Cambridge

Habermas J (1995) Vorstudien und Ergänzungen zur Theorie des kommunikativen Handelns. Suhrkamp, Frankfurt a. M

Habermas J (1998a) On the pragmatics of communication. MIT-Press, Cambridge

Habermas J (1998b) The inclusion of the other. MIT-Press, Cambridge

Habermas J (2003) Truth and justification. MIT-Press, Cambridge

Habermas J (2006) Religion in the public sphere. Eur J Philos 14:1–25

Habgood-Coote J (2019) Stop talking about fake news! Inquiry 62:1033–1065

Hacking I (1999) The social construction of what? Harvard University Press, Cambridge

Hagen K (2020) Should academics debunk conspiracy theories? Soc Epistemol 34:423–439

Hales S (2006) Relativism and the foundations of philosophy. MIT-Press, Cambridge

Hales S, Welshon R (2000) Nietzsche's perspectivism. University of Illinois Press, Urbana

Halpin H, Clark A, Wheeler M (2014) Philosophy of the web: representation, enaction, collective intelligence. In: Halpin H, Monnin A (eds) Philosophical engineering. Toward a philosophy of the web. Blackwell, Malden, pp 21–30

Hammersley M (2011) Methodology: who needs it? Sage, London

Hampton K (2018) Social media or social inequality: Trump's "unexpected" election. In: Boczkowski P, Papacharissi Z (eds) Trump and the media. MIT-Press, Cambridge, pp 159–166

Hanna J (2004) The scope and limits of scientific objectivity. Philos Sci 71:339–361

Hansson SO (2017) Science denial as a form of pseudoscience. Stud Hist Philos Sci 63:39–47

Harding S (1995) "Strong objectivity": a response to the new objectivity question. Synthese 104:331–349

Harding S (2003) How standpoint methodology informs philosophy of social science. In: Turner S, Roth P (eds) The Blackwell guide to the philosophy of the social science. Blackwell, Malden, pp 291–310

Harding S (2015) Objectivity and diversity. University of Chicago Press, Chicago

Hardwig J (1991) The role of trust in knowledge. J Philos 88:693–708

Harman G (1965) The inference to the best explanation. Philos Rev 74:88–95

Hartmann C (2020) Gefangen in der Filterblase? In: Klimczak P, Petersen C, Schilling S (eds) Maschinen der Kommunikation. Springer Vieweg, Wiesbaden, pp 45–62

Haslanger S (1995) Ontology and social construction. Philos Top 23:95–125

Haslanger S (2000) Gender and race: (What) are they? (What) do we want them to be? Nous 34:31–55

Hautamäki A (2020) Viewpoint relativism. Springer, Cham

Hecht D (2018) Pseudoscience and the pursuit of truth. In: Kaufman A, Kaufman J (eds) Pseudoscience: the conspiracy against science. MIT-Press, Cambridge, pp 3–20

Hegel GWF (2018) The phenomenology of spirit. Cambridge University Press, Cambridge

Heidegger M (1998) Pathmarks. Cambridge University Press, Cambridge

Heisenberg W (1958) Physics and philosophy. Harper & Brothers, New York

Hekman S (1997) Truth and method: feminist standpoint theory revisited. Signs 22:341–365

Hendricks V, Vestergaard M (2019) Reality lost. Springer, Cham

Hessen B (1974) Die sozialen und ökonomischen Wurzeln von Newtons 'Principia'. In: Weingart P (ed) Wissenschaftssoziologie II. Athenäum, Frankfurt a. M., pp 262–325

Hetherington S (2005) Knowing (how it is) that p: degrees and qualities of knowledge. Veritas 50(4):129–152

Hetherington S (2011) How to know. Wiley-Blackwell, Malden

Hickethier K (2008) Die Wahrheit der Fiktion. In: Pörksen B, Loosen W, Scholl A (eds) Paradoxien des Journalismus. Springer VS, Wiesbaden, pp 361–374

Hingst K-M (1998) Perspektivismus und Pragmatismus. Königshausen & Neumann, Würzburg

Hintikka J, Hintikka M (1983) Some remarks on (Wittgensteinian) logical form. Synthese 56:155–170

Horwich P (2004) From a deflationary point of view. Clarendon Press, Oxford

Hösle V (2015) Einstieg in den objektiven Idealismus. In: Hösle V, Müller FS (eds) Idealismus heute. Wissenschaftliche Buchgesellschaft, Darmstadt, pp 30–49

Hossack K (2007) The metaphysics of knowledge. Oxford University Press, Oxford

Hossack K (2011) Précis of the metaphysics of knowledge. Dialectica 65:71–73

Hughes E (2001) A cyberpunk's manifesto. In: Ludlow P (ed) Crypto anarchy, cyberstates, and pirate utopias. MIT-Press, Cambridge, pp 81–83

Hume D (1978) A treatise of human nature, 2nd edn. Clarendon Press, Oxford

Hume D (2007) An enquiry concerning human understanding. Oxford University Press, Oxford

Ichikawa JJ (ed) (2017) The Routledge handbook of epistemic contextualism. Routledge, London

Ignatieff M (2001) Human rights as politics and idolatry. Princeton University Press, Princeton

James W (1909) The meaning of truth. Longmans, Green and Co., New York

James W (1959) Pragmatism. Longmans, Green and Co., New York

Jane E, Fleming C (2014) Modern conspiracy. Bloomsbury, New York

Janich P (2018) What is information? University of Minnesota Press, Minneapolis

Jemielniak D (2014) Common knowledge? An ethnography of Wikipedia. Stanford University Press, Stanford

Jerusalem W (1982) Die soziologische Bedingtheit des Denkens und der Denkformen. In: Meja V, Stehr N (eds) Der Streit um die Wissenssoziologie, vol 1. Suhrkamp, Frankfurt a. M., pp 27–56

Joachim H (1906) The nature of truth. Clarendon Press, Oxford

Kahneman D (2011) Thinking, fast and slow. Penguin, London

Kant I (1996) Practical philosophy. Cambridge University Press, Cambridge

Kant I (2004) Prolegomena to any future metaphysics. Cambridge University Press, Cambridge

Kant I (2007) Critique of judgment. Oxford University Press, Oxford

Kavanagh J, Rich M (2018) Truth decay. RAND Corporation, Santa Monica

Kelsen H (2013) The essence and value of democracy. Rowman and Littlefield, Lanham

Kessler G (2021) As president, Trump made 30,573 false claims. Washington Post, 24 January, pp A1, A4

Kessler G, Rizzo S, Kelly M (2020) Donald Trump and his assault on truth. Scribner, New York

Klaus E (2008) Abschied von der Dichotomie. In: Pörksen B, Loosen W, Scholl A (eds) Paradoxien des Journalismus. Springer VS, Wiesbaden, pp 343–360

Klimczak P (2021) Fiction, fake and fact. In: Klimczak P, Zoglauer T (eds) Wahrheit und Fake im postfaktisch-digitalen Zeitalter. Springer Vieweg, Wiesbaden, pp 45–71

Klimczak P, Zoglauer T (eds) (2021) Wahrheit und Fake im postfaktisch-digitalen Zeitalter. Springer Vieweg, Wiesbaden

Koertge N (2000) Science, values, and the values of science. Philos Sci 67(Supplement):S45–S57

Koro-Ljunberg M, Carlson DL, Montana A (2019) Productive forces of post-truth(s)? Qual Inquiry 25:583–590

Krausz M, Meiland J (1982) Relativism. Cognitive and moral. University of Notre Dame Press, Notre Dame

Krebs J (2014) Information transfer as a metaphor. In: Hagengruber R, Riss U (eds) Philosophy, computing and information science. Pickering & Chatto, London, pp 29–40

Kristiansen L, Kaussler B (2018) The bullshit doctrine: fabrications, lies, and nonsense in the age of Trump. Informal Logic 38:13–52

Kuhn T (1970) The structure of scientific revolutions, 2nd edn. University of Chicago Press, Chicago

Kuhn T (1976) Theory-change as structure-change: comments on the Sneed formalism. Erkenntnis 10:179–199

Kuhn T (1977) The essential tension. University of Chicago Press, Chicago

Kuhn T (1982) Commensurability, comparability, communicability. Proc Biennial Meeting Philos Sci Assoc 2:669–688

Küng H (1992) Projekt Weltethos, 4th edn. Piper, München

Kusch M (2002) Knowledge by agreement. Clarendon Press, Oxford

Lack C, Rousseau J (2016) Critical thinking, science, and pseudoscience. Springer, New York

Lackey J (1999) Testimonial knowledge and transmission. Philos Q 49:471–490

LaFrance A (2020) Nothing can stop what is coming. The Atlantic, June, pp 26–38

Lakatos I (1970) Falsification and the methodology of scientific research programmes. In: Lakatos I, Musgrave A (eds) Criticism and the growth of knowledge. Cambridge University Press, Cambridge, pp 91–196

Lakatos I (1976) History of science and its rational reconstruction. In: Howson C (ed) Method and appraisal in the physical sciences. Cambridge University Press, Cambridge, pp 1–39

Laudan L (1981) A confutation of convergent realism. Philos Sci 48:19–49

Laughlin R (2008) The crime of reason. Basic Books, New York

Lee P (2015) Truth wars. Palgrave Macmillan, New York

Lem S (2002) Die Technologiefalle. Suhrkamp, Frankfurt a. M

Leplin J (1981) Truth and scientific progress. Stud Hist Philos Sci 12:269–291

Lévy P (1999) Collective intelligence. Basic Books, New York

Lewandowsky S, Ecker U, Cook J (2017) Beyond misinformation: understanding and coping with the "post-truth" era. J Appl Res Mem Cogn 6:353–369

Lewis CI (1946) An analysis of knowledge and valuation. Open Court, LaSalle

Lewis CI (1956) Mind and the world order. Dover, New York

Lincoln Y, Guba E (2013) The constructivist credo. Left Coast Press, Walnut Creek

Lipton P (2005) The truth about science. Philos Trans R Soc B 360:1259–1269

List C, Goodin R (2001) Epistemic democracy: generating the Condorcet Jury Theorem. J Polit Philos 9:277–306

Lloyd E (1995) Objectivity and the double standard for feminist epistemologies. Synthese 104:351–381

Lockie S (2017) Post-truth politics and the social sciences. Environ Sociol 3:1–5

Longino H (1990) Science as social knowledge. Princeton University Press, Princeton

Loxton D (2019) Understanding flat earthers. Skeptic Mag 24(4):10–23

Lundgren B (2019) Does semantic information need to be truthful? Synthese 196:2885–2906

Lynch M (2017) The internet of us. Liveright, New York

Maasen S (1999) Wissenssoziologie. Transcript, Bielefeld

MacFarlane J (2010) Making sense of relative truth. In: Krausz M (ed) Relativism. A contemporary introduction. Columbia University Press, New York, pp 124–139

MacFarlane J (2014) Assessment sensitivity. Oxford University Press, Oxford

MacMullen I (2020) What is "post-factual" politics? J Polit Philos 28:97–116

Maddalena G, Gili G (2020) The history and theory of post-truth communication. Palgrave Macmillan, Cham

Mahner M (2007) Demarcating science from non-science. In: Kuipers T (ed) General philosophy of science – focal issues. Elsevier, Amsterdam, pp 515–575

Malcolm N (1963) Knowledge and certainty. Prentice-Hall, Englewood Cliffs

Maras S (2013) Objectivity in journalism. Polity Press, Cambridge

Marcuse H (2002) One-dimensional man. Routledge, London

Marino P (2006) What should a correspondence theory be and do? Philos Stud 127:415–457

Massimi M (2018a) Perspectivism. In: Saatsi J (ed) The Routledge handbook of scientific realism. Routledge, London, pp 164–175

Massimi M (2018b) Four kinds of perspectival truth. Philos Phenom Res 96:342–359

Mathiesen K (2019) Fake news and the limits of free speech. In: Fox C, Saunders J (eds) Media ethics, free speech, and the requirements of democracy. Routledge, New York, pp 161–179

Maturana H, Varela F (1992) The tree of knowledge. Shambhala, Boston

May T (2001) The crypto anarchist manifesto. In: Ludlow P (ed) Crypto anarchy, cyberstates, and pirate utopias. MIT-Press, Cambridge, pp 61–63

McCarthy ED (1996) Knowledge as culture. The new sociology of knowledge. Routledge, London

McIntyre L (2015) Respecting truth. Routledge, New York

McIntyre L (2018) Post-Truth. MIT-Press, Cambridge

Meiland J (1980) On the paradox of cognitive relativism. Metaphilosophy 11:115–126

Mejia R, Beckermann K, Sullivan C (2018) White lies: a racial history of the (post)truth. Commun Critical/Cult Stud 15:109–126

Messingschlager T, Holtz P (2020) Filter bubbles and echo chambers. In: Appel M (ed) Die Psychologie des Postfaktischen: Über Fake News, "Lügenpresse", Clickbait und Co. Springer, Berlin, pp 91–102

Meyer K (2018) Das konspirologische Denken. Velbrück, Weilerswist

Meyers C (2019) Partisan news, the myth of objectivity, and the standards of responsible journalism. In: Fox C, Saunders J (eds) Media ethics, free speech, and the requirements of democracy. Routledge, New York, pp 219–239

Mößner N, Kitcher P (2017) Knowledge, democracy, and the internet. Minerva 55:1–24

Mouffe C (2000) The democratic paradox. Verso, London

Munn NJ (2012) The new political blogosphere. Soc Epistemol 26:55–70

Munoz-Torres JR (2012) Truth and objectivity in journalism. Journalism Stud 13:566–582

Myres JD (2018) Post-truth as symptom: the emergence of a masculine hysteria. Philos Rhetor 51:392–415

Nagel T (1986) The view from nowhere. Oxford University Press, New York

Nagel T (1991) Mortal questions. Cambridge University Press, Cambridge

Nehamas A (1985) Nietzsche. Life as literature. Harvard University Press, Cambridge

Nerurkar M, Gärtner T (2020) Datenhermeneutik: Überlegungen zur Interpretierbarkeit von Daten. In: Wiegerling K, Nerurkar M, Wadephul C (eds) Datafizierung und Big Data. Springer VS, Wiesbaden, pp 195–209

Neurath O (1983) Philosophical papers 1913–1946. Reidel, Dordrecht

Newton-Smith W (1983) Trans-theoretical truth without transcendental truth? In: Henrich D (ed) Kant oder Hegel? Stuttgarter Hegel-Kongress 1981. Klett-Cotta, Stuttgart, pp 466–478

Nguyen CT (2020) Echo chambers and epistemic bubbles. Episteme 17:141–161

Nietzsche F (1996) (HA) Human, all too human. Cambridge University Press, Cambridge

Nietzsche F (1999) (KSA) Kritische Studienausgabe in 15 Bänden. dtv, München

Nietzsche F (2001a) (BGE) Beyond good and evil. Cambridge University Press, Cambridge

Nietzsche F (2001b) (GS) The gay science. Cambridge University Press, Cambridge

Nietzsche F (2003) (NB) Writings from the late notebooks. Cambridge University Press, Cambridge

Nietzsche F (2006) (GM) On the genealogy of morals. Cambridge University Press, Cambridge

Nietzsche F (2009) (TL) On truth and lie in an extra-moral sense. In: Writings from the early notebooks. Cambridge University Press, Cambridge, pp 253–264

Nietzsche F (2020) (UF) Unpublished fragments (Spring 1885 – Spring 1886). Stanford University Press, Stanford

Nozick R (2001) Invariances. The structure of the objective world. Harvard University Press, Cambridge

Oreskes N, Conway E (2010) Merchants of doubt. Bloomsbury, New York

Orwell G (1989) Nineteen eighty-four. Penguin, London

Oswald M (2019) Strategisches Framing. Springer VS, Wiesbaden

Pariser E (2011) The filter bubble. Penguin, London

Peels R (2017a) Ten reasons to embrace scientism. Stud Hist Philos Sci 63:11–21

Peels R (2017b) The fundamental argument against scientism. In: Boudry M, Pigliucci M (eds) Science unlimited? University of Chicago Press, Chicago, pp 165–194

Peirce CS (1955) Philosophical writings. Dover, New York

Penrose R (1989) The emperor's new mind. Oxford University Press, New York

Pettenger M (ed) (2007) The social construction of climate change. Ashgate, Aldershot

Popper K (1962) Conjectures and refutations. Basic Books, New York

Popper K (1976) The logic of the social sciences. In: Adorno T et al (eds) The positivist dispute in German sociology. Heinemann, London, pp 87–104

Popper K (1999) All life is problem solving. Routledge, London

Popper K (2002) The logic of scientific discovery. Routledge, London

Poskett J (2019) Materials of the mind. University of Chicago Press, Chicago

Prado CG (2006) Searle and Foucault on truth. Cambridge University Press, Cambridge

Prado CG (2018) The new subjectivism. In: Prado CG (ed) America's post-truth phenomenon. Praeger, Santa Barbara, pp 1–14

Predelli S (2020) Fictional discourse. Oxford University Press, Oxford

Psillos S (1999) Scientific realism. Routledge, London

Putnam H (1975) Mathematics, matter and method. Cambridge University Press, Cambridge

Putnam H (1981) Reason, truth and history. Cambridge University Press, Cambridge

Putnam H (1983) Realism and reason. Cambridge University Press, Cambridge

Putnam H (1987) The many faces of realism. Open Court, LaSalle

Putnam H (1992) Realism with a human face. Harvard University Press, Cambridge

Putnam H (2016) Realism. Philos Soc Crit 42:117–131

Quine WV (1963) From a logical point of view, 2nd edn. Harper Torchbooks, New York

Quine WV (1974) The roots of reference. Open Court, LaSalle

Quine WV (1986) Philosophy of logic, 2nd edn. Harvard University Press, Cambridge

Quine WV (1987) Quiddities. Harvard University Press, Cambridge

Quine WV (1992) Pursuit of truth. Harvard University Press, Cambridge

Quine WV (1995) From stimulus to science. Harvard University Press, Cambridge

Quine WV (1998) Reply to Robert Nozick. In: Hahn LE, Schilpp PA (eds) The philosophy of
   W.V. Quine, 2nd edn. Open Court, Chicago, pp 364–367
Quine WV (2013) Word and object. MIT-Press, Cambridge
Quine WV (2019) Science and sensibilia. The 1980 Immanuel Kant lectures. Palgrave
   Macmillan, Cham
Quine WV, Ullian JS (1978) The web of belief, 2nd edn. McGraw-Hill, New York
Raeijmaekers D, Maeseele P (2017) In objectivity we trust? Pluralism, consensus, and ideology in
   journalism studies. Journalism 18:647–663
Rasmussen D (2014a) The pragmatic enlightenment. Cambridge University Press, Cambridge
Rasmussen J (2014b) Defending the correspondence theory of truth. Cambridge University Press,
   Cambridge
Rasmussen D (2018) Contemporary political theory as an anti-enlightenment project. In: Boucher
   G, Lloyd HM (eds) Rethinking the enlightenment. Lexington Books, Lanham, pp 39–59
Rawls J (2001) Justice as fairness. A restatement. Harvard University Press, Cambridge
Reichenbach H (1961) Experience and prediction. University of Chicago Press, Chicago
Reid T (1818) An inquiry into the human mind on the principles of common sense. Anderson,
   Edinburgh
Rescher N (1973) The coherence theory of truth. Oxford University Press, Oxford
Rescher N (1974) Foundationalism, coherentism, and the idea of cognitive systematization. J Philos
   71:695–708
Rescher N (1992) A system of pragmatic idealism, vol 1. Princeton University Press, Princeton
Rescher N (1999) The limits of science. University of Pittsburgh Press, Pittsburgh
Rescher N (2006) Studies in epistemology. Ontos, Heusenstamm
Riegraf B (2010) Konstruktion von Geschlecht. In: Aulenbacher B, Meuser M, Riegraf B (eds)
   Soziologische Geschlechterforschung. Springer VS, Wiesbaden, pp 59–77
Rini R (2017) Fake news and partisan epistemology. Kennedy Inst Ethics J 27:E43–E64
Rippe KP (1993) Ethischer Relativismus. Schöningh, Paderborn
Risjord M (2014) Philosophy of social science. Routledge, New York
Romele A (2020) Digital hermeneutics. Routledge, New York
Rorty R (1972) The world well lost. J Philos 69:649–665
Rorty R (1979) Philosophy and the mirror of nature. Princeton University Press, Princeton
Rorty R (1982) Consequences of pragmatism. University of Minnesota Press, Minneapolis
Rorty R (1989) Contingency, irony, and solidarity. Cambridge University Press, Cambridge
Rorty R (1991) Objectivity, relativism and truth. Cambridge University Press, Cambridge
Rorty R (1995) Is truth a goal of inquiry? Davidson vs. Wright. Philos Quarterly 45:281–300
Rorty R (1999) Philosophy and social hope. Penguin, London
Rosenberg J (1988) Comparing the incommensurable: another look at convergent realism. Philos
   Stud 54:163–193
Roth G (1987) Erkenntnis und Realität: Das reale Gehirn und seine Wirklichkeit. In: Schmidt SJ (ed)
   Der Diskurs des Radikalen Konstruktivismus. Suhrkamp, Frankfurt a. M., pp 229–255
Roth G (1992a) Kognition: Die Entstehung von Bedeutung im Gehirn. In: Krohn W, Küppers G (eds)
   Emergenz: Die Entstehung von Ordnung, Organisation und Bedeutung. Suhrkamp, Frankfurt a.
   M., pp 104–133
Roth G (1992b) Das konstruktive Gehirn: Neurobiologische Grundlagen von Wahrnehmung
   und Erkenntnis. In: Schmidt SJ (ed) Kognition und Gesellschaft. Suhrkamp, Frankfurt a. M.,
   pp 277–336
Roth G (1997) Das Gehirn und seine Wirklichkeit. Suhrkamp, Frankfurt a. M
Rovane C (2013) The metaphysics and ethics of relativism. Harvard University Press, Cambridge

Rovane C (2016) Relativism and recognition. In: Bell J, Cutrofello A, Livingston P (eds) Beyond the analytic-continental divide. Routledge, New York, pp 261–286

Russell B (1975) My philosophical development. Allen and Unwin, London

Russell B (2001) The problems of philosophy, 2nd edn. Oxford University Press, Oxford

Ryan M (2001) Journalistic ethics, objectivity, existential journalism, standpoint epistemology, and public journalism. J Mass Media Ethics 16:3–22

Salgado S (2018) Online media impact on politics. Views on post-truth politics and post-postmodernism. Int J Media Cult Pol 24:317–331

Scheler M (1982) Wissenschaft und soziale Struktur. In: Meja V, Stehr N (eds) Der Streit um die Wissenssoziologie, vol 1. Suhrkamp, Frankfurt a. M., pp 68–127

Schlick M (1979) Philosophical papers, vol 2 (1925–1936). Reidel, Dordrecht

Schmid CE, Stock L, Walter S (2018) Der strategische Einsatz von Fake News zur Propaganda im Wahlkampf. In: Sachs-Hombach K, Zywietz B (eds) Fake news, hashtags & social bots. Springer VS, Wiesbaden, pp 69–95

Schmidt SJ (1994) Kognitive Autonomie und soziale Orientierung. Suhrkamp, Frankfurt a. M

Schopenhauer A (2010) The world as will and representation, vol 1. Cambridge University Press, Cambridge

Schubert CH (2020) Donald Trump's "fake news" agenda. In: Schneider U, Eitelmann M (eds) Linguistic inquiries into Donald Trump's language. Bloomsbury, London, pp 196–214

Schurz G (2014) Philosophy of science. A unified approach. Routledge, New York

Schweiger W (2017) Der (des)informierte Bürger im Netz. Springer, Wiesbaden

Searle JR (1995) The construction of social reality. Free Press, New York

Sellars W (1997) Empiricism and the philosophy of mind. Harvard University Press, Cambridge

Sextus Empiricus (2000) Outlines of scepticism. Cambridge University Press, Cambridge

Shannon C, Weaver W (1963) The mathematical theory of communication. University of Illinois Press, Urbana

Simmel G (1895) Ueber eine Beziehung der Selectionslehre zur Erkenntnistheorie. Archiv Syst Philos 1:34–45

Smart JJC (1963) Philosophy and scientific realism. Routledge & Kegan Paul, London

Spohr D (2017) Fake news and ideological polarization: filter bubbles and selective exposure on social media. Business Inf Rev 34:150–160

Stagl J (1992) Eine Widerlegung des Kulturellen Relativismus. In: Matthes J (ed) Zwischen den Kulturen? Schwartz, Göttingen, pp 145–166

Stokke A (2019) Lying, sincerity, and quality. In: Meibauer J (ed) The Oxford handbook of lying. Oxford University Press, Oxford, pp 134–148

Stonier T (1990) Information and the internal structure of the universe. Springer, London

Sunstein C (2008) Democracy and the internet. In: van den Hoven J, Weckert J (eds) Information technology and moral responsibility. Cambridge University Press, Cambridge, pp 93–110

Sunstein C (2009) Going to extremes. Oxford University Press, Oxford

Sunstein C (2010) Believing false rumors. In: Levmore S, Nussbaum M (eds) The offensive internet. Harvard University Press, Cambridge, pp 91–106

Sunstein C (2017) #republic. Princeton University Press, Princeton

Surowiecki J (2004) The wisdom of the crowds. Doubleday, New York

Susen S (2015) The 'postmodern turn' in the social sciences. Palgrave Macmillan, New York

Sussman RW (2014) The myth of race. Harvard University Press, Cambridge

Tegmark M (2015) Our mathematical universe. Penguin, London

Tessier D (2020) The needle in the haystack: how information overload is impacting society and our search for truth. In: Dalkir K, Katz R (eds) Navigating fake news, alternative facts, and misinformation in a post-truth world. IGI Global, Hershey, pp 18–35

Tewksbury D, Rittenberg J (2012) News on the internet. Oxford University Press, Oxford

Thalmann K (2019) The stigmatization of conspiracy theory since the 1950s. Routledge, London

Turner S (2014) The politics of expertise. Routledge, New York

Vaas R (2020) Weisen der Wahrheit. Universitas 75(8):39–63

Vaihinger H (2021) The philosophy of 'As If'. Routledge, Abingdon

van Fraassen B (1989) Laws and symmetry. Clarendon Press, Oxford

van Woudenberg R, Peels R, de Ridder J (2018) Introduction. Putting scientism on the philosophical agenda. In: de Ridder J, Peels R, van Woudenberg R (eds) Scientism. Oxford University Press, New York, pp 1–27

Vollmer G (1993) Wissenschaftstheorie im Einsatz. Hirzel, Stuttgart

von Baeyer HCH (2005) Das informative Universum. Beck, München

von Foerster H (2003) Understanding understanding. Essays on cybernetics and cognition. Springer, New York

von Glasersfeld E (1985) Einführung in den radikalen Konstruktivismus. In: Watzlawick P (ed) Die erfundene Wirklichkeit. Piper, München, pp 16–38

von Glasersfeld E (1987) Wissen, Sprache und Wirklichkeit. Vieweg, Braunschweig

von Weizsäcker CF (2006) The structure of physics. Springer, Dordrecht

von Wright GH (2001) Ludwig Wittgenstein. A memoir, 2nd edn. Clarendon Press, Oxford

Walsh A (2013) Science wars. Transaction, New Brunswick

Walter M (2014) Der Kampf um die Wirklichkeit. Mediale Legitimationsstrategien gegenüber Verschwörungstheorien zum 11.September. In: Anton A, Schetsche M, Walter M (eds) Konspiration. Soziologie des Verschwörungsdenkens. Springer VS, Wiesbaden, pp 181–202

Walzer M (1994) Thick and thin. Moral argument at home and abroad. University of Notre Dame Press, Notre Dame

Ward S (2011a) Ethics and the media. Cambridge University Press, Cambridge

Ward S (2011b) Multidimensional objectivity for global journalism. In: Fortner R, Fackler M (eds) The handbook of global communication and media ethics, vol 1. Blackwell, Malden, pp 215–233

Washington H, Cook J (2011) Climate change denial. Earthscan, London

Weiner G (2017) Trump and truth. Nat Aff, Spring, pp 79–91

Weischenberg S, Scholl A (1995) Konstruktivismus und Ethik im Journalismus. In: Rusch G, Schmidt SJ (eds) Konstruktivismus und Ethik. Suhrkamp, Frankfurt a. M., pp 214–240

Whorf BL (1957) Language, thought and reality. MIT-Press, Cambridge

Wight C (2018) Post-truth, postmodernism and alternative facts. New Persp 26:17–29

Willaschek M (2015) Der mentale Zugang zur Welt, 2nd edn. Klostermann, Frankfurt a. M

Williams M (2001) Problems of knowledge. Oxford University Press, Oxford

Winch P (1964) Understanding a primitive society. Am Philos Q 1:307–324

Winston B, Winston M (2021) The roots of fake news. Routledge, London

Wisnewski G (2005) Lügen im Weltraum. Knaur, München

Wittgenstein L (1967) (RFM) Remarks on the foundations of mathematics. MIT-Press, Cambridge

Wittgenstein L (1969a) (OC) On certainty. Blackwell, Oxford

Wittgenstein L (1969b) (NB) Notebooks 1914–1916. Harper Torchbooks, New York

Wittgenstein L (2001) (TLP) Tractatus logico-philosophicus. Routledge, London

Wittgenstein L (2009) (PI) Philosophical investigations, 4th edn. Wiley-Blackwell, Malden

Yearley S (2005) Making sense of science. Sage, London

Zeilinger A (2005) Einsteins Schleier. Goldmann, München

Zimmermann F, Kohring M (2018) "Fake News" als aktuelle Desinformation. Medien und Kommunikationswissenschaft 66:526–541

Zimmermann F, Kohring M (2020) Aktuelle Desinformation – Definition und Einordnung einer gesellschaftlichen Herausforderung. In: Hohlfeld R et al (eds) Fake News und Desinformation. Nomos, Baden-Baden, pp 23–41

Zoglauer T (1993) Das Problem der theoretischen Terme. Vieweg, Braunschweig

Zoglauer T (1995) Der Informationsgehalt empirischer Modelle – Zur Logik des semantischen Informationsbegriffs. In: Max I, Stelzner W (eds) Logik und Mathematik. de Gruyter, Berlin, pp 484–495

Zoglauer T (1996) Can information be naturalized? In: Kornwachs K, Jacoby K (eds) Information. New questions to a multidisciplinary concept. Akademie, Berlin, pp 187–207

Zoglauer T (2016) Verständigungsprobleme mit Außerirdischen. In: Weber K, Friesen H, Zoglauer T (eds) Philosophie und Phantastik. Mentis, Münster, pp 141–166

Zoglauer T (2018) Technikkritik als Kritik an der Moderne. In: Zoglauer T, Weber K, Friesen H (eds) Technik als Motor der Modernisierung. Alber, Freiburg, pp 26–56

Zoglauer T (2020) Wissen im Zeitalter von Google, Fake News und alternativen Fakten. In: Klimczak P, Petersen P, Schilling S (eds) Maschinen der Kommunikation. Springer Vieweg, Wiesbaden, pp 63–83

Zoglauer T (2021) Wahrheitsrelativismus, Wissenschaftsskeptizismus und die politischen Folgen. In: Klimczak P, Zoglauer T (eds) Wahrheit und Fake im postfaktisch-digitalen Zeitalter. Springer Vieweg, Wiesbaden, pp 1–26

Printed in the United States
by Baker & Taylor Publisher Services

Printed in the United States
by Baker & Taylor Publisher Services